Winning Strategies
for the
Indian Market

Winning Strategies for the Indian Market

EDITED BY

Anuradha Dayal-Gulati
and
Dipak Jain

Northwestern
University Press
Evanston, Illinois

Northwestern University Press
www.nupress.northwestern.edu

Printed in the United States of America

10   9   8   7   6   5   4   3   2   1

Library of Congress Cataloging-in-Publication Data

Winning strategies for the Indian market / edited by Anuradha Dayal-
    Gulati and Dipak Jain.
        p. cm. — (Kellogg School of Management)
    Includes bibliographical references and index.
    ISBN 978-0-8101-2695-4 (pbk. : alk. paper) 1. Consumption
(Economics)—India. 2. India—Economic conditions. 3. India—Social
conditions. I. Dayal-Gulati, Anuradha. II. Jain, D. (Dipak) III. Series:
Kellogg School of Management (Series)
HC440.C6W56 2010
330.954—dc22
                                                                    2010008955

∞ The paper used in this publication meets the minimum requirements of
the American National Standard for Information Sciences—Permanence of
Paper for Printed Library Materials, ANSI Z39.48-1992.

CONTENTS

PREFACE

India is experiencing enormous changes, which are affecting everyone in the country. At every socioeconomic level, growth is bringing change—favorable or unfavorable, wanted or not. India has the world's fastest-growing markets in several sectors, such as airlines, telecom, and organized retail. In several other sectors, such as credit cards, it has the fastest-growing market in the Asia-Pacific region. India's consumer goods market is among the ten largest markets in the world, and it is expected to be among the five largest in the next few years.

With GDP growth exceeding 7% in the last several years, India has finally witnessed the emergence of an Indian consumer population that is no longer restricted to the small percentage of people at the top of society. Private consumption now accounts for 64% of GDP—significantly higher than in China (42%), but also higher than in Europe (58%) and Japan (55%). Some observers believe that the broadening foundation of consumer support in India could cause a shift in underlying GDP growth toward the upper end of a 7% to 8% range. This increasingly powerful domestic demand is, for the first time, providing the basis for sustainable growth and development. And therein lies the excitement and future of India. A country that has for so long struggled with social and political conservatism has gone from an emerging market with latent potential to the place where everyone wants to be.

While the popular press has used the terms "India" and *Bharat* to describe the divergence between the urban, middle-class India that has primarily benefited from growth ("India"), and the rural, largely illiterate, impoverished India that has thus far been marginalized (*Bharat*), the truth is that there are more than two types of India.

Several Indias coexist; the India we see depends on the parameters we use in segmenting and aggregating the target population. But any way we look at India, with its remarkably diverse demographics, the country not only poses interesting challenges but also offers extraordinary opportunities for those willing to take the leap.

More than 95% of India's population is under the age of sixty-five, 70% is under thirty-six, and half that percentage is under eighteen. With rising income levels, the standard of living has been increasing: only 26% of the population is below the poverty line now, compared to over 50% in the mid-1970s. The young, mobile segment of the population earns more and is willing to spend more than previous generations. These Indians have more job opportunities and higher pay scales than their parents ever did. Furthermore, a high percentage of these Indians are still living at home and saving their salaries. Thus, they can spend a large percentage of their income, and changes in consuming habits and patterns have created a class for whom rising aspirations can become a reality.

In the industries we examine here, the growth observed in recent years is only in its nascent stages, and consumption is accelerating off a low base. Low penetration rates for a whole range of consumer products and services—credit cards, cell phones, and banking, to name a few—all point to the enormous market potential in all these sectors. Domestic and multinational companies have all jumped into the fray to reach the growing Indian market. Domestic companies have aggressive expansion plans to establish a national footprint and capture market share and even go global. Multinational corporations (MNCs), in response to liberalization of regulations, are not far behind. And firms are no longer restricting themselves to the select urban metropolises where they traditionally focused. The vast rural market, long considered impoverished and logistically challenging, has become the new frontier in the battle to capture the hearts, minds, and wallets of the Indian consumer. Nowhere is this focal shift more visible than in the telecom sector, where increased competition has meant a dramatic reduction in prepaid pricing points for mobile subscribers. The same dynamic applies to a whole range of durable goods now being offered to different target segments by domestic and international companies alike, all attempting to capture a piece of the market of the aspiring Indian consumer. Price wars are rocking almost every consumer product category in an attempt to capture market share. As afford-ability increases, in some sectors profitability requires scale to make up for lower prices and revenues per consumer. As a result, in some industries, we are beginning to see inevitable consolidation and the emergence of partnerships to ensure survival in an increasingly competitive environment.

While India has become a new frontier for growth, it also remains challenging for the intrepid companies operating in this market. Inadequate infrastructure, such as power and roads, and red tape continue to raise the costs of doing business in India, despite tremendous opportunities in the marketplace. But successful firms are finding ways to work through these constraints. Their major challenge still remains how to compete in an increasingly demanding marketplace. Reaching the value-conscious Indian consumer, who wants quality at an affordable price, demands creative solutions. We see again and again that to reach first-time consumers, successful companies are rethinking their products and services—be they cell phones, microwave ovens, credit cards, cars, or tubes of toothpaste. Consumer education, grassroots marketing, longer product life cycles, innovative financing, and advertising are also key in this market. Creativity even extends to the provisions of microfinance and rural elementary education to harness the poten-tial the rural consumer now offers. Lessons learned by MNCs, some painful and others prudent, have repeatedly shown that in India, successful business models are often those that are tailor-made to local markets and customs.

India is now poised for flight. And the Indian government, despite political pressures, has over the past two decades remained committed to its efforts to undo the restraints of the past and modernize the Indian economy. The economic reforms begun with India's balance of payments crisis in 1991 have been furthered by numerous initiatives. India joined the World Trade Organization (WTO) in 1997, signaling a firm commitment to opening its economy to foreign investment and to participating more completely in the global economy. With its WTO membership, India placed a greater focus on meeting regulated trade policies and made a stronger commitment to intellectual property protection. Thus, the economic changes India has undergone over the last fifteen years have created significant growth opportunities. But the government has moved forward cautiously, trying to integrate the reform framework with a domestic political imperative that stresses broad-based economic development. This caution has caused the government to move slowly in certain areas, including multibrand retailing, privatization of infrastructure, price controls in the pharmaceutical sector, and opening access to foreign direct investment. The political imperative does not pose a fundamental setback to reform. As we see in the chapters ahead, the Indian government has set the stage for growth by liberalizing and in certain cases responding to the changing environment. Despite the challenges, change will continue, even if the reality of Indian politics requires it to be slower than companies would like.

This book, then, is about change and the implications of change experienced by all Indians. To give the reader some perspective on the dramatic shifts taking place, we have focused on an array of industries that span different consumer segments, ranging from the urban wealthy to the rural poor. The chapters provide analytical insights into the retail, credit card, microfinance, hospitality, airline, telecom, and pharmaceutical sectors. Each chapter provides an overview of the competitive and growth dynamics in a key sector of the economy and examines innovative strategies adopted by the major players in that sector. We hope that this book will give the reader a glimpse of the shifts and emerging trends. The implications of this transformation can be seen in price wars, razor-thin margins, increasingly demanding consumers, new consumer segments, business strategies for the challenging Indian market, and innovative products and services. As India strides onto the world stage, the astonishing growth that it has experienced thus far appears to be only the beginning.

This book is a continuation of a series from the Kellogg School of Management. Like prior publications, this too is based on first-hand research conducted by Kellogg students under the supervision of Kellogg faculty as part of Global Initiatives in Management (GIM), a program offered by Kellogg for the last decade. Each year, the GIM program offers courses that span the globe; recent courses have focused on China, Japan, India, South Africa, Chile, Brazil, Southeast Asia, the Middle East, and the European Union. Kellogg students in the GIM program have capped their classroom experiences with visits to the countries of focus over spring break. In addition to the lectures and country visits, the students undertake in-depth research on the issues they examine, basing their findings on firsthand, in-country interviews. For this book, all research was conducted by students as part of a semester-long course followed by a field trip to India. Many of the chapters are based on a composite of research by multiple teams on different facets of the same sector. We synthesized the research to create a single chapter on that sector.

The book is organized as follows. Chapter 1 provides an overview of the Indian consumer. Based on current research, it provides key insights into effective strategies for the Indian market. Chapter 2 examines the dramatic changes in the retail industry, particularly in the area of organized food retail, while also highlighting challenges of the industry. Chapters 3 through 6 analyze the changes that are occurring in four dynamic sectors: credit cards, telecommunications, airlines, and the hospitality industry. These chapters examine how companies are raising penetration rates, reaching out to new customer segments, and increasing affordability—and doing so innovatively in the face of challenges and constraints. Chapter 7 looks at the transformation of the Indian pharmaceutical industry in the wake of India's decision to accept product patents according to the WTO guidelines on Trade-Related Aspects of Intellectual Property Rights (TRIPS). These changes are providing a springboard for Indian companies to look outside of domestic borders and become increasingly innovative to meet the opportunity of the global marketplace. Finally, chapters 8 and 9 look at organizations that employ innovative strategies to reach consumers at the bottom of the pyramid. These strategies have the potential to fundamentally transform India's society and economy. Chapter 8 looks at social entrepreneurship in India, particularly at recent developments in the microfinance industry and trends in public-private partnerships for elementary school education. Chapter 9 looks at the Tata Nano, the world's cheapest car, and at the innovative methods and processes used to design the car for consumers at the bottom of the pyramid. These innovative approaches exemplify a shift in thinking of companies and individuals who are driving change in India.

An important cultural pillar at the Kellogg School is teamwork; this book too is the product of teamwork at many levels. It began with student teams that worked together diligently in conducting the primary research that went into this book. We would like to thank the authors for their time and effort in making revisions and meeting deadlines. We are deeply grateful to faculty advisors for the India class—Bala Balachandran, Raj Gupta, Mark Finn, Ed Wilson, and Sunil Chopra—for their input on this project. A number of other people have also been instrumental in making this book a reality. Mark Finn, director of the Global Initiatives in Management program, has played a key role in driving and supporting this project. Other people, too innumerable to mention, have generously given of their time in meeting with the students and us in India and the United States. We thank all of you for your continuous support for our program.

We gratefully acknowledge Donna Shear, the former director of Northwestern University Press, for her patience and her commitment; and Rich Honack, Assistant Dean and Chief Marketing Officer, Kellogg School of Management, for his enthusiastic commitment and backing. We would also like to thank Lindsay Kadish-Williams for providing administrative support. Our editors have played an important part in bringing this book to fruition. We would like to thank Nandini Chowdhury for her incisive comments and editing, delivered frequently with quick wit and humor; Tom Truesdell, for his infinite patience and quick turnaround times; and Franz Wohlgezogen, who played a key role in bringing this book to completion. We have indeed been fortunate to have such a wonderful team to help us pull this book together.

Anuradha Dayal-Gulati

Dipak Jain

KELLOGG SCHOOL OF MANAGEMENT
EVANSTON, ILLINOIS

Chapter 1

THE EMERGENCE OF THE INDIAN CONSUMER

*Shilpa Borkar, James Chen, Adam Grablick,
Kim Hickey, Amy Hsiao-Hung Hsiao,
Sunil Kapadia, Leigh Katcher, Stephen Moffat,
Lebbonee Price, Eugene Youn*

Historically, India's explosive population growth has been viewed as a major obstacle to prosperity. Yet, in a short span of ten years, this vast pool of humanity (1.1 billion people, or roughly one-sixth of the world's population) now represents an invaluable, virtually untapped consumer market, ripe with growth opportunities. The single biggest cause for this dramatic shift in perception has been the emergence of a true Indian consumer class, no longer limited to the top 2% to 3% of the population (1.2 million affluent households) concentrated in the eight major cities, who constitute the top of the consumption and income pyramid. Even while 30% of the population (about 150 million households) does not possess sufficient incomes to make regular purchases, approximately 67% (close to 700 million people) signifies a potential consumer base more than double that of the United States.

As the twelfth-largest global economy, India has enjoyed a sustained economic growth above 8% since 2003. This GDP growth has materially benefited millions of aspiring Indians for whom higher incomes have led to higher purchasing power, which has translated into higher consumption. Rising incomes are projected to account for 80% of consumption growth in the next twenty years and will continue to drive the increase in overall discretionary spending, which rose from 35% of average household income in 1985 to 52% in 2005. Over the next twenty years, discretionary spending in India is expected to reach 70% of average household consumption. Even a cursory look at credit card statistics reveals that both the volume of purchases and average purchase size has significantly increased in a short period of time. In fiscal year 2007 to 2008 the monthly average expenditure per card was Rs 4000 ($87), up from Rs 1500 ($33) three to four years ago. And credit card growth has been in the double digits since 2000. Furthermore, an estimated 50% of the population is under age twenty-five, and 81% is under age forty- five, accounting for a large portion of the annual consumer spending increase over the last ten years. Employment opportunities for women are on the rise, and many households benefit from dual incomes. These statistics all point to the average Indian becoming more interested in consumer goods and becoming more capable of paying for a wider variety of products.

Several Indias Coexist

The real driver of India's growing consumer goods market is the growing middle class. Several estimates of the number of households that compose this middle class exist, including labels to denote their potential purchasing power, but the size of this group has been changing rapidly. To put the speed of this change into perspective, we begin by looking at changes in poverty levels. The bottom two income quartiles, estimated at 40 to 60 million households, have been classified as destitute. These two quartiles—comprising those earning less than Rs 16,000, or about $1 a day, and those earning Rs 16,000 to Rs 22,000, or $400 to $5,000 annually—can only afford basic necessities for some time to come. Yet the number of households in these lowest two income quartiles fell from a total of 57 million households in 2002 to about 37 million households in 2007—a dramatic decline in poverty. This group, consisting of subsistence farmers and unskilled laborers, can be found in India's villages and urban slums. If growth continues at the pace it has been, these destitute households will move to the next income quartiles.

The dramatic decline in poverty can also be seen in the next two income quartiles. Households with annual income levels ranging from Rs 45,000 to Rs 200,000 ($977 to $4,340) increased from 46 million to 75 million from 2002 to 2007, while the income quartile just below (Rs 22,000 to Rs 45,000, or $477 to $977) showed a smaller increase—from 74 million households to 82 million. While households in the lower of these two income quartiles may still struggle to meet basic necessities, the majority of these households have money for other areas of consumption. Typically, these households spend half their budget on necessities for basic sustenance, but that amount is falling each year. Over the coming years, many of the households in these two quartiles will move into the middle class. These households consist mainly of small shopkeepers, farmers with small landholdings, and semiskilled industrial and service workers. They have been called "aspirers" or "struggling India." With rising incomes, the consumer market is expected to grow in proportion overall, with increasing numbers of consumers able to afford higher-priced and more discretionary products.

The number of households in the highest income segment (with an annual income of more than Rs 200,000 or approximately $4,300) doubled from 2.6 million households to an estimated 5.2 million from 2002 to 2007. This segment has been further classified into "seekers" (with incomes from Rs 200,000 to Rs 500,000, or $4,300 to $10,800) and "strivers" (with incomes from Rs 500,000 to Rs 1 million, or $10,800 to $21,500). Seekers include young college graduates, midlevel government officials, traders, and businesspeople. Strivers, also called "global Indians," are in the upper end of the middle class (an estimated 1.2 million households) and have been growing at 20% per year. They tend to be senior government officials, managers of large businesses, professionals, and rich farmers. These are households that buy branded products, vacation abroad, and behave like their counterparts in developed countries in terms of lifestyle and ownership of goods. By 2025, the spending power of this group will be 20% of total Indian consumption. The middle class numbers about 50 million people, and by 2025 it is estimated to expand to nearly 600 million.

Indians also constitute a fifth of the world's citizens below age twenty, and this generation, nurtured on success, is joining the ranks of Indian consumers. The challenge facing manufacturers is to come up with products and services that appeal to this group of consumers, who have a short attention span coupled with rapidly changing needs and preferences. Additionally, youth often spend beyond their means. They are willing to experiment with high-end brands, because they have a high level of disposable income.

A Changing Rural Market

India's consumer market is defined not just by income and age, however, but also by geography. While India's urban centers receive attention for their rapid growth, the majority of the population resides, and will continue to reside for some time, in rural areas. About 70% of India's population, approximately 790 million inhabitants, lives in areas with a population density under 400 per square kilometer, and over the next twenty years, the rural population is projected to grow by 116 million. Even with increased growth in the urban population over the next two decades, a study by McKinsey & Company, a management consulting firm, projects that 63% of Indian inhabitants will still live in rural areas in 2025.

Rural India has not been the locus of any significant market growth and has traditionally been characterized as an impoverished, predominantly agrarian population with virtually no purchasing power. First, the volume of potential customers, based on income, is small as a proportion of the total rural population. "Tier 1 and 2 cities will continue to control and drive approximately 62% of consumption of high-end products in 2025," says Rajeev Karwal, founder of a venture capital firm based in Delhi. Second, the rural population is scattered over a vast geographic area, making these people hard to locate and expensive to target, given the country's poor infrastructure. However, according to Karwal, "New technologies like the Internet and wireless broadband can solve both these problems, making it economically viable for companies to offer a range of services, such as banking, distance education, and health care to rural India. This, in turn, will transform the expectations, aspirations, and economy of the rural consumer."

The idea of rural India as predominantly agricultural has given way to a different reality as employment has gradually shifted away from agriculture. Employment in agriculture declined from 75% in 1987 to 67% in 2004. Manufacturing, construction, trade, transport, and communication are on the rise, and they accounted for 34% of rural employment in 2004, up from 25% in 1987. Rural India now accounts for 48% of India's economy and accounts for more than $100 billion in consumer spending, making it a significant contributor to India's gross domestic product.

Although rural India shares a common geography, the rural population is not homogeneous. Certainly, rural India can no longer be described as solely impoverished. Distinct household income brackets also exist within the rural market, and awareness of these income groups provides a better understanding of the consumers. A 2007 McKinsey report on India's consumer market identifies five different economic groups in rural India. These groups range from very poor to very wealthy and illustrate the importance of the decline in extreme poverty and the increase in disposable income in the rural market.

Mirroring the changes at the national level, the rural poor decreased from 96% of the population to 65% from 1985 to 2005, and this group is projected to decline to 29% by 2025. The decline of the poorest income group simultaneously leads to growth within the next two higher economic groups, and by 2015 these two groups are projected to be 47% of the rural population, or 80 million households, and will control 55% of spending in the rural market. Significant growth is also anticipated to take place among households in the higher income bracket ($4,300 to $10,800 in annual income). The low end of this group constitutes the floor of the "middle class" in India, and projections show this group will grow from 3% in 2005 to 20% by 2025. By 2025, this group will constitute a fifth of the rural population and a third of its spending power. On the opposite end of the spectrum from the poor are the rural wealthy, whose annual incomes range from $10,800 to $21,500+. This group includes landowners, wealthy farmers, businesspeople, and traders. In twenty years India's rural market is projected to be larger than the consumer market in South Korea or Canada and almost four times the size of India's urban market. By 2025, rural consumption will nearly triple, creating a potential market of more than $577 billion. As millions of the lowest-income households move into the second tier, they will begin to afford products and services beyond immediate needs.

Can Multinationals Profit from Rising Income and Changing Consumption?

India's sizable consumer base has an added allure for multinational corporations (MNCs) faced with the challenge of saturated global consumer markets. Its growing market for consumer goods is already among the top ten global markets and could be among the top five in the next few years. Until recently, several MNCs had defined the Indian market exclusively in terms of the premium segment (top 2% to 3% of the population). Their concentration on urban higher-margin consumer segments—who can tolerate premium pricing and who have a purchasing power equivalent to those of consumers in developed countries—has been an extremely successful and profitable strategy. Companies such as Colgate-Palmolive, Unilever (with its Hindustan Unilever Ltd. [HUL]), Procter & Gamble (P&G), and Kraft have established strong footholds in India by aiming at high-income consumers.

But, with growing incomes, rising consumption, and a growing middle class, both multinational and domestic companies are battling for market share across various consumer categories. Firms are pushing into the lower-income groups in the urban, semiurban, and rural areas to offset declining profitability and capture market share. India will be a critical growth market for many MNCs, but not without challenges. Companies that fail to understand the unique needs of the Indian consumer will miss out on one of the most important growth opportunities in the next two decades.

Caution: "India Is Different, India Is Different, India Is Different"

To even begin to approach India's large, relatively low-income, mostly rural, and young consumer market—often concentrated in harder-to-reach places—companies must better understand the consumers it comprises. As K. M. S. Ahluwalia, founder of India's largest market research firm (now ACNielsen ORG-MARG), repeatedly warns his Western clients, "India is different, India is different, India is different." Large and potentially long-term returns await those companies willing to understand and approach these diverse segments, but the challenges cannot be underestimated.

The companies that failed in India did so because they attempted to sell global products at global prices and, assuming that their brands were strong enough to draw customers, chose not to establish well-planned marketing and sales channels. The companies that have succeeded, on the other hand, understand the country's rapidly changing consumer goods landscape and the diverse needs and cultural beliefs of the various segments. That knowledge has been critical in helping them tailor products and production methods to Indian market conditions and in helping them fit the budgets and tastes of Indian consumers, sometimes slashing prices by even more than 50%.

How Culture Influences Consumption

While Indians across various income groups and locations show a marked eagerness to change their consumption patterns in response to rising disposable incomes, they also remain rooted in cultural traditions and belief systems that continue to have a marked influence on their consumption choices and preferences. Although Indians aspire to have Western products, the biggest mistake firms can make is to assume that Indians across all segments will take to a large, global brand solely because of its international image and brand associations. An interesting example from the premium segment illustrates how sensitivity to social values can change positioning and influence marketing strategy. The leading diamond seller De Beers has long used the message "A diamond is for love" to associate the precious stone with romance, engagement, and marriage. But this positioning may be less relevant to the Indian market, where most marriages are still arranged, at least to some degree, so that most couples "get married and then fall in love." Thus, De Beers initially developed a unique marketing platform for India, focusing consumers on a "value for money" proposition and providing information to aid the new diamond purchaser. Similarly, the company takes Indians' strong family values into account by marketing diamonds to both grooms and their mothers, who play a larger role in the engagement decision than their Western counterparts. In general, Indian families are known for being close-knit, with most Indians endorsing the value of family ties. This cultural feature carries several implications for marketing, including the need for companies to reconsider their global marketing strategy and align their products and advertising with family values.

Often, MNCs have to rethink not only their products and advertising but, more fundamentally, how they interact with their customers. Providers of luxury goods and high fashion, for example, have found that the usual routine of glitzy stores, celebrity endorsement, and glossy ads does not work as effectively in India to attract the country's highly brand-conscious, high-income clients as does personal client-to-client interactions. Adapting to the new elites' desire to be served and fussed over, Moët Hennessy organizes luxurious yet intimate dinner parties at local socialites' houses, where the upwardly mobile can sip its wines and spirits; Hugo Boss has its staff call on clients in their offices, where salespeople provide advice on style and color and tailors make adjustments; and Mercedes brings its entire range of cars to wealthy towns around the country and invites the local elite for a test-drive. To win in the lucrative customer segment of India's $100,000 millionaires, foreign companies need to go all out and find the right personal touches.[1]

Even mundane articles and categories require firms to understand Indian consumers' preferences and practices. For instance, the Kellogg Company introduced its corn flakes in India in 1995, but the product failed miserably, achieving less than 20% of its initial sales target because it did not fit into the country's tradition of fresh, homemade breakfast foods. Indians like hot milk with their cereal, and Kellogg's cereal, which is made for cold milk, couldn't stand up to hot milk. Only after revamping its product and making a cereal suitable for hot milk did Kellogg's became profitable in India.

In contrast, McDonald's Corporation's revenue in India has grown 50% annually since 1997, even though 20% of India's population is completely vegetarian, and about 82% does not eat beef. McDonald's has enjoyed this success because it introduced an array of vegetarian choices and indigenized its flavors to suit the spicy Indian palate. McDonald's came up with the Maharaja Mac, a 100% ground lamb burger; the Chicken Maharaja Mac; the McVeggie; and the McAloo Tikki (with potatoes). The vegetarian items are advertised with a 100% PURE VEG stamp on them. In fact, 75% of the McDonald's menu in India is Indianized. In 2001, when McDonald's introduced the Veg Surprise burger, a veggie burger with Indian spices, sales volume shot up 40%. The flagship Maharaja Mac and the McVeggie are not only profitable, they are also politically correct burgers. Indian political activists are always eager to protest against so-called "cultural imperialism," and foreign-based fast-food chains are easy targets.

KFC was a completely different story. In the mid-1990s, KFC opened its first store in Bangalore, India's most cosmopolitan city, with plans to open sixty more stores in the country. But the day it opened, protests erupted: KFC was accused of using illegally high amounts of monosodium glutamate (MSG), a flavor enhancer, and frying its chicken in pork fat (India's 150 million Muslims do not eat pork). Activist groups protested outside the restaurant in Bangalore, holding placards reading QUIT INDIA and STOP PLAYING FOUL. Because of these protests, KFC scaled back its expansion plans and maintained a low profile. It again started expanding in late 2005, when the economy was booming and people were exposed to the Western influences of fast food and shopping malls. Currently, it has opened multiple outlets in cities like Bangalore, Mumbai, and New Delhi and is opening many more in tier 2 cities without opposition.

Interestingly, fast-moving consumer goods (FMCGs), such as laundry products, represent another arena in which companies have faced strongly established cultural infrastructure. Contrary to the expectation of easy adoption, companies had to deal with considerable resistance because of traditional lifestyle preferences. Until recently, washing machines were uncommon in India, with most laundering performed by hand, often by *dhobis* (launderers) hired specifically for this task. *Dhobis* typically scrubbed wet clothes with "washing cakes" (bars of detergent). Not surprisingly, studies have shown that washing cake sales exceeded powdered detergent revenues in the 1990s, often by 50%. But modernity is intruding on tradition, and for the first time, India's *dhobis* see their livelihood, and their very existence, threatened as the automatic washing machine creeps into modern Indian homes.

Finally, toothpaste is a product category with significant household-related cultural dimensions, especially in rural areas, where many residents have never handled tubes of the product, instead cleaning their teeth with charcoal powder or neem-tree bark. Consumer education therefore has been a major challenge for toothpaste marketers in India, but many have made significant progress. Colgate-Palmolive's Colgate toothpaste, for instance, was not widely accepted in India until Colgate began using road shows to help educate people throughout India about oral care. But it took about three years for the product to gain popularity.

Clearly, then, raising consumer awareness is critical for the successful launch of a new product. For instance, MNCs targeting fast-moving consumer goods have to anticipate a lengthy product life cycle in India that involves a slow uptake because consumers may take a long time to gain awareness of, try, and adopt the product. Because there is a general lack of additional market research, owing to low initial cost and ease of product launches, most FMCG companies have a "ready, fire, and aim" approach: market research consists primarily of trial and error during launch. FMCG companies entering India should therefore factor in additional investment in time and capital before pronouncing product launches successes or failures. They must not only find ways to offer products relevant to the diverse tastes of Indian consumers but also grapple with the challenges of cultivating consumer insights and developing products in India's lengthened product life cycle.

In the case of consumer durables, such as washing machines, refrigerators, and microwave ovens, market research largely means understanding the cultural habits, constraints, and lifestyle preferences of the Indian household and understanding the Indian housewife, who would be the primary user of such products. In the case of color televisions and other luxury items, market research means understanding the needs of the whole family unit and developing marketing strategies that are directed to the entire family.

Success requires MNCs entering the Indian market to truly understand the environment, desired experience, attitudes, and behaviors of the Indian consumer. Vikram Bakshi, managing director of McDonald's India, stresses that no brand—not even a big global brand like McDonald's—can take the market lightly but has to make itself relevant to the consumers in the country. He also emphasizes that translating the value proposition to India needs to be consistent with the brand's heritage and its potential: "Our menu is 'Indianized,' and the McAloo Tikki burger is our highest selling product [but] the McDonald's experience around the world is consistent, offering quality, great service, cleanliness, and value."[2]

Balancing Globalization with Customization: Product Development with a Local Flavor

One of the greatest struggles that companies entering India face is trying to meet the competing demands of globalization and customization. Such companies must determine the right balance, trying to achieve cost-efficiency while trying to customize and sell global products in an extremely diverse, multilingual country of predominantly lower-income people often located in remote, inaccessible areas.

In the quest for balance, we see different companies opting for different strategies, depending on the products they are trying to sell and the segments they are trying to reach. Representing one end of the spectrum is Proctor & Gamble's P&G India. Leveraging its parent company's global scale to achieve cost-efficiency, P&G India does not attempt to tailor products to the diversity found throughout the Indian market; instead, it utilizes market insights that apply to India as a whole. When P&G introduced its leading diaper brand, Pampers, into the Indian market, it took into account consumer feedback and came up with a bikini design that suited the country's tropical climate. It also incorporated an easily resealable fastening system that replaced conventional tapes, which wear out more quickly. In addition, the diapers were priced as low as Rs 20 ($0.40 per diaper), which won over middle-class Indian consumers. Similarly, Ariel—P&G's global powerhouse detergent brand—was adapted by including ingredients that combat the unique dirt and debris on Indian clothes.

Whirlpool has also been a leader in introducing products targeted specifically at the needs of the Indian consumer. One of its earliest refrigerator innovations, the Flexigerator, addressed the needs of India's space-constrained consumers. The Flexigerator offered drop-down shelves and flexible shape options—features now standard in almost all refrigerators sold in India. Additionally, recognizing that Indian consumers need to store large quantities of water, Whirlpool introduced refrigerator doors that could adequately shelve 1.5-liter water bottles.

Other companies, such as Wyeth (now a subsidiary of Pfizer), a global pharmaceutical and consumer health-care company operating in India since the 1960s, have adapted their product formulations and are constantly exploring product reformulations for the Indian market. These include reformulating its Anacin brand so that it is available in topical ointment form, which has been very well received by the Indian market. Johnson & Johnson offers Band-Aids with turmeric, Colgate has added ayurvedic herbals to its toothpaste, and SC Johnson offers its Glade air freshener in incense sticks.

General Mills demonstrates another successful approach to customization in India. Although leveraging globally developed product and manufacturing concepts in India, General Mills has concentrated on developing completely customized products, such as its Pillsbury Chakki Fresh Atta flour, a basic food need for many Indians. The company produces its packaging with India's seven most widely spoken languages to ensure understanding among India's largest linguistic groups. To address the diverse tastes in

India, General Mills tailors its flavors. For instance, in 2006 it introduced Pillsbury Punjabi Atta, a flour product customized to suit the Punjabi palate. General Mills pitted the product against other regional players, such as Roshan da Atta and Shakti Bhog Atta, carrying the slogan "Sadda Taste, Saadi Roti" (My Taste, My Roti). In addition, it priced the product lower than the prices of competing brands.

General Mills believes that segmentation is key in a market like India, because one cannot be all things to all people. Rather than fit India into P&G's low-cost global strategy, General Mills focuses on working with Indian tastes and customs to ingrain the company into the Indian marketplace.

While the enormous variety of Indian consumers' tastes and customs—and the sheer range of pricing categories, from extreme low cost to überpremium—can be a challenge to marketers, it also yields important learning advantages to companies willing to embrace the variety and range of Indian consumers. Companies like Microsoft and Nokia, for example, have discovered India to be the perfect testing ground for high-tech products aimed at emerging markets. Microsoft has initiated a number of projects in India's agricultural, textile, and education sectors. It has usability-tested new hardware and software that allows entrepreneurs to better track their deliveries and payments, helps farmers share farming practices and expertise, and enables schools who cannot afford one PC per child to have multiple pupils use one PC simultaneously. The company also runs focus groups in many rural and small urban communities and lets individuals with little or no previous exposure to computer technology experiment with PCs. Observing these interactions, Microsoft gains insights on how to approach the millions who make up the bottom of India's economic pyramid and tap them as a business opportunity in the future, when they emerge to join the middle class.[3]

Nokia already has a strong position within a large segment of India's low-income consumer segment. The company currently holds a 70% share of the country's cell phone market. To gain this, Nokia has invested heavily in developing products for the low-end handset market in India, in customizing its handsets' features (e.g., integrating a flashlight and adding an antislip grip), and in providing low-cost mobile services (e.g., sending local market prices and weather forecasts to farmers' and traders' phones). In a recent interview, Nokia's CEO highlighted the benefits of his company's experiences in India: "I think we have learned a lot in these markets, which have been applied in others, particularly Africa. We are seeing things happening in Africa from the mobile-communications-market point of view that we saw happening in India maybe five or six years ago."[4]

Best Practices: Consumer Insights

Despite their different approaches, each company has used consumer insights to drive product and brand development. HUL and P&G India both require management teams to visit and stay in rural villages at different times in the year. General Mills obtains their consumer insights by conducting "observationals," in which marketers go into the field and observe consumers in their private kitchens. Godrej, an Indian company, leverages its employees and their personal knowledge of local consumers.

However, one of the key challenges with developing consumer insights in India is trying to understand the daily challenges facing Indian consumers. In the words of Vidur Behal, vice president of R&D Homecare Asia at Unilever, "Employees' significantly higher incomes relative to common Indian households are a major barrier to consumer understanding. Understanding poverty is difficult for those who don't live it; there is little ability to empathize."

Balancing Pricing and Aspiration with Value for Money

Price has always been one of the most critical factors in determining success in developing markets, and pricing for Indian consumers is a particularly tricky task. Among the psychological factors that play a role in their purchasing behavior are an orientation toward savings and value for money (VFM). As consumers become more educated, pragmatic, and demanding, the focus on low prices has been replaced by a VFM perspective.

Indians have traditionally been savers, often banking one-third to one-half of their incomes and preferring to pay off credit card balances in full. In the last ten to fifteen years, however, these trends have shifted to reflect the sharp rise in the number of Indians with greater disposable income. These "aspirational" Indians are much more willing to purchase luxury items and services. Nonetheless, conservatism is reflected in the mantra "value for money," spoken by Indian consumers of all strata. Indians present MNCs with the frustrating combination of price sensitivity and brand seeking, with every purchase a carefully considered decision based on much lower levels of impulsiveness than in the West. Advertising, then, must present a strong VFM proposition, and several MNCs have erred in this regard, misperceiving the Indian consumer as simple and naive rather than savvy and demanding.

Being compulsive savers, the Indian consumer is extremely price conscious. Merely having a premium product and brand is not sufficient to justify a premium price in the Indian market. Many brands that have been successful internationally have failed in India, because they were perceived to be priced too high. For example, Colgate Total, an international success, failed in India as a premium brand at its initial price. However, when it was relaunched at a lower price, it became a huge success.

To appeal to the cost-conscious Indian, successful companies have also reduced the consumer's cost of entry into product categories by providing payment options such as financing, pay per use, and community ownership. In segments as diverse as motorcycles, durable goods, and apparel, for example, companies have representatives from banks and other financial institutions in stores to process loans in just a few hours. Game console makers are considering pay-per-use formats, including prepaid cards. Along with PC makers, they are also studying ideas for community ownership (e.g., schools) as a way to drive penetration and consumption.

Still, although Indian consumers are price conscious, the increase in their purchasing power has made value, for Indians who can afford more, no longer only a function of price. With a proliferation of products, consumers are willing to pay a premium for quality or branded products, but only if they perceive such products to have additional value. And it might take consumers considerable time to appreciate the value that a product or brand provides. Therefore, pricing strategies must consider the time needed for consumers to appreciate the value a product or brand provides. For example, the launch of HUL's Rin Supreme, a significantly superior product based on new technology, took more than three years to succeed, because consumers were slow to realize that the product had additional value.

To complicate matters further, the typical value-added growth strategies that MNCs use to sustain market growth have had little success in India because of consumer aspiration for new luxury items that have so far remained unaffordable to the middle-income Indian household. An HUL executive has proposed that instead of spending more money for value-added products, Indian consumers are more likely to spend the additional money to explore previously untapped categories. With the rise in disposable income, more luxury goods, such as cosmetics, cell phones, and cable television, are becoming available to consumers in India. Consumers are not willing to spend money to upgrade commodity products when they can use additional income for newfound luxury products. In fact, some consumers have downgraded commodity items, like some FMCG products, in order to purchase a luxury good.

Best Practice: Addressing Income Differentials with Product Variety

To convert latent buying potential into a real purchase, pricing has emerged as a front-runner. Price wars are rocking almost every major consumer category, from FMCGs to automobiles, airline fares, cell phones, and even credit cards. To negate the squeeze on profit margins, firms are aggressively entering into semiurban and rural markets to push volumes. To fully capitalize on the opportunity in the Indian market, companies must offer distinct products to different income segments, trading off between price points and product features.

Firms are designing products to reflect local usage patterns, thereby reducing costs to achieve a price point that creates demand. LG, for instance, has successfully developed products that help it maintain its premium brand positioning while appealing to lower price point consumers. It reengineered its color television (CTV) product specifications to develop three models specific to the Indian market. These included an entry-level, no-frills model to expand the market at the low end as well as a premium flat-screen CTV for the middle segment. By keeping the price of the flat screen within 10% of the price of comparably sized conventional CTVs, LG was able to persuade consumers to purchase it, quickly stealing market share from other manufacturers.

Philips Electronics India not only offers different products based on consumer economic class, but it also brands them distinctly. Philips' consumer segmentation classifies their consumers as either pride/performance oriented (mainly urban consumers) or price oriented (largely rural consumers). For the pride/performance-oriented consumers, the Philips brand name is used. According to company executive S. Sukumaran, the Philips brand is positioned primarily around superior picture quality. Philips tries to attract these consumers by continually innovating on features, such as Ambilight technology, which provides a hue of color around the television to complement what is on-screen. For the price-oriented consumers, the brand name Vardaan is used to signify a boon, or "God's blessing" for the rural markets.

Ensuring Affordability for Lower-Income Groups: Low Pricing and Downsized Packaging

Given the primarily low incomes throughout India, the focus for pricing is not on discounts for large packages, but on low prices and massive sales volume through package downsizing. To keep prices low, many FMCG companies have used cost-saving technologies. For example, HUL and Nirma developed low-priced, mass-market detergent powders by using dry mix technology—simply combining key ingredients in large vats—rather than the costlier spray dry manufacturing system used for premium detergents. P&G sells Ariel in affordable single-use sachets. The mass-market detergents, while inferior in quality to premium brands, are much more afford-able. Similarly, detergent manufacturers have kept prices down by removing features irrelevant or of low value to mass-market consumers: special cleaning enzymes, perfumes, stain-removing capabilities, and colored speckles that make the product look more effective while offering no actual cleaning benefits. Proctor & Gamble, Wyeth, and others have defied the corporate tradition of "trading up" consumers to larger packages by introducing affordable miniproducts, revising product formulations, and concentrating sales efforts on volume in lieu of strong margins.

When packaging helps lower the price of products, it can powerfully boost their ability to penetrate the consumer market. For example, the sachet introduced by numerous shampoo manu-facturers (e.g., the makers of Pantene, Velvette, Sunsilk, and Nirma) on "low cash ring" packaging has allowed many Indian consumers to purchase shampoo for the first time, with estimated annual growth of sachet revenues at 25% to 30%. What was a luxury is now affordable to many Indian consumers, who can now satisfy their aspirations at a lower price. The sachet, designed for one-time use, was originally priced at one to three rupees, making it much more affordable, at least on occasion. Sachet packaging is also very compatible with Indian retail settings, which are often limited to tiny kiosks or general stores, many of them less than eight square feet. This packaging innovation makes these products accessible to a large segment of India's population that otherwise could not afford it. In ten years, the share of the population buying shampoo has increased from 18% to 45%, with sachets driving almost all of this growth *despite* their premium price per unit of volume.

In addition to helping make products affordable, packaging can be a key product attribute for the consumer market. For instance, in the early 1980s Parle Agro used Tetra Pak packaging—small, vacuum-packed cardboard containers for juice—to grow the market for its Frooti fruit drinks, especially in the children's segment. The new packaging allowed storage of the product without refrigeration at a time when penetration of refrigerators was no more than 20% in urban areas, and less than 1% in rural areas. In addition, the Tetra Pak packaging removed the need for preservatives, and it looked good. This example clearly indicates that products must be packaged to reflect India's varying climate and consumer tastes.

The Challenge of Building Brand Loyalty in the Indian Consumer

All of the companies interviewed agreed that as Indians become more savvy consumers, quality is the first and most important step in the branding of companies and products. "Quality is not a qualifier but a differentiator" was a common refrain of all interviewees. Whether through a "house of brands" or a "branded house" approach, MNCs wishing to enter the Indian market must select an appropriate strategy to build their brands. Although Indians do not associate additional value with products simply because they are branded, established brands help legitimize products. Even though Indians are price conscious, they are also extremely brand loyal. The Indian consumer is moving up from unbranded to branded goods in packaged foods and cleaning products, and demand for nascent categories such as breakfast cereals, hair coloring, cosmetics, and health and hygiene products is growing. To address the Indian population's strong focus on value for money, consumer advertising is often product, not image, driven.

Corporate Branding Versus Product Branding

While both Indian companies and MNCs agree that branding is important, they have all pursued different paths in building their brands. Godrej, like other Indian companies, has pursued a policy of a "branded house," which emphasizes trust, reliability, and quality. In fact, through its corporate brand, the company guarantees all its products. As noted by the CEO of Godrej Consumer Products,

"The brand equity that Godrej has built in areas such as air conditioners is leveraged to extend the trust the company has built with its customers to their toilet [bathroom] soaps. This allows Godrej to move into new products and have an established and recognizable brand with the Indian consumer." Additionally, for smaller, local companies like Godrej, it is more cost-effective to build a corporate brand to increase brand loyalty than to build product brands.

Many MNCs have pursued a "house of brands" strategy, which reflects their philosophy toward the mature markets to which they are accustomed. HUL, P&G, and General Mills take little interest in creating a singular corporate brand to carry their products; instead, they focus on differentiating multiple brands in order to reach various segments. According to an executive at General Mills India, "The creation of a singular corporate brand limits the ability to create value-added products and premium products."

These approaches not only reflect the difference between Indian companies and their Western competitors, but also reflect the different markets they target. Godrej targets value-oriented, mass-market consumers, whereas MNCs prefer to target affluent, urban consumers initially. The difference between the two target markets is significant, resulting in different branding strategies. Still, no matter which strategy is used, companies must look to build differentiated and consumer-relevant brands to gain consumer loyalty. According to Nirmal Gupta, professor of management at Ryerson University, if companies can build loyalty among these consumers, they will ultimately be able to migrate existing customers to higher-margin products and capitalize on the aspirations of Indian consumers. For brands with multiproduct offerings, a consumer that has a good experience with one category is more likely to "stay in the brand family" for additional purchases. This is especially true for first-time purchasers.

MNC Branding Strategies

While the MNCs all subscribe to the "house of brands" strategy, differences remain in their approaches to brand building in India.

The divergence in branding philosophies is part of the fundamental difference in the way they approach global expansion. As previously noted, P&G uses a largely global brand-building strategy with few, if any, resources dedicated to creating new brands in a country. Brands are almost exclusively developed by corporate resources with a global perspective and then implemented locally by using local expertise and perspectives. General Mills India, on the other hand, allows local teams to develop customized and unique brands, such as Pillsbury Chakki Fresh Atta flour.

Brand Building and Brand Communication: Using Multiple Media to Promote Consumer Education and Raise Brand Awareness

The increasing importance of branding has also increased the importance of brand exposure and marketing in the Indian market. However, constraints in retail space prevent the use of displays and limit visibility of a product. According to the CEO of Godrej Consumer Products, "There is very little interaction between the consumer and the brand at traditional retail spots, which account for 93% of the Indian retail market." Therefore, the opportunity for interaction between the consumer and the brand is primarily via the mass media and word of mouth.

Television is the largest mass medium in India. As such, the high penetration rates of television—more than 80% in urban areas—have helped MNCs advertise their products to the Indian market. Over a three-month period, TV is estimated to be six to nine times more cost-effective as an advertising medium than print, generating stronger impact and recall. Though radio has greater reach, its ability to engage potential customers is limited, motivating many advertisers to use this medium only supplementally.

The recent explosion in cable television use has only added to the importance of using television as the major avenue of brand interaction with the consumer. Cable television now provides more ways to segment the market. For example, some cable stations are now targeting various regional populations with local-language programming. This practice provides means to target specific brand messages to the diversity of Indian consumers and also provides the most cost-effective way to raise consumer awareness of a product. While it may be difficult to cut through the clutter of televised messages, cable TV provides the easiest way for brands to reach consumers. But even as the largest mass medium, television reaches only about 50% of the Indian population. Companies cite word of mouth and other delivery devices as being equally important in building brands and educating consumers in India.

A major challenge of introducing new product categories into India is consumer education, especially in rural markets. Here, forms of mass communication (e.g., television) are not as available as in urban markets and literacy rates are low, so companies must rely on visual ads, retailer relationships, and shelf-space displays. The cost per contact of rural promotions is four to five times higher than that of comparable urban promotions, but the investment may be worth making, since growth of the rural personal care and household product market is estimated to be three times that of the urban market. One of the most ingenious modes of rural customer education and advertising in India is Video on Wheels (VOW). VOW vans with a screen mounted on the roof or in the vehicle's rear drive into villages, usually blaring film music. There they show entertainment features interspersed with commercials. Colgate, which used VOW to air thirty-minute infomercials and distribute free toothbrush and toothpaste samples to rural residents, estimates that VOW helped double toothpaste consumption in rural India in the 1990s. Partly because of its significant cost, VOW has been used primarily for stimulating trial use rather than for more basic recurrent advertising.

Regardless of the advertising form used, marketers must effectively address the diversity of India's consumer market. They must consider the number of languages spoken in the country. According to the 2001 Indian census, more than 50% of urban consumers speak Hindi or English, but nine other languages are spoken by more than 2% of the population, or by at least 20 million consumers. As a result, companies developing national ad campaigns often film ads in three basic languages (English, Hindi, and Gujarati) and then record voice-overs in several other languages. For enhanced effectiveness, ads must be reinforced at the retail level by shop owners, largely because getting consumers to try a product is the main challenge for market entry.

Best Practice: Developing Grassroots Marketing Efforts

Leading companies created a market for consumer durables, especially for new products such as microwave ovens, through education and grassroots marketing. A market shaper often reaps advantages in terms of brand recognition and consumer insights that help it stay ahead of the competition. For example, microwave ovens have traditionally had very low penetration levels in India. Most Indians place a high value on home-cooked meals and therefore do not see a need for a microwave. To generate demand in this category, Godrej launched a nationwide educational campaign. It gave free product demonstrations and cooking demonstrations to let consumers learn firsthand about microwave ovens. Each microwave oven came with free microwave-safe cookware as well as an Indian cookbook, which included recipes from famous local five-star chefs. Godrej also advertised its products in Indian lifestyle magazines. The company's intimate knowledge of Indian cooking habits—coupled with a directed, educational marketing strategy—led to increased sales and market share in this growing category.

Product Delivery: The Distribution Challenge

In a country of more than one billion people, most of whom live in rural areas, distribution presents unique challenges that have been used to create competitive advantages. India's lack of infrastructure makes distribution one of the most critical variables for India in our marketing mix framework. India has two dozen cities with more than one million residents each, and the majority of India's population resides in rural villages. These facts suggest that the long-term growth of the consumer market depends heavily on MNCs' ability to reach the rural segment.

The dichotomy between the urban and rural populations underscores the need for manufacturers to take a two-pronged approach in India, aiming to reach these two very distinct consumer segments. The large urban centers lend themselves to an autonomous distribution system directed by the manufacturer, using a network of distribution centers and distributors ("stockists") to ensure placement of the manufacturer's goods in the retail channel. Stockists, who can be affiliated with manufacturers or independent, operate in localized territories and act as the conduit to the retail trade for several FMCG manufacturers. They have acute knowledge of their local marketplace and maintain strong relationships with each independent retailer in their territory, allowing MNCs sufficient reach in the highly disaggregated and predominantly independent retail circuit.

The distribution of packaged goods to rural villages requires one intermediate step in the distribution network. India has more than six hundred thousand villages, 44% of which have fewer than five hundred people each. Stockists cannot efficiently reach all of these villages. Instead, they pass along their goods to independent wholesalers, who are equipped with high-capacity trucks that can store mass quantities of goods from a wide variety of manufacturers. These wholesalers travel from village to village and act as a mobile retailer, effectively expanding the vast reach of FMCG manufacturers and making a wide variety of necessary goods available to the people of remote villages.

The consumer reach of a multinational FMCG corporation in India depends on how broadly established the MNC's operation is in India. MNCs new to India have initially targeted consumers within the urban centers and eventually expanded to more remote locales as they evolved along the life cycle to maturity. For example, HUL and P&G, each boasting a consistent presence in India for several decades, have penetrated the consumer market from the bustling urban center of Mumbai all the way down to the most remote villages of rural India. Gayatri Yadav of General Mills India notes, "General Mills is relatively new to India (since 1994) and has thus far focused efforts on building distribution and brand

equity in urban centers in western India." This evolution of distribution networks for MNCs closely follows the path of profits. In
other words, MNCs are first attracted to the urban markets, where
they can set higher prices and navigate the retail network more
easily. Once saturation is attained in urban markets, they progress
down the profitability pyramid toward more remote areas with
more complex distribution requirements and less profitable pricing
scenarios. This evolution results in diminishing profits, further
emphasizing manufacturing and cost efficiencies to drive earnings.

While distribution networks are a competitive advantage for
established MNCs such as HUL and P&G, the wide availability of
local expertise and talent makes the development of a broad-reaching
distribution network for less-established firms less daunting. One
HUL executive has suggested that effective proprietary distribution
networks can be established in approximately three to five years.
Given the initial focus of MNCs on urban markets, this time frame
should easily suffice for developing internal distribution networks to
smaller or rural markets before saturation of urban markets occurs.
Alternatively, firms may choose to use existing networks of independent stockists and wholesalers if they see no advantage to developing
their own distribution systems. While the costs and logistics of
distribution remain a challenge, new entrants to the Indian market
will find it easier to distribute their products to rural consumers
than MNCs did a decade ago. However, they may find it more
difficult to establish the local ties and presence in rural communities that early-moving MNCs have built up over the years.

Consumers in rural environments have personal relationships
with the owners of their local mom-and-pop retailer; the majority of
them do not have the means to travel into the cities to obtain their
durables. LG developed a penetrative distribution strategy that ensures
products are available even in smaller towns and cities, breaking the
trend of urban dependency that plagues most white-goods manufacturers. In fact, a significantly higher percentage of its sales came
from nonurban sources than the industry average. LG achieved this
success by setting up a pyramidal sales structure that encompasses
fifty-one branch offices in larger cities, eighty-seven central offices in
smaller towns, and seventy-eight offices in even more remote areas.

Best Practice: Create Distribution Network Capabilities

Indian consumers place a good deal of faith in their retailers, and families often buy most of their goods over many years from the same retailer. The retailer not only recommends goods but also prescribes goods. Furthermore, because the rural population accounts for 70% of all Indians and is growing at a rate of 25% per year, it is clear that developing an extensive distribution network will be extremely important in the coming years. More than 50% of growth for FMCG companies will come from rural and semi-urban segments by 2010.

Companies like HUL, ITC Limited, and Colgate have good distribution networks. HUL's model, based on an intricate network of small-scale stockists, gets goods on shelves in even the most difficult-to-reach places. For instance, with the stockist's aid, HUL can deliver products to remote areas without road access, often relying on donkeys. The stockist develops relationships with retailers to take their orders, stock their shelves, and merchandise their products. Thus, use of stockists affords HUL better distribution breadth and depth, as well as better control over pricing.

Conclusion

Facing saturation of the premium Indian consumer segment, MNCs and large local companies have focused increased attention on the 67% of the consumer market that has previously not been considered significant. In terms of volume and growing incomes, these consumers have significant purchasing power, representing a substantial market opportunity. Many estimates suggest that the mass market's rural segment, the majority of the market, is growing at least three times faster than more-urban segments. And the growth of India's economy renders the mass market more accessible than ever. But companies wishing to penetrate this market face significant challenges. To understand mass-market consumers, they must recognize this group's cultural and psychographic features, many of which differ widely from those of Western consumers. For example, Indians' emphasis on family ties is very strong, and they are simultaneously price sensitive and brand seeking, resulting in an overwhelming focus on value for money. Although increasing numbers of Indian consumers, especially younger ones employed by MNCs, are willing to spend impulsively, the predominant financial mind-set is oriented toward saving. Marketers must also address India's cultural and linguistic diversity, adapting products, packaging, and marketing to a variety of groups with disparate preferences and practices.

To promote trial use, MNCs must engage in extensive consumer education, especially in rural areas, where household goods taken for granted in the West (e.g., toothpaste and shampoo) are still relative novelties. Companies may leverage established and newer education vehicles in this regard, but a thoughtful approach is required, given the complexities of accessing and penetrating rural markets. Similarly, TV has led to greater access to the mass market via advertising.

Even when companies have strong manufacturing and marketing capabilities, their success in India depends largely on distribution. Distribution challenges include the fragmented retail universe, expensive and wide-ranging provincial taxes, and poor infrastructure. To address these challenges, creative distribution models, including the use of stockists and direct-to-wholesaler selling, have emerged.

As India's economy has bloomed and consumers' purchasing power has increased, new retail formats have arisen, including the Western-style mall, department store, and supermarket. The proliferation of such outlets has made India's urban retail landscape resemble that of the West more than ever before. Organized retailing in urban markets will help drive demand for premium products and increase value growth, but it is rural regions that will drive consumption with higher penetration. Already, urban areas are experiencing changes in social dynamics because of the growth in retail. In addition, media penetration has brought an escalating awareness of brands and lifestyle products to tier 2 cities, resulting in a gap between aspiration and availability. With the rise of hypermarkets and malls, rural areas will be exposed to global trends, consumer packaged goods, and consumerism. As these changes sweep across the vast tracts of rural land between the country's major cities, increasingly savvy consumers may well make or break the fortunes of the many global and domestic players seeking their rupees.

Notes

1. Nandini Lakshman, "India's Rich Get the Personal Touch," *BusinessWeek,* July 2, 2008, http://www.businessweek.com/globalbiz/content/jul2008/.

2. Niti Bhan and Brad Nemer, "Brand Magic in India," *BusinessWeek,* May 8, 2006, http://www.businessweek.com/innovate/content/may2006/id20060508_952455.htm.

3. Megha Bahree, "In Pictures: Microsoft's India Lab," *Forbes,* September 10, 2008, http://www.forbes.com/2008/09/10/.

4. *BusinessWeek,* "Nokia's Big Plans for India," August 31, 2007, http://www.businessweek.com/globalbiz/content/aug2007/.

Bibliography

Ahluwalia, K. Montek Singh. 2006. Personal interview, March.

Bahree, Megha. 2008. "In Pictures: Microsoft's India Lab." *Forbes,* September 10. http://www.forbes.com/2008/09/10/.

Banerjee, Rajiv. 2006. "The Importance of Being Traditional." *Economic Times,* April 20.

———. 2006. "Traditional Trade Channels Still a Draw for Retail Biggies." *Economic Times,* October 26.

Bharadwaj, V. T., Gautam M. Swaroop, and Ireena Vittal. 2005. "Winning the Indian Consumer." *McKinsey Quarterly* (September). http://www.mckinseyquarterly.com/.

BusinessWeek. 2007. "Nokia's Big Plans for India," August 31. http://www.businessweek.com/globalbiz/content/aug2007/.

Businessworld. 2004. "Chain Gangs," October 25.

Chatterjee, Purvita. 2006. "Pillsbury in India." *Foodie Rant,* May 31. http://foodierant.blogspot.com/2006/05/pillsbury-in-india.html.

Economic Times. 2006. "Retailing: Electronic Bazaar to Have In-House Brands," April 21.

———. 2006. "Retailing: Retail Chains Eye Strategic Investors," April 13.

———. 2005. "Brand-Equity: Shoppers Without Borders," March 16.

———. 2005. "Indian Kitchens Make Microwaves," February 6.

Economist. 2005. "Growing Pains," April 16: 54–55.

Ernst & Young. 2006. "The Great Indian Retail Story," April 19.

Financial Times Limited. 2006. "In Retail, Wins Are at Back-End," June 1.

———. 2005. "Spencer's, Smarter," October 27.

Godrej & Boyce Manufacturing Company. 2007. http://www.godrej.com/.

Gupta, Rakesh. 2006. Personal interview, March.

Hindu Business Line. 2005. "Retail Boom: FDI Can Give the Extra Thrust," May 27.

Hindustantimes.com. 2005. "Small Screen: Bust or Burst?" January 22. http://www.hindustantimes.com/.

ICRA. 2005. *Consumer Durables Research Report, 2005.*

Jain, Kuldeep P., Nigel A. S. Manson, and Shirish Sankhe. 2005. "The Right Passage to India." *McKinsey Quarterly* (February). http://www.mckinseyquarterly.com/.

KPMG International. 2005. *Consumer Markets in India—The Next Big Thing?* http://www.kpmg.fi/Binary.aspx?Section=174&Item=2249.

Lakshman, Nandini. 2008. "India's Rich Get the Personal Touch." *BusinessWeek,* July 2. http://www.businessweek.com/globalbiz/content/jul2008/.

LG Electronics. 2007. www.lgezbuy.com/.

Motwani, Shyam. 2006. Personal interview, March.

National Council of Applied Economic Research. 2004. *India Rural Infrastructure Report.*

Signapore Economic Development Board. 2007. "P&G Looks to Win Over Asian Consumers by Meeting Basic Needs," January 11. http://www.sedb.com/edb/sg/en_uk/index/.

Sukumaran, Suresh. 2006. Personal interview, March.

Vietor, Richard H. K., and Emily J. Thompson. 2004. *India on the Move.* Watertown, Mass.: Harvard Business Publishing.

Chapter 2

THE PROMISE OF ORGANIZED
FOOD RETAIL IN INDIA

Leslie Carroll, Eileen Chao, Philip Cooksey,
Diane Gojkovic, Michael Rosskamm

The Indian retail industry is in the midst of unprecedented change—a retail revolution. India has the highest density of retail outlets of any country in the world—twelve million outlets— yet the vast majority of the retail sector consists of unorganized vendors. In fact, compared with the retail sector in other emerging economies, India's is dramatically underdeveloped. Modern, organized retail accounts for just 3% of total retail in India— compared with 20% in China, 40% in Thailand, and 85% in the United States. That is about to change. Existing retail chains have begun to aggressively expand their retail operations throughout the country, and deep-pocketed players like Reliance Industries have entered the market in a big way. Organized retail sales, currently only a small fraction of the total retail landscape, were estimated at $25 billion in 2008. However, analysts expected that figure to grow 30% for the next five years, reaching more than $90 billion by 2013, owing to significant changes in economic and demographic factors and a relaxing of foreign direct investment regulations. This growth is primarily fueled by a growing consumer base—more than 600 million by 2010—and rising consumer spending. These conditions lead many industry observers to predict that India's retail sector will be the fastest growing globally over the next five years, pushing India past Russia as the top retail investment destination among the top thirty world emerging markets.[1]

The retail revolution is driven by the growing wealth and disposable incomes of Indian consumers, a demand for convenience, a faster-paced lifestyle, and an increasing consciousness and concern about the health and quality of products. Correspondingly, diverse retail formats are emerging to offer Indians across all segments a unique combination of service, price, and choice to accommodate their new lifestyle goals. Heavily concentrated in the large urban centers, organized retail can take on many faces—from single-brand stores to open-air malls, from traditional grocery stores to hypermarkets and bazaars. It is this area that the world's eyes are on, watching how the sector will develop over the next five to ten years. But while the maturing of organized retail will undoubtedly have a positive impact on quality, pricing, production, and distribution across all retail segments, there are numerous challenges for retailers in this developing industry. These challenges include public and political pressure against organized retail and liberalization of the industry, a fragmented supply chain with innumerable intermediaries, a complex sales tax regime, inhibiting property regulations, and cultural and regional spending differences that impede the growth of uniform, national retail formats. In the face of these constraints, it is critical for retailers to make the right decisions concerning locations, operations and scale, and diversification in order to gain both substantial market share and profits.

In this chapter, we look at recent trends and various retail formats that are emerging in organized retail. We discuss various challenges that retailers confront in the changing marketplace and examine how major national players, such as Reliance, Pantaloon Retail, and Subhiksha Trading, have driven innovation in organized food retail and have shaped the future of the industry.

Indian Retail: A Can't-Miss Opportunity

Historically, social and political conservatism has encouraged tremendous resistance to change in the retail industry. Foreign direct investment (FDI) has been restricted in the retail trade to private-label, high-tech, and medical items. Because of these strict regulations, multibrand international retailers have not been able to enter directly into the Indian market. However, in 2006, 51% FDI was allowed in single-brand retailing, and in just a couple of years, the urban marketplace has become filled with single-brand retailers as companies scramble to reach the massive population base. A variety of stores selling everything from food (e.g., McDonald's and KFC) to apparel (e.g., Nike and Chanel) have taken hold, and their impact is highly visible in the retail landscape. Currently, Indian regulations allow multibrand retailers to enter only through franchises and in the cash-and-carry segment, where retailers provide a business-to-business channel for other retailers and other companies. Despite these restrictions on companies, the Indian retail market—deemed a can't-miss opportunity—has recently seen the entry of several companies that are determined to leverage what opportunity there is.

The Retailing Legacy

Traditionally, retailers in India have been either small, localized operations known as *kirana* stores—which sell perishables and provisions—or mobile retailers (pushcart vendors), who primarily sell fresh foods. The *kirana* network has been the mainstay of Indian retail for more than one hundred years, and it still dominates organized retailing. An estimated twelve million *kirana* stores exist in India today, and they constitute 96% of all organized retailing. They usually occupy less than 550 square feet, operate on a small scale, and offer a limited range of merchandise. They are typically family owned, run by independent entrepreneurs who maintain personal contact with customers, and have virtually no bargaining power with suppliers and merchants. *Kiranas* operate with extremely low overhead costs. The real estate is "free," since most *kiranas* are extensions of houses. Labor costs are low because *kiranas* are typically managed by family members on shifts. The *kiranas'* operational strengths include a no-cost home delivery service, an ability to cater to impulse buying on short notice, early opening and late closing times, and a willingness to extend informal microcredit in the form of monthly bill settlement. Most importantly, *kiranas* have strong roots in their communities. They have a clear understanding of local consumer needs and offer a high level of customer intimacy, which strengthens customer loyalty.

Emerging Formats and Major Players

Although organized retailers began appearing in India in the early 1990s, they showed little growth during the next decade. Throughout the 1990s, organized retail added only one million square feet of space per year as consumers remained tied to their local *kirana* stores. However, the pace of growth increased significantly after the new millennium began: in 2003 the retail industry added an estimated ten million square feet of space, and more than sixty million square feet between 2005 and 2008. Increased international media penetration, favorable real estate opportunities, falling interest rates, increased availability of credit cards, a booming Indian economy, and sharply increasing consumer spending have fueled the growth of national retailers and sparked investors' optimism for the Indian retail sector.

Traditional markets are making way for convenience stores, supermarkets, hypermarkets, and department stores. Western-style malls have been set up not just in the largest metro areas but also in the tier 2 cities. These different formats have introduced the Indian consumer to a wide variety of shopping experiences. At one end of the organized retail spectrum are specialty and department stores. These aim to provide a luxury, service-based shopping experience for their clientele, who tend to be more focused than other consumers on apparel and personal care and less concerned about pricing. Specialty stores for books, apparel, health-care products, home furnishings, and electronics are proliferating, and they often cater to shoppers' aspirational impulses. For instance, with its air-conditioning, wide aisles, and modern designs, Shopper's Stop creates a luxury shopping experience for its customers. Catering primarily to the upper middle class, Shopper's Stop emphasizes service. It hires college graduates for frontline sales staff and creates value through its customer loyalty program. Customer intimacy will remain most important for the high-end market, as lifestyle customers will continue to demand service-oriented, upscale outlets. Thriving on customer loyalty, high margins, and cachet, specialty and department stores will form a small, profitable sector of the overall retail industry. However, it is the food and grocery retail sector that has attracted the largest investments and has experienced the most dramatic growth.

Convenience Stores and Supermarkets

Food and grocery retailers are the staple of retailing, accounting for 75% of overall retailing value sales. Until recently, however, organized food retailing had experienced a concentration of growth in southern India, through food retail chains in Chennai, Hyderabad, and Bangalore. With rising investment in this sector, chained grocery stores are now on the rise throughout urban India. Convenience stores and supermarkets offer the greatest competition to the *kiranas,* as they are usually located directly in residential neighborhoods and compete directly with *kiranas* on convenience and price. Newly opened stores attempt to attract shoppers with higher-quality fresh foods, with special low prices on basic items like grains or flour, and with extended business hours.

While independent retailers accounted for almost half of retail sales in 2007, giants such as Reliance Retail, Pantaloon Retail, Bharti Retail, and Subhiksha Trading Services have pursued aggressive national rollouts of new retail outlets, substantially increasing their retail space. Until 2008, when it found itself overextended during the global economic downturn, Chennai-based chain Subhiksha Trading Services ran India's largest chain of supermarkets, pharmacies, mobile stores, and vegetable stores. It had set up more than sixteen hundred stores across the country since 1997. Bharti Retail is planning to invest $2 billion to $2.5 billion by 2015 to set up retail outlets in supermarket and hypermarket formats pan-India.

Hypermarkets

Indian hypermarkets are perhaps the most westernized retail format in India and the most radical departure from traditional shopping habits for Indian consumers. These warehouse-style, big-box retail stores are closely modeled after their American counterparts, often offering more than 150,000 square feet of shopping space, airy layouts, a wide selection of groceries, fresh food, and nonfood items (such as kitchen equipment, consumer electronics, and clothes), discount prices, concessionaries, and inviting coffee bars.

What makes hypermarkets such a departure for Indian retail, however, is less their merchandise than the shopping habits they call for. Indian consumers are used to buying small quantities of groceries and fresh food frequently and locally, in their immediate neighborhood, or even having them delivered directly to their own doorstep. Convenience shopping has been ingrained into Indian consumers' psyche for generations. Hypermarkets, however, require consumers to travel to less-than-convenient locations, which—given the ever-congested roads in urban areas and the lack of infrastructure in rural areas—can be a time-intensive undertaking. While enterprising auto rickshaw operators offer transportation to and from hypermarkets, some commentators maintain that the majority of Indian consumers would not buy from hypermarkets even if a free shuttle bus took them there. Yet, while consumer surveys show that Indian consumers purchase relatively fewer perishables than groceries, beverages, frozen foods, and nonfood items in hypermarkets, operators and market observers attest to healthy traffic and sales in many hypermarkets. However, analysts are also concerned that lower incomes in rural areas and tier 2 cities and high land costs will make it difficult for hypermarkets to achieve Western-scale profits.

These concerns notwithstanding, five national retailers are operating hypermarkets and are rapidly expanding the format beyond the metros to tier 1 and 2 cities. Pantaloon Retail, the country's biggest retailer and a subsidiary of Kishore Biyani's Future Group, now runs more than 100 Big Bazaar hypermarkets in India (up from twenty-four in 2006) and is adding new hypermarkets every month, primarily in nonmetro areas. Together with

Pantaloon's 150 Food Bazaar supermarkets, these outlets generated revenue of $720 million in fiscal year 2007 to 2008 (a 60% increase over the previous year) and are estimated to reach almost $4 billion in the next three to four years, according to Biyani.

Cash-and-Carry

A few international retail chains, particularly Wal-Mart and Metro, have decided to seize the opportunity to enter the Indian retail market through the less-regulated cash-and-carry segment. In 2007, Wal-Mart began joint operations in India with Bharti Retail to enter the cash-and-carry market. While Bharti Retail is a 100% owned supermarket chain, it will be supported by Wal-Mart's logistics and supply chain technology through a franchise agreement. The fifty-fifty joint venture between Bharti and Wal-Mart will be a wholesale cash-and-carry business that will use Wal-Mart's back-end logistics technology, inventory systems, cold chain infrastructure, truck tracking, and fuel management. The German Metro Group entered the market in 2003, when it set up two distribution centers (about 110,000 square feet each) in Bangalore. Since then, Metro has opened cash-and-carry stores in Hyderabad, Mumbai, and Kolkata.

Growth of Alliances and Partnerships

While the cash-and-carry segment has seen a number of high-profile partnerships between foreign and Indian companies, strategic alliances play an important role in the other segments too. For example, the Indian conglomerate Tata has indicated that it also is looking to set up supermarkets in India, partnering with the Australian retail giant Woolworths. Tata subsidiary Infiniti Retail is already working with Woolworths on a cash-and-carry basis and is considering expansion into other formats. Bharti Retail is also looking at partnering with existing local store owners across India through a franchise model. Pantaloon Retail has joined hands with ITC Limited for the food and grocery business. ITC, which operates a retail chain of Choupal Fresh stores for both wholesale and retail of farm-fresh produce, will help Pantaloon get a much-needed rural presence and provide direct linkages to farm products. In exchange ITC will be able to expand into urban areas.

The retail boom is just the beginning of future opportunities in India. Foreign companies are lining up, waiting for the government to take the next step in expanding foreign direct investment to multibrand stores. Anticipating such changes, foreign companies are working to develop active partnerships with Indian companies to gain a foothold. The Bharti–Wal-Mart partnership is a prime example of such an alliance. If regulations change, however, the nature of the market will change drastically: relationships like Bharti's with Wal-Mart may become obsolete, and many foreign players will try to enter in a big way. This situation will add to the already sizable investments made in the Indian retail industry and will have significant consequences for the current players. Unmistakably, as competition increases, strategic alliances between firms providing capital, expertise, and reach will remain invaluable in helping to counter challenges facing the industry.

The Retailing Challenge in India

There are numerous challenges retailers have to overcome to profitably grow their business in India. These challenges primarily relate to sourcing, infrastructure, politics, and labor. It is necessary to look at those challenges and examine their implications for retailers.

Consumer Behavior and Expectations

Many countries have seen their economies develop and their retail sectors go from small one-off shops to large national players. India is expected to follow that route, but the largest roadblock to that effort lies within the hearts and minds of Indian consumers. For many years, Indian consumers have been shopping in specific ways. They know their local shop owners and turn to them for delivery services, credit, and convenience. If the large national players want to win over these customers, they are going to have to fundamentally change the buying habits of a substantial portion of the population. For many Indian consumers, organized retail involves a full cultural shift. Indeed, some market observers suggest that for a large part of the rural population, shopping in one of the new, bright, handsomely equipped, and bountifully stocked retail stores will remain for some time to come an alien and uncomfortable experience such consumers would rather avoid.

Major national retailers have recognized the challenges of changing consumer habits and aim to present consumers with an appealing value proposition that balances the novelties and benefits of modern retail with the convenience and familiarity of traditional retail. These marginal steps are a good way to accustom consumers to a new way of shopping. Pantaloon's Big Bazaar and Food Bazaar stores, for example, try to emulate the layout and atmosphere of traditional bazaars by presenting many products in the open at stalls, allowing customers the familiar "see-touch-feel" shopping experience. Even the highly westernized HyperCity stores offer Western-style prepared luxury foods side by side with typical Ganesh figurines.

While some Indian consumers may be reluctant to shop in modern retail establishments, a large section of the population is ready to embrace modern retail to satisfy their newly developed shopping aspirations—and they demand low prices, high quality and availability, and a broad selection of merchandise. Thus, to attract both the reluctant and the demanding consumers, large retailers will need to leverage their scale to drive merchandise costs down, broaden their assortments of SKUs, and increase stock turns. Lower costs of retailing, combined with better choice and quality, can be of clear benefit to the value-conscious Indian customer and stimulate demand.

Sourcing

Generally speaking, large national retailers rely on large national suppliers to stock their shelves with products. At present, suppliers in India are not consolidated, and no national players have emerged. In food retail and perishables, the supply chain connecting farmers to existing organized and unorganized retail is highly inefficient: it includes several intermediaries and manual handling, which lead to high wastage and low remuneration for the farmers. In addition to wastage, the number of intermediaries means produce travels slowly, leading to markups, loss of quality, and inefficiency. This situation makes it difficult to run an efficient national retailer, and it hurts all supply chain partners' margins. One opportunity for large national retailers is not only to reduce their own procurement costs with their negotiation power, but also to lower logistic costs and increase margins for their partners by consolidating the supply chain and improving its efficiency. According to a recent study, organized retailing could increase farmers' incomes by as much as 37%, lifting families out of poverty.

Without larger suppliers, however, such opportunities are difficult to seize. Other options exist for national retailers, but none of them has proved effective yet. Regional suppliers are an option, but they complicate coordination of product offerings and back-end operations. Global sourcing—importing merchandise from large foreign suppliers—is another option; however, in many product categories, the Indian consumer has not sufficiently warmed up to global products (see chapter 1). Besides, stringent import rules can make global sourcing difficult and expensive.

Infrastructure

Infrastructure in India has been inadequate for large-scale retail expansion. Carl Nordenberg, a shopping center developer with JJ Gumberg, explains that in approaching the Indian shopping center market, his firm has had to plan and pay for various contingencies it has not had to deal with in other countries. JJ Gumberg is currently planning to build all of its centers in India with its own water and power supplies, to keep its projects from shutting down. In addition, JJ Gumberg has had to develop the roads in the immediate vicinity of their centers to ensure that they remain accessible. These infrastructure issues complicate the building of centers and raise costs. Moreover, Nordenberg notes that, although corruption has declined, the efficiency of the public-service sector is dismal, resulting in project delays and making large-scale retail rollout very difficult.

Despite these problems, however, India is witnessing explosive growth in retail real estate, at an estimated rate of more than 300% from 2005 to 2007. While some analysts are concerned that the current "mall mania" will result in an oversupply of retail space—in vacant and ultimately failing malls and shopping centers—national retailers are scrambling to sign every square foot of space available now or soon. And despite the three-digit growth of retail square footage, available land in convenient locations—close to or in residential areas—remains a bottleneck. Pantaloon Retail alone has signed approximately 25% of all modern retail space that is expected to become available until 2009.[2] National retailers' ambitious growth plans often even outpace the rapid growth of retail space: Reliance had to reschedule its expansion plan because of development delays for some of the spaces it had optioned for. A few national players, such as Reliance, try to work around these limitations by acquiring and converting existing retail outlets.

Most of India's top retailers, such as Pantaloon and Reliance, already employ sophisticated distribution and logistics systems, including real-time inventory planning, replenishment, and tracking. However, real-time notification, while valuable, cannot fully compensate for the infrastructure deficiencies that make transportation difficult—and for the underdeveloped logistics systems farther upstream in the supply chain with merchants and farmers. To complicate logistic issues further, as retail expands beyond tier 1 cities into diverse regions of the country, individual outlets must accommodate the distinct cultural, religious, and linguistic features of each region. Different stores will demand small lots of specialized products, and successful retailers will have to find a cost-effective way to source and transport these goods. How to source an ever-widening variety of goods and deliver them to an increasing number of outlets will become an important consideration as retailers determine where to locate both their stores and their distribution warehouses. While major retailers invest heavily in facilities and infrastructure, public investment in transportation infrastructure is required in the long run, to further enhance efficiency of organized retail throughout India, especially in the rural areas.

Political Environment

FDI in retailing remains a heated issue in India. Wal-Mart's planned foray into India was accompanied by protests from small-store owners and political parties. However, opposition that was mainly restricted to FDI and the entry of multinationals has shifted to domestic business houses. With chained grocery retailers opening small stores in residential neighborhoods, the major impact has been felt among the traditional food retailers. The market share of these independent small shops has been eroding in favor of the major organized retail stores since the mid-1990s. That trend is likely to accelerate, given the massive expansion of retail space by the major national retailers. The strong growth in organized retailing in 2006 to 2007 was met by public opposition, especially in tier 2 cities and rural areas.

Such opposition is one of the main reasons that the relaxation of foreign direct investment restrictions is likely to be slow. Many independent shopkeepers, street vendors, and middlemen in the distribution chain expect that the move to organized retail and the growth of chain food retail will destroy their livelihood, and they have made their interests clear to their elected officials. Some politicians have used these concerns as a political platform, but such populism remains sporadic. Many within the government recognize that for India to keep pace with the rest of the world, liberalization must occur, and the benefits will accrue over time. Under pressure from both Indian and international businesses to open up retailing, the central government is unlikely to impose restrictions on retailing or retailers. It may impose zoning restrictions for grocery retailers as well as for hypermarkets in residential areas. It is currently exploring possibilities of allowing FDI in multibrand retail in just a couple of sectors, like electronics and sporting goods, where opposition is expected to be lowest.

Lack of Trained Manpower

As organized retail grows, more than a million people (and an additional 1.5 million, including back-end operations) will need to be hired and trained to staff the new retail ventures. According to the consulting firm Technopak, this number is only representative of the direct employment by the retail sector. Modernization will create additional demand for jobs staffing warehouses, supply centers, and transportation routes. While the employment creation potential of modern retail is very high, it poses a significant challenge in terms of access to such high numbers of trained manpower in such a short time period. A key issue facing chained retailers is the availability of manpower—from shop floor to senior management personnel. Only 5% of India's population was employed in retailing in 2007, and few people had specialized knowledge of retailing. In addition, with senior management moving from one competitor to another, turnover is high. Given the limited pool of talent, this turnover is likely to remain high in the near term. Attrition rates in the sector are at 40%, and staff costs at large companies have nearly doubled over the past year. Retailers will need to examine their human resource management policies to offer training, career progression, and incentives. As employment opportunities are growing, more and more retailers are indeed providing training. Still, while retail growth will provide training of the middle segments of the labor force in the long run, the lack of skilled personnel is likely to remain an issue for some time to come.

The Entry of Reliance into the Food Retail Market

Reliance Retail has been a major player in the Indian retail landscape since its entry into the market in 2006. Since then Reliance has launched a number of retail formats: convenience stores, hypermarkets, and specialty stores for electronics, apparel and jewelry, books, and health and wellness products. The company pursues a multibillion-dollar investment strategy to create almost 2,000 supermarkets and 500 hypermarkets across India. It plans to capture 5% of India's severely fragmented retail space by 2010. By 2008, Reliance had established 590 outlets in fifty-seven cities, amounting to 3.5 million square feet of trading space for its Reliance Fresh supermarket chain alone. We will focus closely here on Reliance's rollout of its Reliance Fresh stores—first, because Reliance is the large industrial conglomerate entering the sector, and others are expected to follow; and second, because Reliance's solutions and approaches, especially its supply chain solutions to deal with the unique challenges of retailing in India, are on a much larger scale than the solutions of its competitors.

Understanding the Indian Consumer

One of Reliance's key objectives is to build the brand loyalty of customers early on. It hopes to build a strong brand by providing unprecedented affordability, quality, and choice. It also wants to establish a benchmark of hygiene and quality with its stores and the merchandise. Reliance Fresh offers products that consumers would buy three or four times a week, to increase frequency of visits (some stores carry fresh flowers that are purchased every day). Stores also carry products unique to a region, such as spices. To achieve this level of specialization, Reliance conducts market research and runs pilot tests with various products. For instance, executives never thought precut vegetables would work with the Indian consumer, but a pilot test revealed great success with the product and Reliance introduced it. Contracting with local farms facilitates regional diversity.

In addition, Reliance strives to achieve convenience for the customer through store design. The Reliance Fresh stores are easy to navigate: rather than putting the most desired products at the back of the store (so customers must walk by all other products to get to the product they want), the high-turnover products are placed in the front of the store, to maximize convenience. Prices are set so that bargaining is unnecessary. To create an enjoyable shopping experience, the store is modern and hygienic, and Reliance aims to offer the consumer consistent quality.

All details of design and customer experience are determined very carefully, given that organized retail is such a new development and an unfamiliar experience for the typical consumer. The first several players will be able to exert tremendous influence on how the shopping experience unfolds for the customer. Retail is a very high-touch business, and any company that can define how that experience feels to consumers early on will enjoy substantial gains over companies that enter later and rush to replicate the moves of their predecessor. If Reliance can establish the linkage between its brand and the consumer's shopping experience, then subsequent players in this market will have a much more difficult time penetrating the market and stealing share.

Location

A key element in defining the customer experience is the location of the store. Reliance positioned the Reliance Fresh stores as a neighborhood grocery convenience store. The chain operates small and medium-sized stores, ranging from two thousand to five thousand square feet (supermarkets typically range from eight thousand to ten thousand square feet). According to Jai Bendre, head of food marketing at Reliance, each store aims at catchments of only about two thousand households in a 1.25- to 2-mile radius. Consumers are expected to visit the stores at least twice a week, so the model is engineered to clock a fast turnover of inventory. Consequently, Reliance Fresh stores are typically located right in the middle of residential neighborhoods, often next door to traditional *kiranas*. Given the scarcity of available land and given land development costs, Reliance, like other national retailers, grew some of its retail space inorganically through acquisitions. The company acquired Adani Supermarkets in 2007 and converted the fifty Adani retail outlets to the Reliance Fresh format. To approach smaller towns and villages, Reliance has opened "all under one roof" hypermarkets that spread over fifteen thousand square feet and offer a wide variety of food and nonfood items.

In some regions, Reliance has encountered protests to its store openings. Public and political opposition in Kolkata and in the northern state of Uttar Pradesh, for example, forced the company to adjust its plans for expansion. One approach Reliance has taken to soften opposition is to better integrate its cash-and-carry Ranger Farms stores with the local communities. These stores buy in bulk from the farmers, and in the early-morning hours, they allow street vendors to buy at wholesale prices from the Reliance supply chain, thereby increasing the vendors' margins.

Building the Supply Chain

Reliance achieves quality and affordability by setting up its own integrated supply chain. While its investments currently focus on the front end, its long-term infrastructure goals include building a pan-India supply chain connecting Indian farmers to Indian consumers and to the global market. To this end, Reliance has begun to establish distribution and processing centers that procure directly from the farmers and that grade and standardize produce. As of this writing, Reliance had more than one hundred locations for collection and processing of produce. The company has also been setting up deals with state governments to establish rural hubs to buy fruit, vegetables, pulses, and dairy goods from the farmers. By disintermediating the supply chain and buying directly from the farmers rather than the wholesaler (*mandi*), prices are reduced by at least 15% to 20%, achieving the firm's objective of higher quality at lower prices. While a few hundred farmers supply directly to Reliance, that number is expected to increase to several million, partly through contract farming. According to reports, a quiet revolution is taking place in the countryside as farmers receive higher returns and are seeing the benefits of selling their produce directly to the retail chains. As the supply chain improves, Reliance estimates cost savings to be in the range of 30% to 35% above current levels, particularly for perishables like flowers and vegetables.

In addition to procurement and processing, Reliance uses a precooling infrastructure, including refrigerated vans for transport of perishable products to the retail outlets. This infrastructure significantly reduces loss of produce, which is at around 40% in traditional retail. Reliance is considering using its supply chain and logistic infrastructure to enter the cash-and-carry format and supply to the retail industry at large.

Creating efficiencies in large-scale distribution in turn facilitates mass production for small and medium-sized suppliers. Reliance is identifying geographical clusters—rural business hubs—that would implement farm initiatives and create an infrastructure to collect, process, and distribute products at the district level. The company is planning to set up 1,600 hubs across the country that would provide agricultural inputs, financial services, veterinary care, and education to the farmers.

Staffing

Reliance wants to be known as the partner of choice for Indian farmers and to be known for its attractive employment opportunities. The company expects to employ five hundred thousand staff and create an additional one million jobs indirectly. So far, it has hired several thousand managers for its new stores. To reduce staffing costs and find people to manage and operate its stores, Reliance is turning to couriers, newspaper delivery people, and roadside vendors for its retail operations, as they can be employed at lower salaries than conventional retail staff. Reliance Retail isn't the first company to try to tap such unconventional sources for employees. Pantaloon Retail plans to hire housewives and senior citizens. Spinach, the Mumbai-based supermarket chain, has hired sales staff from among pushcart vendors on Mumbai's streets. Some industry analysts have suggested, however, that training these employees and helping them develop crucial soft skills for customer service could be a challenge.

Next Steps

Most of the national retailers, such as Pantaloon, RPG Enterprises, and Bharti Retail, have aggressive expansion plans and are rapidly opening stores to capture consumer spending. Reliance's major foray into retail seems to signal the beginning of a new wave of major industrial conglomerates entering the retail sector in a big way. After the Future Group and Reliance, Tata has recently announced major expansion plans and investments of about $500 million for its Star India Bazaar chain of large supermarkets.

Reliance now has to ensure its differentiation from the other players while increasing the efficiency of the back-end operations of its stores. It also needs to fix the remaining glitches in its supply chain management. For instance, in India's hot summer, Reliance has found it difficult to ensure the quality of its fresh produce and now realizes that it needs to add more refrigerated warehouses. In addition, Reliance is continuously adjusting and improving the assortment of merchandise offered in its stores. The company is now widening its stock to include more household items across all its stores to compete more effectively with the *kiranas*. Furthermore, Reliance aims to tap into the market for premium food and is in advanced talks for alliances with at least four foreign food companies: United States–based fresh fruit and vegetable suppliers Dole and Chiquita and meat retailers Sadia of Brazil and Doux of France. Such alliances will also give the company access to knowledge of logistics and technology—a critical requirement for a company seeking a larger share of the growing market.

Creating Profitability in the Food Retail Segment

Expansion Across Segments

Most national retailers choose to exist in more than one format, as they seek to capture consumers across multiple customer segments. For example, leading retailer Pantaloon owns the lifestyle-oriented department stores Pantaloons and Central as well as value-oriented Big Bazaar hypermarkets and Food Bazaar supermarkets. It has also made an entrance into wholesaling through a business-to-business format modeled after Wal-Mart's Sam's Club. Similarly, Tata-owned Trent attempts to service both the lifestyle category, with its

Westside department stores, and the mass market, with Star India Bazaar. To expand into new formats and offer a wider variety of products, retailers have actively scouted for joint venture opportunities and acquisitions. Bharti Retail is also opening smaller stores, larger front-end stores, and the cash-and-carry with Wal-Mart. On the heels of the announcement of the Bharti–Wal-Mart joint venture for wholesale cash-and-carry, Reliance Retail announced its plans to enter the same business segment, supplying to *kirana* stores and institutional buyers.

According to Gibson Vedmani, chief executive of Retailers Association of India (RAI), "Food and grocery retailing normally takes around three to five years to break even, and scaling up becomes difficult if the retailers lack the wherewithal."[3] The financial strain these aggressive scaling efforts puts on companies has been most visible with Subhiksha. Formerly one of the largest retail chains in India, Subhiksha grew frenetically from 150 stores in 2006 to more than 1,600 stores in 2008, and it grew its sales more than tenfold to $800 million in the same period. This expansion, however, burdened the company with a 22:1 debt equity ratio and depleted the company's cash reserves. In December 2008 Subhiksha sent the majority of its employees on leave without pay, defaulted on its rent and supplier payables, and has since been attempting corporate debt restructuring.

The Rise of Private Labels

Historically a value-conscious society, Indians are becoming increasingly susceptible to both private and international brands. While the introduction of premium brands like Levi's and Arrow has been successful at the department store or lifestyle segment of retail, private-label products have also been quite successful. Trent's department stores sell almost exclusively its own "quality at a reasonable price" Westside-branded products. This trend is now gaining traction in the food retail segment.

Nearly half of the fast-moving retail products in India are food items, and more than half of these are unbranded, including perishables like fruits and vegetables. This situation holds great potential for retailing—to brand such products and sell them through large, organized retail outlets. Most of the chained grocery stores are introducing their own private labels. The Reliance Fresh stores sell products under the premium food brand Reliance Select. This brand covers pulses, rice, spices, and vegetables.

Pantaloon's hypermarket, Big Bazaar, and supermarket, Food Bazaar, expanded their private-label offerings to products such as detergents and soaps, and they are expanding the number of categories overall. Big Bazaar, for instance, will soon launch thirty-nine more categories under its food brand Fresh and Pure. Star India Bazaar uses private labels to reach out to its most price-conscious customers. Bharti Retail plans to sell the products of relatively unknown small manufacturers under its own private labels.

Indian retailers have not yet positioned themselves to excel in product leadership. Even at the department store level, Pantaloons and Shopper's Stop, which have strong private brands, compete most effectively on price, not product. Only Trent, with its own in-house design team, has successfully created a differentiated, value-oriented product offering with its Westside brand. As the Indian middle class continues to grow, private branding could give new entrants into the market a competitive advantage.

Loyalty Programs, Store Credit, and Promotions

Beyond branded products, however, retailers are attempting to brand their outlets' shopping experiences as well, styling themselves as either weekend destinations or one-stop shops. Whether to each store's brands or experience, consumers have begun to demonstrate loyalty toward particular outlets. Savvy retailers have fostered this loyalty with the introduction of programs that offer reward points and discounts for repeat visits. Shopper's Stop's First Citizen Club is the largest loyalty program in Indian retail. Pantaloon offers loyalty programs for its different retail store formats.

Another approach to attract consumers to a particular chain of stores and foster their loyalty is a store credit card program. Big Bazaar

stores have introduced a "Shakti Credit Card" exclusively for housewives in association with ICICI Bank. Pantaloon Retail is currently
considering such an approach to tap into the 60% bottom of the
pyramid (BOP) consumer segment in India. The company argues
that most BOP consumers currently pay a 100% to 200% "poverty
premium" on the products they consume and would thus benefit
immensely if store credit enabled them to shop at lower prices at
Pantaloon outlets. Such a credit program would credit new business
for Pantaloon Retail and for its parent's financial services subsidiary.

Finally, retailers have devised innovative promotion schemes to
lure customers to their stores and counter the recent surge in food
prices. Subhiksha aimed to adapt an "everyday low price" policy,
Big Bazaar ran promotional schemes such as offering discounts on
a customer's food bill, and Spinach was introducing weekend offers
for products whose prices have shot up significantly.

Lowering Procurement and Supply Chain Costs

With Reliance's big push into building its supply chain infrastructure, other retailers are also looking into integrating their back-end
supply chains. Wadhawan Retail—owner of Spinach, Sabka Bazaar,
and Home Store formats—is now integrating its back-end supply
chain into a single entity. Although Pantaloon, recognized as a
dominant player in the Indian retail industry, has developed mainly
the nonfood sourcing infrastructure, it is now trying to strengthen
its sourcing infrastructure for its hypermarkets and supermarkets.
New players are emerging to become suppliers to the chained grocery
stores. For instance, ITC Limited is entering into partnerships with
other retailers to supply their fresh produce needs. It was also the
first organized retailer to establish fresh vegetable and fruit supply
chains through partnerships with smallholder farmers. In addition,
chained grocery stores such as Big Bazaar and Food Bazaar are
focusing on lowering procurement costs through purchase volumes
as they expand the number of outlets.

As many national retailers dramatically increase their number
of retail outlets, many will probably need to shift their investments

from the front end to the back end, to improve operational efficiency and lower costs. Reliance, for example, has set itself comprehensive infrastructure goals to better connect Indian farmers to consumers and the global market, to construct distribution centers, and to improve its cold chain of refrigeration vans and warehouses for perishable products. An increasing number of companies will probably attempt to disintermediate their supply chain or integrate backward within the grocery/produce sector to facilitate the integration and efficiency of their suppliers' operations.

Expansion into Tier 2 Cities

The six largest Indian cities account for 66% of total organized retailing, but aggressive expansion is under way in other tier 1 and 2 cities to attract new customers and benefit from more-favorable real estate conditions. As industrial-use conversions and reasonable rents become increasingly scarce in larger cities, tier 2 cities become more attractive. With the economic boom in India spreading to tier 2 cities and towns, reaching out to prospective consumers in these cities is high on the agenda of most retail companies.

Retailers consider market presence in these cities and towns to be key to their growth and profitability. In addition, media penetration has led to a gap between consumers' aspirations and availability of products. For instance, even RPG's lifestyle-oriented Spencer's stores, currently spread across twenty-five cities in India, are now moving aggressively into tier 2 and 3 cities. To get over the property challenge, retailers are also looking to franchisees to help scale up their business in smaller cities.

Conclusion

A fundamental lesson of a growing market is that companies can grow largely without direct competition with each other; a rising tide lifts all ships. For instance, according to Business Monitor International (BMI) estimates, hypermarket sales are set to increase by a phenomenal 260% (to $1.35 billion) by 2011, thanks to the expansion efforts of existing players and new market entrants alike, while supermarket sales will witness growth of 132.9% (to $1.63 billion). Such projections suggest that there may be sufficient room for national retailers to grow profitably without having to steal share from one another. When asked if Bharti's foray into retail was late vis-à-vis its competitors, Bharti's chairman and CEO Sunil Mittal said that India offered huge potential: "Even six to seven years down the line, no one player will be able to dominate the Indian retail market."[4] However, this may not remain the case for too long: at the Indian Retail Forum in 2008, some retailers said they were beginning to feel the rising competition and a resulting dilution of catchment areas in urban locations.[5] However, most national retailers' focus will not be on establishing niche markets, but will be on simply capturing as much of the overall growth within the different geographical areas and consumer segments of the market.

Given a market whose growth can support the entrance of numerous players, it is only natural for many companies to enter. This situation will likely spur development and improvements more rapidly than if only a few companies were operating. It will foster creativity in design and execution of the retail formats and provide the consumer with a greater variety of shopping options. Eventually, however, there will be a shakeout as the market starts to mature. Inefficient investments and weak execution will give way to companies with stronger operational effectiveness, larger financial resources, and properly tailored alignment between strategy and operations.

As the organized retail sector grows in the next five years, the impact will also be felt in industries connected with retailing, such as agriculture and consumer goods manufacturing. Improvement to the retailers' back-end infrastructure will significantly reduce the 40% produce spoilage rate for perishables, and costs will be reduced for suppliers, retails, and consumers alike. Competition in the retail industry will increase availability and variety throughout, and it will encourage suppliers and manufacturers to innovate and provide more-differentiated products. Furthermore, as more retailers become organized on a large scale, supplier power will decrease and larger retailers will be able to counter food price inflation. In a time of rising food prices, they can help combat inflation more effectively than local vendors and can devise innovative ways to battle the surge in food prices. Through bulk buying and offsetting losses in perishables with profits made on other products, big retailers can consistently offer fruits and vegetables at 15% to 20% lower (30% to 40% for vegetables) than local vendors can.

Given the value proposition of modern retailing, Indian consumers may thus find their loyalties shifting soon. While the *kiranas* and local vendors will continue to play an important role in Indian retailing, the lure of lower prices, better quality, and wider selection offered by larger retailers may be more attractive than the convenience of proximity and the customer rapport that local vendors have thus far relied on. Retail giants like Pantaloon and Reliance are certainly making it their business to deliver on this value proposition and to usher in the era of modern, organized retail throughout India.

Notes

1. George MacDonald, "Indian Store Chiefs Are Divided over Arrival of Foreign Retailers," *Retail Week,* September 15, 2006.

2. Pantaloon Retail (India), Investor relations presentation, May 2, 2006, http://www.pantaloon.com/investore_presentation.pdf (accessed March 22, 2009).

3. Quoted in Saumya Roy and Sagar Malviya, "Tata Plans Supermarkets with Woolworth's," July 5, 2007, LiveMint.com, http://www.livemint.com/2007/07/05002943/Tata-plans-supermarkets-with-W.html.

4. *Economic Times,* "For Bharti–Wal-Mart, Three Isn't Crowd," March 7, 2007, http://economictimes.indiatimes.com/retail-rush/For-Bharti-Wal-Mart-three-isnt-crowd/articleshow/1751331.cms.

5. Hemant Patel and Akhil Kejriwal (Enam Securities), Indian Retail Forum 2008, analyst report.

Bibliography

Asia Economic Outlook. 2007. "The History and Future of India's Retail Sector," February 9.

BBC News. 2006. "Wal-Mart to Enter Indian Market," November 27. http://news.bbc.co.uk/.

Bharadwaj, V. T., Gautam M. Swaroop, and Ireena Vittal. 2005. "Winning the Indian Consumer."*McKinsey Quarterly* (September). http://www.mckinseyquarterly.com/.

Bharti Enterprises. 2007. "Bharti Announces Strategic Roadmap for Its Retail Venture," February 19. http://www.bharti.com/.

Business Monitor International. 2007. "Bharti Confirms Wal-Mart Plans," April 1.

Business Standard. 2006. "Reliance Retail Eyes Pan-India Footprint in 5 Yrs," November 4.

CNN Money. 2007. "India's Bharti Eyes Big Expansion, Wal-Mart Deal," February 19. http://money.cnn.com/2007/02/19/news/international/.

David, Ruth. 2007. "Carrefour Near Indian Deal." *Forbes,* February 2. http://www.forbes.com/markets/2007/02/02/.

Economic Times. 2007. "For Bharti–Wal-Mart, Three Isn't Crowd," March 7.
———. 2006. "Reliance Fresh to Open Its Doors from Nov 3," October 30.

Euromonitor International: Country Market Insight. 2008. "Retailing—India," April.

Financial Express. 2006. "Reliance Opens a 'Fresh' Chapter in Retail with Outlet in Hyderabad," October 30.

Financial Times Limited. 2005. "Foreign Direct Investment: India," January 5. http://www.fdimagazine.com/news/.

Gupta, Vikram. 2007. "India at 60: Retail and the Indian Economy." *South Asia Monitor,* no. 108 (July 5). http://www.csis.org/media/csis/pubs/sam108.pdf.

Hindu Business Line. 2006. "Reliance Kicks Off 'Fresh' Retail in Hyderabad," October 28. http://www.thehindubusinessline.com/2006/10/29/.

Hindustan Times. 2007. "French Retailer Geant Sets Up Mumbai Store," April 17.

Jain, Sunil. 2006. "Cash 'n' Carry: Bharti Style." *Rediff.com,* December 4. http://www.rediff.com/money/2006/dec/04/.

MacDonald, George. 2006. "Indian Store Chiefs Are Divided over Arrival of Foreign Retailers." *Retail Week,* September 15.

Madaan and Company. 2007. "Sector Specific Foreign Direct Investment in India: FDI in India," April 20. http://madaan.com/sectors.html.

Mishra, Mridula, and Umakant Dash. 2008. "Importance of Retail Service Attributes: A Case Study of Indian Consumer." *ICFAIAN Journal of Management Research* 7 (2).

Mumbai, Sagar. 2007. Streets to Shops: Reliance Retail to Hire Courier, Paper Delivery Boys." *Wall Street Journal*, June 20. http://www.livemint.com/2007/06/.

Pantulu, Chitti, and Sindhu Bhattacharya. 2006. "A Fresh Start for RIL Retail." *Daily News and Analysis*, October 29. http://www.dnaindia.com/.

Pradhan, Debasis, and B. K. Mangaraj. 2008. *Reliance Fresh Stores in Food Retailing*. London: London Business School. http://www.london.edu/assets/documents/facultyandresearch/Reliance_Fresh.pdf.

Reuters. 2007. "Wal-Mart, India's Bharti 'Very Close' to Deal," February 23. http://www.reuters.com/.

Roy, Saumya, and Sagar Malviya. 2008. "Tata Plans Supermarkets with Woolworths." *Wall Street Journal*, June 3. http://www.livemint.com/.

Sarma, M. K. 2000. "Some Issues in Retail Management in India." *Vision* 4, no. 1:35–40.

Sinha, Piyush Kumar, Arindam Bannerjee, and Uniyal Dwarika. 2002. "Deciding Where to Buy: Store Choice Behaviour of Indian Shoppers." *Vikalpa* 27, no. 2:13–27.

Sudhir, Agrawal, Bhatia Monica, and Kalra Rameesha. 2008. "Organized Food Retail Is More Effective Than Unorganized Food Retail for Customer in India at the Time of Sky Touching Inflation." *IndianMBA.com*, May 17. http://www.indianmba.com/Faculty_Column/.

Times of India. 2006. "Reliance Fresh Set to Debut in Hyderabad," October 30. http://timesofindia.indiatimes.com/.

Tribune India. 2007. "Reliance Fresh Gets Industry's Support," September 3. http://www.tribuneindia.com/.

Tuhina Pandey. 2006. "Reliance Launches Retail Stores." *NDTV*, November 3. http://www.ndtvprofit.com/.

Vora, Hiral, and Himangshu Watts. 2006. "Reliance to Invest $5.6 Billion in Retail." *Reuters India*, June 27.

Zeenews.com. 2006. "RIL Unveils First Retail Format Store Brand," October 29. www.zeenews.com/.

Chapter 3

TOWARD A CREDIT-DRIVEN CONSUMER CULTURE: CREDIT CARDS' INFLUENCE ON THE INDIAN LIFESTYLE

Anwei Li, Krista Plaisted, Cara Sylvester, Megha Vora

With a population of 1.1 billion people, rising per capita incomes, and a rapidly growing middle class whose consumption patterns represent a marked departure from traditional consumer spending behavior, India is certainly well positioned to embrace massive credit card growth. In fact, it's no surprise that India has become the third-biggest card market for Visa International in the Asia-Pacific region, after Japan and Korea, and is among the fastest-growing markets for Visa in the region. According to GE Money—which was formed when GE Capital partnered in 1998 with State Bank of India, India's largest public-sector bank—the size of the Indian credit card market is growing at 35% annually, and spending is expected to grow 50% annually over the next four to five years, according to an article in *BusinessWeek* (February 23, 2006). Maninder Kohli, vice president of Citibank India, also highlights growth in individual wealth and disposable incomes, liberalization, job creation, and increased consumer spending as factors that "have led to the annual double-digit growth in the number of credit cards issued in India since 2000." The outlook continues to be optimistic. Unquestionably, growth of the credit card market could bring in its wake greater transparency within the Indian economy and a shrinking of parallel economies. It could also make payments more efficient and cost-effective both domestically and globally. Industry growth will enable Indian consumers to borrow more easily, which in turn will generate greater consumer spending and economic stimulus.

However, all is not what it seems with the blue-skies forecast. While credit card issuance has been growing at impressive double-digit rates, penetration has been extremely low, and, not surprisingly, restricted mainly to the wealthy and the middle class in the metro areas and tier 2 cities.

Consider that the United States has around three hundred million cards for a population of 280 million people. Compare that with the number of credit cards issued in India at the end of 2007, which was only twenty-five million—a penetration rate of less than 2% of the Indian population. We are immediately struck with the number of consumers that still remain out of reach (even when we discount approximately 60% of the agrarian rural population not targeted by credit card companies).

Naturally, issuing and acquiring banks are aggressively trying to take advantage of this amazing opportunity for expansion and to maximize this growth potential. Industry players have realized that they have to come up with creative solutions to increase penetration and reach market segments that have not been focused on before. Key providers are faced with a complicated set of challenges if they want to take advantage of this aggressive growth environment. As we shall see, some of these challenges are typical of cash-based economies in developing countries and some are unique to the Indian culture and mind-set. This chapter explores the following issues: the key factors that have kept penetration at such low levels despite an environment conducive to growth; the impact of new players entering the credit card business, which has until recently been dominated by multinationals; the specific marketing strategies and expansion tactics used by key players to increase merchant acceptance and reach different target segments to differentiate themselves; and finally, the urgent need for more standardized/regulated risk assessment tools that can facilitate information sharing across the industry to facilitate growth of the credit card market.

An Environment Conducive to Growth

An Urban Population Acclimatized to Electronic Payments

In contrast to the fast but limited growth in credit cards in India, debit cards have experienced far greater growth in a much shorter period. Debit cards, which were first introduced in India in 1999, are attributed with fueling India's card market. According to a report by the Economist Intelligence Unit (EIU), as of January 2007, there were around seventy million debit cards, making up nearly 75% of the payment cards that are currently issued. The primary reason for this is because it is much easier to qualify for a debit card than for a credit card, since all that is required is a bank account. Approximately 150 million people in India have some sort of bank account, making the current market potential for debit cards much larger than that for credit cards. Most banks offer free debit cards to customers that open personal bank accounts. These debit cards can also be used as ATM cards.

Interestingly, while there are nearly four times as many debit cards as credit cards in India, debit cards are still used mostly for cash withdrawals at ATMs rather than for purchases. Banks have been pushing ATM usage aggressively because of the administrative cost savings for banks and convenience to customers. According to the EIU, there were more than twenty-one thousand ATMs across the country in March 2006—more than seven times the figure in 2001. And in the last few years, the point-of-sale (PoS) usage of debit cards has dramatically increased, and it is expected to continue to increase. Debit cards are viewed as the tool for getting consumers used to the concept of electronic payments, since more people are eligible for debit cards than for credit cards, and even consumers who are averse to credit can still use debit cards since payments are instant. As the EIU report notes, although the volume of credit cards is lower, the volume and value of transactions are nearly five times higher than that of debit cards—estimated at about Rs 335 billion (US$7.5 billion) in the first ten months of fiscal year 2006 to 2007. Prepaid cards are also on the rise, as Indian consumers are generally debt averse. The growth of e-commerce is also fueling the growth of this segment, as prepaid cards provide greater safety for transactions on the Internet.

Rising Consumerism and an Organized Retail Market

Specific consumer trends are playing a significant role in the astonishing growth of India's credit card market. In addition to the rise in consumer spending—primarily due to the rise in personal income and the growth of the middle class—India also has a large, relatively young, educated population that is drawn to the consumerism found in younger generations in the West. In fact, 50% of India's population is under age twenty-five, and this population has more disposable income than ever before. Since most of the individuals in this segment still live at home, their income becomes largely disposable income.

Additionally, India has seen tremendous growth in the organized retail market, as shopping malls and retail stores are being developed in most of the major cities. With liberalization has come increased availability of foreign and domestic consumer goods and greater affordability. Organized retail has been one of the key drivers of increased consumer spending. As a result, "Credit cards are riding the boom," says Rajiv Lochan, analyst at McKinsey & Company, a management consulting firm. Consumerism has increased credit card usage and acceptability. Yet another trend is the rise of retail consumer finance. Retail consumer finance is still relatively nascent, being only four to five years old. "Customers are [still] relatively ignorant in terms of their financial needs, but the area of retail consumer finance is very much growing as both consumers and businesses are still exploring different market opportunities," says Lochan.

Why Is Penetration Persistently Low?

Despite these consumer trends, a complicated nexus of institutional, merchant, consumer, and cultural factors has historically kept penetration at low levels. First, because India has primarily had a cash-driven economy, no personal credit bureaus existed until recently. Consequently, it was very difficult to quantify an individual's creditworthiness, and very few individuals had sufficient documentation to qualify for credit.

Second, because credit card growth has been limited to major metro and tier 2 cities, merchant acceptance, while growing at double-digit percentages, also remains relatively low and limited to the tier 1 and 2 cities. Cost has also been a significant challenge to merchant acceptance. Most merchants in India are still small family businesses, which may not see the value in accepting credit cards and may not see how credit card sales could balance out the costs for the PoS terminals and transaction fees, especially since most of their customers are still not demanding to pay with credit. In addition, few merchants currently pay taxes, and credit card receipts would create a sales record that could be used by tax authorities.

A report by India's National Council of Applied Economic Research notes that India remains an overwhelmingly cash-based economy, with more than 90% of personal consumer expenditures made with cash or check. There are a number of reasons for this. Technological advances in the banking sector, which have made electronic payments easier and more economical, have only been recent. Indeed, some of the smaller cities are still not wired for the necessary terminals for card transactions, as electronic payment systems are relatively new to India

In addition, the underground economy—the unregulated, informal portion of the economy that produces goods and services for sale—is still very much present in India. This situation has led to substantial tax evasion by Indian consumers and small businesses. As Lochan points out, "Roughly only 2% to 5% of the Indian population pays taxes." Because such a large tax-evasion culture exists, many consumers and small businesses are still reluctant to use electronic payments, which are traceable and leave a clear audit trail. The government has recently taken various initiatives to hold both individuals and businesses accountable, requiring tax returns if more than a certain amount is spent and tracked on a credit card, as well as taxing goods that more and more people now own, such as cell phones.

Finally, Indians have traditionally had an aversion to the idea of credit, valuing thrift and frugality. Although attitudes on the concept of credit have been changing rapidly as more and more individuals have been making larger purchases that they once could not afford (e.g., cars and homes), credit aversion is still an issue to many Indian consumers. The current credit card market in India consists primarily of the upper middle class, which, because of tax implications, uses credit cards mainly for large purchases. However, because of the rapid growth in wealthy and middle-class households, as well as in the number of young adults, the potential customer base is expanding and challenging traditional values. This growing affluence is likely to erode the aversion to credit.

Thus, while credit card companies have positioned themselves for expected growth and changes in consumer behavior due to growing affluence, they continue to grapple with several challenges: difficulty establishing credit eligibility, inadequate infrastructure outside of tier 1 cities, a strong underground economy, and a desire to stay below the tax radar in a population that has traditionally been credit averse. We see next how the various players compete for shared space, try to implement innovative solutions and marketing strategies to deal with these persistent challenges, and provide a host of incentives to encourage use of credit cards where people would ordinarily favor cash transactions.

The Changing Competitive Landscape

In the past, multinational banks had the strongest and largest presence in India's credit card industry. Diner's Club introduced the first credit card in India in 1980, and the card remained the only one until Citibank took it over in 1990 and launched Visa and MasterCard.

While Citibank has historically led the credit card market in India, primarily targeting the upper educated classes in tier 1 cities, in the last few years domestic banks have also gained tremendous ground, and they are competitively positioned to capture market share in smaller Indian cities. The private domestic banks have offices throughout India; the most prominent players include ICICI Bank, Housing Development Finance Corporation (HDFC), and Bank of Baroda. Among the public domestic banks, which are government owned, the most prominent player is State Bank of India (SBI). Citibank's Kohli notes that although ICICI currently leads the market in terms of number of cards, Citibank still leads the market in terms of card spending. In the last few years, the domestic players have been very aggressive in acquiring new card members.

One reason that domestic players have been so successful and are expected to increase penetration substantially is that they have more bank branches and a much larger customer base throughout India than the multinationals. Local banks are located in both the larger and smaller Indian cities, while multinational banks are primarily located only in the largest cities. Consequently, domestic banks' presence throughout India is much stronger, which has allowed them a larger client base for retail banking. To increase reach, they are now focusing on advertising and promotions, a trend unheard of in India a few years ago. These banks are currently penetrating the middle class throughout tier 1 and 2 cities, and credit card penetration in midsize cities in India, though low, is increasing. The public bank SBI is consolidating its presence in tier 2 and 3 cities, where it is rolling out new ATM terminals.

Thus, expansion tactics and marketing strategies vary among different players in the industry. We will see how large multinationals are focusing on product and portfolio management to offset marketing barriers owing to traditional bottlenecks, while domestic private and public banks focus largely on volume and distribution.

Gaining Market Share, Increasing Card Usage, and Battling Bottlenecks

Product Diversification Versus a "One Card Fits All" Strategy

Product diversification is a priority for the large foreign players and less of a priority for the domestic banks. All the large players (both domestic and multinational) are attempting to move toward offering a large variety of different cards to cater to increased segmentation and targeting of consumers. They have realized that one card does not fit all in India, and the rising segments have reacted positively to the more targeted marketing techniques. Research by McKinsey & Company has indicated that Indians in their twenties and thirties are far more likely to consider credit than older generations have been. Banks are therefore using a variety of marketing tactics specifically to target the up-and-coming youth of India as well as growing middle-class segments.

As competition for the same market increases, one key initiative that credit card companies in India have undertaken is overall product line expansion, particularly with cobranded cards. This strategy has been enormously successful in encouraging higher credit card usage across several segments. Most of the card-issuing companies now have cobranded credit cards—primarily with airlines, petroleum companies, and retail stores—as they aggressively try to differentiate themselves. Cobranding implies that a card is branded with a particular company that may offer some sort of reward to the cardholder (e.g., miles, discounts, or reward points) according to spending. Currently, the most widely used credit card in India is SBI's card cobranded with the Indian Railways. With more than fourteen million passengers per day using the railway in India, many travelers use the card to buy their daily train tickets. Other popular cobranded cards include the Citibank Jet Airways Card (a card cobranded with India's leading airline) and the Citibank Indian Oil Card (a card cobranded with the largest provider of fuel in India). These cobranded cards have fairly specific target markets (e.g., consumers aged eighteen to twenty-one who are interested in music), and the response of consumers has been overwhelmingly positive. Issuers are also moving toward new segments, such as grocery chains, hospitals, and utilities, as the new launch pad for growth within the cobranding market. Similar to cobranding, another popular marketing technique used by card issuers is the use of affinity cards, which are branded with the name of a charity. Typically, a donation is made to the charity based on a percentage of card spending. For instance, Citibank launched an affinity card with a popular NGO, the Child Relief Fund. Cobranded cards have been doing extremely well and have been instrumental in fueling growth in the industry.

Companies have also started offering "premium" cards for the upper-tier Indians who have owned credit cards for longer periods of time. Large multinationals are focusing their product suite on specific gold and platinum cards similar to the premier cards that exist in the United States today. Similar reward structures exist, such as travel assistance and cash-back rewards for high-volume users.

Two smaller product areas gaining acceptance in the marketplace are corporate and international cards. Corporate cards were the driver of growth in 2006, with the strongest presence in this area by foreign banks. Issuers have also begun to focus on issuing international cards because of increased international travel by Indian consumers. Government regulations, lifted in 2003, abolished restrictions that prevented Indians from using international credit cards for travel expenses. So far, only the large multinational banks and large Indian banks—private and public—have entered these product areas aggressively. Most travel cards are prepaid, and with the growth in overseas travel, the prepaid travel card is expected to compete strongly with traveler's checks.

Most private Indian banks, however, have not yet tackled the premium segment and continue to have the "one card fits all" mentality. They focus on volume of cards (market share) rather than breadth of product suite, because for these smaller players, trying to appeal to different segments is far too costly.

The "Findability Issue": Locating Consumers Who Fit the Market Segments

As marketing becomes more sophisticated and more easily segmented into specific targets, there is still the issue of how to locate the individuals who make up that segment. Given the increasing push toward a diversified product offering, one of the most pervasive issues the industry faces is what Anil Vinayak, vice president of account management for MasterCard, refers to as the "findability issue." The issue is that there is no unique identifier for an Indian citizen, so it is very difficult to locate a particular segment of the market. For instance, frequent travelers are relatively easy to locate, as marketers can use frequent-flyer information from the airlines to locate these individuals. But as Vinayak points out, beyond the obvious classifications, it becomes very difficult to locate individuals.

Most credit card firms in India at least use a basic income classification breakdown to segment and target their population. In addition to basic income classification, marketers within most issuing and acquiring banks use the socioeconomic classification (SEC) to segment their markets. This is an internationally recognized economic classification that breaks down individuals according to educational level and occupation. For instance, a credit card company may decide that it would like to target postgraduates who are self-employed and have one hundred or more employees. The groups SEC A and SEC B represent educated urban consumers, making up nearly six million households in sixteen cities. According to Streamline India, a domestic consulting firm, more than 75% of SEC A and B homes live in eight cities of India and receive the greatest attention regarding trendy and lifestyle products. While this is a very attractive market for credit card companies, there are still challenges in actually locating these people. The industry has established the India Cards Council—a group of major banks and credit card issuers—partly to tackle this findability issue.

Vinayak also points out that within the SEC, credit card companies have historically targeted only SEC A (ten to fifteen million households), which is the top segment in India, consisting primarily of salaried employees. The SEC A market is fairly saturated at this point, and companies are trying to move into SEC B (forty to fifty million households), which consists of a higher number of self-employed individuals, who are more difficult to locate. Because of the findability issue, many credit card companies, especially the domestic players, have resorted to a "one card fits all" mentality, as the psychographic cards are simply too costly to market.

In addition to using income level, education, and occupation to segment and target markets, many companies are also beginning to use geographic segmentation to move from tier 1 cities into tier 2 and 3 cities, because credit card issuers view the tier 1 markets as fairly saturated and are looking for new and creative ways to penetrate the tier 2 market. The major multinational players in the industry are focusing heavily on about thirty top cities, but they are extending their reach. Indian banks have an advantage in this area because they have a greater presence in some of the smaller cities.

Grappling with Distribution

Distribution is a current challenge within the Indian credit card industry, owing to the lack of penetration beyond tier 1 cities as well as to several infrastructure challenges. Because of inefficiencies in the postal system, unreliability of the telephone network, and extremely limited access to the Internet, banks cannot rely solely on traditional means of marketing in India. Therefore, credit card issuers must resort to fairly primitive means of marketing.

Most of the issuing banks employ direct sales agents (DSAs) to conduct the majority of their sales activities. DSAs are contracted employees who go door-to-door attempting to persuade Indian consumers to sign up for a credit card. Multinationals also employ a smaller in-house sales team that focuses on the upper-tier, premium card market. While these strategies are not ideal, McKinsey's Lochan does not see any infrastructure changes occurring within the next several years that would strengthen the Indian postal service and therefore open up direct mail marketing. Additionally, since Indians are used to the personalized door-to-door sales techniques, Lochan was not even sure that the typical Indian consumer would understand the direct marketing techniques.

Because of these marketing challenges, portfolio management is gaining momentum in the industry. While many of the domestic banks continue to focus on gaining market share, many of the multinationals are focusing on how to strengthen relationships with their current customers. Large multinational banks have instituted a "supply and demand" management system within their portfolio management group. On the supply side, they are wrestling with whether they should be issuing second cards to their current cardholders or doubling the cardholders' credit limit. On the demand side, they continue to look at various promotions to urge their cardholders to use their cards more often. For instance, Citibank launched an initiative offering cardholders cash loans up to their credit limit. Currently, card companies are focusing on increasing card use—by educating cardholders and promoting card use—rather than on increasing the number of cards in circulation.

Dealing with Debt Aversion

Because of India's natural aversion to debt, a large proportion of cardholders pay their credit card balances, so that only 35% to 40% of credit card issuers' revenues are generated from revolving balances (i.e., interest margins). Moreover, with the Indian aversion to credit-fueled consumption, the average expenditure per card is relatively low. In fiscal year 2007 to 2008, the monthly average expenditure per card was only Rs 4000 ($87), although up from Rs 1500 ($32) three to four years ago. Historically, the low revenue from revolving credit has meant an increased emphasis on annual and vendor fees. This, in turn, has created new challenges, because Indian consumers are very hesitant to pay additional fees. Because of increased competition in the industry, for many types of credit cards, banks no longer charge an annual fee. Consequently, the focus has shifted toward other sources of revenue.

Since only a small share of revenues comes from revolving balances and reduced fees, and because banks rely on a small proportion of cardholders to generate income, credit interest rates are very high. Cardholders who make large purchases can pay for these over a period of time through equated monthly installments (EMIs), on which the interest rate is lower than the normal credit card rate. Reports on interest charged have varied from 24% to 30%, which can soar to more than 50%, while charges for late payments can be as high as 20% of the overall balance.

The shift away from large fees has particularly affected some foreign multinationals. According to Kohli, "These banks are turning toward other sources of revenues, such as focusing on premium product lines and cross-selling tactics." Cross-selling is becoming more and more important, especially for the large multi-nationals within the industry. Citibank, for instance, has launched a new initiative to promote cross-selling of credit cards to people who have either a mortgage or another personal loan with Citibank. This new sales technique has had tremendous success, and other multinationals are also employing the technique.

To combat the pricing issues within the industry, many of the large players have started examining their operations for ways to streamline them and increase efficiencies. The credit card industry has traditionally maintained all of its operations in-house, competing primarily on economies of scale. Currently, the large players in the industry do all processing in-house, except for that done by DSAs. This situation has made it somewhat difficult for smaller banks to enter the market. But companies like Venture Infotek, a consumer payment processor, have begun to provide transaction processing services that would allow credit card companies to outsource some of their more expensive operations. With economies of scale, companies like Venture Infotek can process transactions more cheaply than an individual bank. The emergence of this type of company, Lochan notes, has begun to change the playing field, because the bigger companies can no longer compete on lower operational costs alone. Smaller players are actually pioneering outsourcing by contracting certain services, such as collections, to an external agency. To remain competitive, banks are slowly moving toward this outsourcing mentality. Third-party transaction processors (i.e., back-end processors) like Venture Infotek are now becoming more prevalent within the industry. For instance, ABN AMRO, one of the smaller multinationals, pioneered the use of the third-party processor in their partnership with Electronic Data Systems India (EDS India), a technology services company.

The India Cards Council: Coming Together to Combat Barriers

Even as they compete for the same market, major banks and credit card issuers have realized the importance of sharing information to meet the challenges of growth. One step that MasterCard in India took to deal with some of the pervasive issues within the industry was to develop the India Cards Council (ICC). The ICC was founded in 1992 by MasterCard, and currently nearly all major banks and credit card issuers in India are members. The few who are not members are banks not yet using the MasterCard network. The ICC meets quarterly to discuss noncompetitive issues that can help to promote the industry's growth—issues including the need for a credit bureau, a common "do not call" registry, and best practices in emerging credit card categories. The ICC was responsible for creating the first negative file in 1999, and it continues to tackle the tough issues in the industry to unite all parties in pursuing sustained growth. Nitin Gupta, head of MasterCard India, spoke of the ICC as one of the "key initiatives in the industry which is knocking down barriers and fostering continued growth."

Developing a Merchant Network

Although growing quickly, overall merchant acceptance of credit cards in India is still low. Over the past few years, the number of PoS terminals in India has grown significantly, and by 2006 it stood at 306,000—roughly ten times the number in 2001. Yet as Monica Agrawal, vice president of strategic alliances at MasterCard India, points out, these merchants are concentrated in the top twenty cities (although some form of payment card is now accepted in at least 150 towns and cities).

When a bank creates a new credit card, it must first decide which of the acceptance networks, Visa or MasterCard, through which to issue the card. Banks then acquire card customers and merchants who will accept the card. Acquiring banks sell PoS terminals to the merchants and charge a per transaction fee, or merchant discount rate, of 1.1% to 1.7%, which is shared by the merchant and the acceptance network. So far, merchant penetration has been driven primarily by HDFC and ICICI, although Citibank and Bank of Baroda have also played an important role. The largest public bank, SBI, has historically stayed away from merchant acquisitions, riding the current network and focusing on ATMs instead. However, in mid-2007, SBI announced its intention to install one million credit/debit card PoS terminals at retail establishments throughout the country.

The types of credit card–accepting merchants also illustrate where the growth opportunities lie. Current accepting merchant segments are still heavily concentrated in travel and luxury goods, including retail fashion. This fact reflects current cardholders, many of whom are wealthier and can only use their cards while traveling, since their cities may not have accepting merchants yet. However, according to Kohli, this situation is changing. Smaller purchases, as well as insurance, cinema, and direct marketing, are among the fastest-growing categories. In fact, average spending per card has increased because a host of services, such as airline or railway tickets, hotel bookings, and movie tickets can be purchased through the Internet.

Offering Financial Incentives to Increase Merchant Acceptance

To break the cycle of low consumer demand for credit cards due to low merchant acceptance and vice versa, Agrawal argues that acceptance must support issuance. And since the merchant must pay for the PoS terminal, connectivity to the accepting network, and a per transaction fee, banks have to confront the immediate problem of reducing the cost for the merchant to increase acceptance, particularly since there seems to be no urgent demand from the customer to accept credit cards.

Acquiring banks must continue to train sales representatives to grow the number of accepting merchants. To this end, both Visa and MasterCard are supporting initiatives to produce low-cost PoS terminals in India. Visa aided the development of indigenously made PoS terminals with Linkwell Telesystems in Hyderabad. These terminals, which entered the market in 2004, cost about 50% less than imported ones. The cost of PoS terminals will probably continue to drop, primarily because of increased competition for the Indian market. In addition, improved technology in mobile telecom has significantly increased connectivity options for many merchants and lowered costs to increase merchant penetration.

Agrawal also notes that new segments are being targeted and are among the fastest growing, including areas of nondiscretionary recurring expenditures, such as utilities, groceries, medical care and hospitals, insurance, and even taxes. She further notes that MasterCard believes acceptance should be high in these areas, and that acquiring banks should give special discounts and incentives to the merchants involved.

Large international players have already been undertaking specific market expansion strategies to persuade retailers in tier 2 and 3 cities to start accepting credit cards. Both Visa and MasterCard have been running large training and promotion programs in tier 2 cities, such as Mangalore, Jaipur, and Pune. These programs offer free installation and waived fees. E-commerce offers another growth opportunity for the credit card industry, with Indian Railways as the first and largest successful example. Agrawal notes that e-commerce has been growing at a rate of 100% per year as more people gain access to the Internet, yet e-commerce accounts for less than 5% of acquiring volumes. If the trend continues, she argues that, "in the next three years, there may be as many as one million merchants accepting credit cards."

The Problem of Risk Assessment: Developing a Credit Bureau

The vast majority of industry participants agree that the establishment of a trusted credit bureau is essential to accelerate the growth of the credit card industry in India. A growing middle- and upper-class population, coupled with increased availability of high-quality products and services, has created significant demand for consumer credit. Along with this increased demand, however, credit delinquencies have also grown, heightening the need for risk assessment in India's credit card industry. According to Jin Montesano, vice president of GE Consumer Finance in Asia, "The lack of a well-established credit bureau is a big dampener as of now. A start has been made toward establishing a credit bureau, but we are still a long way off from the advanced credit bureaus that we see in the West. There is also the lack of a strong legal framework in terms of collections and recovery of bad debts."

Until recently, Indian lenders had undertaken risk assessment independently, but their assessment was largely flawed because information on total credit exposure was not maintained at any central point. In more-developed credit industries, credit bureaus collect personal financial data on individuals, such as credit history, public records (e.g., court judgments and bankruptcies), and report inquiries (i.e., the number of credit granters who have received a credit report), and sell the information to businesses to help them decide whether to issue credit to an individual and at what rate. According to the Credit Information Bureau (India) Limited (CIBIL), credit bureaus in developed countries have facilitated market penetration of credit to more than 66% of GDP (versus India's current 3%) while keeping nonperforming loans in check. Similarly, comprehensive credit information is required in India to facilitate credit issuance decisions and pricing.

Using Proxies to Assess Eligibility

In the absence of a well-established credit bureau, credit card issuers have established numerous surrogate methods of establishing creditworthiness. Without access to a centralized file of credit risk information on applicants, credit card issuers must use a range of proxies to assess the creditworthiness of individuals. These proxies include salary slips to indicate income levels, income tax returns (limited in usefulness because of the low percentage of Indians who pay taxes), and "lifestyle" documentation (e.g., car or house title, boarding passes, and club memberships). In tier 2 cities, DSAs will often meet credit card applicants at their home before deciding whether to grant credit. While this labor-intensive method has facilitated the initial growth of India's credit card industry, it is clear that a more objective, quantitative, and scalable method is required for the industry to realize substantial growth.

Establishing CIBIL: The First Step to a Credit Rating Scheme

India only recently began to establish a credit rating agency; progress has been steady but slow. The first attempt at an Indian credit bureau was launched in January 1999, when the ICC, the MasterCard-led group for the Indian credit card industry, launched the Negative File Project. Twenty-five MasterCard member banks agreed to contribute to a shared database of cardholders with delinquent balances (i.e., more than 180 days outstanding). While negative information is certainly useful in preventing further credit issuance to high-risk consumers, it lacks the comprehensiveness required for accurate credit ratings. CIBIL was created in August 2000 with a broader goal: "to fulfill the need of credit-granting institutions for comprehensive credit information by collecting, collating and disseminating credit information pertaining to both commercial and consumer borrowers, to a closed user group of Members." While the concept of CIBIL was launched in 2000, the bureau is still in a nascent stage, having only begun collecting consumer information in 2004.

Arun Thukral, CIBIL's COO, is optimistic about the organization's growth, however, noting that it has obtained fifty to sixty million consumer records and attracted 121 members (reportedly 90% of financial institutions in India) in its first year of data collection. CIBIL translates consumer data into credit information reports (CIRs), which member banks can access to make informed lending decisions. Unlike credit reports in developed countries, a CIR contains only subjective information and does not classify any accounts as default accounts or attempt to comment on whether credit should be granted. While Thukral admits that a rating system is an essential component of CIBIL's future strategy, broadening access to consumer data is a higher priority. This access will contribute to the historical data that will be an input into a future rating scheme.

Ensuring Future Growth

The future growth of the credit card industry hinges on the ability of India's credit bureaus—whether CIBIL or a competitor—to overcome significant challenges. First, data quality must improve to gain the trust of both lenders and consumers. The quality of information provided by a credit bureau can only be as accurate as the quality of data entering the system. While India's technology infrastructure is certainly improving, many banks are still moving toward a comprehensive and centralized data collection system for retail banking customers. Thukral highlighted the extreme example of SBI, a bank with nine hundred thousand customers spread throughout the country: many SBI branches still use a paper-based system to record transactions. While centralizing data within one bank is challenging, centralizing it across banks is even more challenging, since India has no unique identifier (such as a social security number) that can be used to link a consumer's information across institutions. This issue is magnified by many consumers' practice of splitting their savings among multiple bank accounts to minimize tax liabilities. The introduction of a national identification system in India would remove a significant roadblock in developing a thriving credit bureau, but it is wrought with logistical challenges.

Second, value-added services must be introduced to transform the raw data into usable decision-making inputs. Once the data reach a sufficient level of accuracy, credit bureaus must establish value-added products to interpret the data and facilitate efficient lending decisions. For example, CIBIL plans to add customized/ generic scoring, default probability/prediction products, and risk/ profitability models to further their relationship with their credit-granting partners.

Third, fraud prevention measures must be further implemented to increase data accuracy. Credit card fraud is increasing in India. Until recently, consumers could be denied credit on the basis of their credit report but had no way to access or refute any information in the report. To counter potential unfairness in credit assessments, the RBI issued a ruling in April 2006 to allow customers to access their credit history as maintained by credit information companies. In addition, the RBI will require that credit-granting institutions send denied credit applicants a written rejection notice including reasons for rejection and a copy of the credit report within thirty days of the decision.

While S. Santhanakrishnan, CIBIL's chairman and CEO, states that banks have already begun using CIBIL's system in a "substantial way" for lending decisions, our conversations with issuing banks and industry analysts indicate limited dependence on bureau information despite strong support for its continued evolution.

Protecting the Consumer: Regulatory Concerns in an Expanding Market

The Reserve Bank of India (RBI), India's central bank, is the primary regulatory body for the banking, debt and securities, and credit card industries. The RBI initially played a relatively benign role regarding credit cards because of the relatively small size of the existing market, but industry experts point out that the RBI is now tightening regulations for nonbanking financial companies (NBFCs) and trying to bring greater transparency to the credit card market.

In 2005, the RBI drafted new consumer protection regulations that prohibited unsolicited credit cards and increasing credit lines without customer consent, required issuing banks to communicate all charges and interest rates clearly, and established a "do not call" list. High interest charges have met with strong criticism from cardholders and consumer advocates such as the Credit Card Holders Association of India, a nationwide group. The Monopolies and Restrictive Trade Practices Commission, the Indian government's trade watchdog, also started investigating card-selling practices of the major multinational and domestic private banks, and in 2007 indicated that Citibank and HSBC had violated RBI guidelines. In May 2007, the RBI issued a warning to all commercial banks against charging "usurious" interest rates and asked them to make sure costs to the borrowers were justifiable.

The head of Citigroup's cards in India, T. R. Ramachandran, commented in an interview that many cardholder problems resulted from a lack of consumer awareness, since many people were first-time borrowers. Consumer education in India was an ongoing challenge, he added. By some estimates, about one in ten credit card accounts in India is written off, indicating that payments on the account are not expected. In the United States, according to Standard & Poor's data, about one in twenty-five accounts is written off. The default rate on credit cards is the highest across different loan categories in India, rising from 7% to 9% of total outstanding payments in 2006 to about 10% to 12% in 2007. Industry analysts attribute this to overleveraging, rising EMIs on existing loans, and an increase in penetration in smaller towns.

Conclusion

Each constituent in the credit card circle faces different challenges. Issuers must figure out how to expand their customer base and understand consumer behavior. Acquiring banks must find a way to increase merchant acceptance. And consumers need to become educated in making electronic payments and become used to utilizing credit for purchases. How and when these challenges are addressed will determine if the industry continues to grow at the same pace or grows explosively.

Clearly, the number one priority in the industry should be to increase vendor acceptance and PoS penetration. Acceptance is a key driver of growth for the credit card industry. Apart from issuing cards to consumers, it is also important to expand the merchant base that accepts these cards. Given that the industry is still a push market (i.e., issuers are reaching out to consumers to sign up for cards rather than consumers reaching out to banks), it is even more critical to have merchants with whom consumers can use their cards. Without greater acceptance throughout the tier 2 and 3 cities and rural areas where credit cards are issued, usage will be limited only to the group of consumers who are wealthy enough to travel and use their cards in other cities. The decreasing PoS and connectivity costs, as well as the expansion to new, nontraditional, and online merchant segments, will drive this expansion, and merchant resistance will decrease significantly. The entry of a large player like SBI on the acquiring side, a player that has ATMs in many cities and could put PoS terminals in these cities as well, would further accelerate the industry's expansion. Currently, merchant acceptance appears to be the bottleneck, and ultimately, we believe acceptance of credit cards by small businesses will drive growth.

Another industry priority is solidifying credit bureau capabilities and establishing a reliable national ID. A national ID would improve credit bureau capabilities in the long run and allow the industry to reach target segments that may be good credit risks but have been hard to find. For now, taxpayers' permanent account number (PAN) and surrogates may suffice as proxies. As banks get better technology and become educated so they are willing to share their information with CIBIL, a huge push could make the underground economy more transparent. However, although CIBIL is very optimistic, most other parties we spoke to are still skeptical about the bureau's immediate effectiveness.

Could the entry of a large player, such as Reliance Communications or Life Insurance Corporation of India (LIC) cause a huge industry growth spurt in tier 2 and 3 cities? Reliance has a strong cell phone network along with a sales force, debt collection process, and bill collection boxes in more than five hundred towns. LIC has 150 million policyholders and one million agents in more than one thousand towns. Given their current infrastructure, these firms could find significant synergies. LIC, for instance, plans to enter into a joint venture with GE Money for the launch of a credit card. Furthermore, back-end transaction processing firms, such as Venture Infotek or EDS, partnering with banks to create low-cost players could lead to a shakeout of the current firms in the industry. Moreover, lowering processing costs could help acquiring banks lower merchant acquisition costs and thus spur growth in merchant acceptance.

In general, industry penetration will trail consumer educa-tion. The shifting demographics in India, with seven million people entering the age twenty to thirty-four bracket every year, present a huge opportunity for the credit card industry. As an increasing number of people shift from the aspiring class to the consuming class, they will become more educated and comfortable with having bank accounts, ATM cards, debit cards, and finally credit cards. Venture Infotek research shows that as cardholders become comfortable with making electronic payments through debit cards, they do start converting to credit cards as well. Consumers will also need to get accustomed to paying taxes, which many believe will become unavoidable as income levels rise and increasing numbers of people own houses, automobiles, and cell phones. All individuals are now required to give their PAN to get a credit card. Indeed, new tax regulation will make tax evasion more difficult for consumers, as credit card spending of more than Rs 20,000 (around $4,400) makes a person a target for taxes. According to Montek Ahluwalia, deputy chairman of the Indian government's Planning Commission, developments in the credit card industry can be viewed as posi-tive, because they strengthen the country's ability to monitor tax evasion.

While it is clear the credit card industry has significant room to grow in India and will likely continue to grow at its current pace, tipping points like those discussed above could boost that growth significantly.

Bibliography

Agrawal, Monica. 2006. Personal interview, March 24.

Alexander, George Smith, and Shweta Jain. 2005. "Swipe War Sweeps Credit Card Mart." *Rediff.com,* January 31. http://in.rediff.com/money/2004/jan/31.

Bansal, Rashimi. 2004. "A New Face of Youth Consumerism." *Businessworld,* June 28. www.businessworld.in/bw/.

Cardbhai. 2007. "Citibank and HSBC Violate RBI Norms," April 25.

Chakravarti, Rita, and Beng-Hai Chea. 2005. "The Evolution of Credit Bureaus in Asia-Pacific." *Citibank Asia Pacific Consumer Bank Regional Business Analytics Unit,* August.

Chatterjee, Paramita. 2008. "Plastic Money Use Jumps 50% in FY08." *Economic Times,* March.

Credit Information Bureau (India) Limited. "The Benefits of a Credit Bureau." http://www.cibil.com/web/benefits.htm (accessed April 2006).

———. "FAQs." http://www.cibil.com/web/faqs.htm (accessed April 2006).

———. "Overview." http://www.cibil.com/web/overviewin.htm (accessed April 2006).

———. 2006. "RBI Allows Bank Customers Access to Credit Profile," February. http://www.cibil.com/web/press_room.htm.

Dayal, Somesh. 2006. Personal interview, March 24.

Economic Times. 2006. "India 3rd Biggest Market for Visa in Asia Pacific," June 17.

Economist Intelligence Unit. 2007. "India: Charge It," April 17. http://globaltechforum.eiu.com/index.

Euromonitor International. 2007. "Financial Cards in India," March.

Financial Express. 2006. "Economy—Railways Join Hands with SBI to Launch Co-Branded Credit Card," February 21.

Gupta, Nitin. 2006. Personal interview, March 24.

Kohli, Maninder. 2006. Personal interview, March 15.

Lafferty Ltd Cards International. 2005. "Country Report—India: Indian Card Growth Exceeds 50% per Annum," February 24.

———. 2005. "Country Survey—India: India's Card Growth Set to Soar," February 28.

Lochan, Rajiv. 2006. Personal Interview, March 16.

Mishra, Gaurie. "India Goes Plastic but Can't Repay." *Economic Times,* September 17.

National Council of Applied Economic Research. 2005. *Emerging India: Transition to a Cashless Economy,* January.

Sender, Isabelle. 2006. "Cashing In on India's Banking Boom." *BusinessWeek,* February 23. http://www.businessweek.com/investor/content/feb2006/.

Streamline Consultants. 2006. "Market Profile." *Streamline India,* April 5. http://www.streamlineindia.com/economy/market.htm.

Thukral, Arun. 2006. Personal interview, March 16.

Timmons, Heather. 2007. "In India, Credit Card Terms Prompt Indignation." *New York Times,* July 6.

Vageesh, N. S. 2006. "So, What's Your Credit Score?" Credit Information Bureau (India) Limited, February 3. http://www.cibil.com/art03_02_06 .htm.

Venture Infotek Research. 2004. *Indian Payment Card Industry, 4th Annual Industry Survey.* http://www.ventureinfotek.com/industryresearch.asp#.

Vinayak, Anil. 2006. Personal interview, March 24.

Chapter 4

THE CHALLENGE OF INDIA'S MOBILE TELECOM MARKET

*Todd Benigni, Aditya Bhashyam, Boaz Cohen,
Jonathan Dreyfus, Adeel Kheiri, Bryan Kim,
Suveer Kothari, Suresh Madhavan*

Since the mid-1990s, the Indian mobile telecom market has experienced phenomenal growth. It is one of the fastest-growing mobile markets in the world and has overtaken Japan as the second-largest mobile market in the Asia-Pacific region in terms of subscribers. According to the Centre for Monitoring Indian Economy, the number of mobile subscribers in India increased from approximately 5.5 million at the end of 2001 to approximately 290 million by 2008. Mobile operators have been adding nearly 6 million subscribers a month, and mobile services revenues are projected to grow at a compound annual rate of about 18% until 2011. Industry estimates also indicate that the Indian mobile market will top 500 million subscribers in the next few years.

The dramatic growth in the market can be attributed to three distinct forces: a marked liberalization of the telecommunications sector over the last decade; aggressive pricing by operators to capture market share; and the burgeoning incomes of India's middle class. This extraordinary growth has revolutionized the life of the common citizen. The enormous potential of mobile telecommunications is often illustrated by the story of a fisherman calling ahead from boat to shore to ascertain the likely price of his catch and to establish where he can maximize value. Still, while this example paints a promising picture, questions remain about its reliability. Who will drive mobile subscription growth in the future? What are the impediments to such growth? Finally, given the interplay of the various forces driving growth in the sector, what are the implications for mobile operators? These questions require a more thorough examination of the mobile telecommunications sector in India.

From Market Potential to Market Penetration

Such extraordinary growth to date has made many wonder whether it can continue. One pointer to still latent market potential in the mobile market is the relatively low penetration rate for Indian cell phone users—approximately 18% as of 2008. This percentage is significantly lower than that of most developing Asian economies. China, for example, has a mobile teledensity (number of phones per hundred people) of 28.3, while Malaysia has a rate of 77. If India is to attain China's mobile teledensity, a staggering increase in the demand for additional cell phones is needed.

So far, a key factor driving expansion in the market has been a steady decline in tariff rates achieved through changes in regulation. Government regulations through the Telecom Regulatory Authority of India (TRAI) have fostered increasing competition, leading to a concomitant fall in tariffs. Since the first licenses were granted in 1995, rapidly changing regulations—such as raising the maximum FDI limit from 49% to 74%, eliminating the access deficit charge (the share of call revenue that operators pay the government to help fund expansion in rural areas), and introducing unified licensing for mobile services and telecom—have all been directed at making telecom services increasingly accessible and affordable to the subscriber. More recently, the Indian government's Department of Telecommunications (DoT) has considered implementing mobile number portability (MNP). If implemented, India will be the first country to have MNP at a penetration level of less than 20%.

Today India has the lowest call rate in the world, at $0.02 per minute—compared with $0.33 in Japan, $0.11 in Brazil, and $0.24 in Australia. Correspondingly, monthly minutes of usage per subscriber has increased, and India now has the highest monthly usage in the Asia-Pacific region. With continual reductions in prepaid pricing points, 80% of incremental subscribers are now prepaid subscribers. This development has led to a shift in the composition of the wireless subscriber base, as prepaid subscribers account for nearly 75% of all subscribers.

With such aggressive pricing policies already in place, will future increases in mobile teledensity also depend on declining tariffs? Is there room for further decline in tariffs to increase affordability? How are key players positioning themselves to secure subscriber market share in such an aggressively competitive environment?

Impact of Unified Licensing

The most significant and far-reaching move in the liberalization of Indian telephony has been the unified licensing regime (ULR), which has radically simplified the licensing procedure and enabled new players to enter the market and level the playing field by offering a range of competitively priced services.

Introduced by the Indian government in 2003, unified licensing allows service providers to offer both fixed and mobile services under one license. Consequently, while operators that once provided full mobile telecom services (global system for mobile communications [GSM]) can now offer basic services as well, operators that once provided only a limited form of mobility service (wireless local loop [WLL] or code division multiple access [CDMA]) can now offer full mobile services. Unified licensing has allowed any operator to provide any service using technology in any area in which the company currently operates. More simply, this has meant the delivery of all telecom services—including voice, data, cable TV, direct-to-home TV, and radio broadcasting—through a single wired or wireless medium, covered by a single license.

GSM operators were unhappy with the regulatory change because the new single-license regime allowed basic operators such as Reliance Communications and the Tata Group to become full mobile carriers and cheaply enter a booming market in which GSM operators such as Bharti Airtel had invested heavily. GSM operators paid huge license fees to provide mobility, while CDMA operators came in as fixed-line service providers with far lower entry tariffs. Reliance Communications is the only major CDMA player, while the Tata Group has a stake in both GSM and CDMA.

To put the licensing conflict in perspective, CDMA uses the entire frequency spectrum and can broadcast at very high signal strength spread over a large radius. CDMA, a proprietary technology of Qualcomm, is used where mobile service providers have to serve large areas, such as the United States. GSM technology is preferred in areas with a concentration of mobile service providers (more than two providers in a 310-mile radius), where individual base stations are the best option. Basically, the two technologies address the same fundamental problem of mobile communication in different ways: how to divide the finite frequencies of airwaves among multiple users at the same time, or how to allow more than one party to hold a conversation on the same frequency without causing mutual interference. For a city like Chennai, with a population of nearly seven million, the GSM grid requires approximately 130 base stations to cover the city, which calls for heavy initial capital investment though operating costs are negligible. WLL, on the other hand, requires only about ten base stations, because they beam all frequencies received by everyone and use CDMA to loop to cell phones. An individual handset, which incorporates the code, deciphers the signal. The relatively light initial capital investment enables CDMA operators to offer lower tariffs, although the cell phone cannot be reused when providers are switched. Under unified licensing, GSM operators invest more in upgrading their networks for better data access services, while WLL operators invest in technologies that enable them to offer prepaid cards and SIM-based phones (phones activated by a subscriber identity module [SIM], a smart card containing all of a subscriber's key user data).

The economic impact of unified licensing has been far-reaching, with the consumer as the ultimate beneficiary. The change in government regulations has made India's mobile telecom market fiercely competitive—between players as well as technologies. CDMA operators—particularly Reliance Communications—entered the market and grew rapidly. After launching its service in December 2002, Reliance took only ten months to become a formidable player in terms of subscribers, through low tariffs and heavy capital expenditure. Reliance currently owns about 70% of the CDMA market. Bharti Airtel, Bharat Sanchar Nigam Ltd. (BSNL), and Vodafone Essar control the largest parts of the GSM market and have been adding subscribers at an impressive pace.

Maximizing Cost-Efficiency

Converged telecom services and networks allow operators in India to maximize cost-efficiency and offer pricing that promotes market growth. Using the most cost-efficient technology, operators can deploy services at a lower cost, with a reduction in tariffs for mobile and other services. Lower prices due to economies of scale have led to greater affordability for the masses, and competition in offering roaming services has meant lower roaming charges. In 2006, the country's nine GSM-based network operators added nearly 50 million subscribers, almost doubling their base, while the four CDMA-based operators added 25 million new subscribers, up from 12 million the previous year. Of the estimated 250 million subscribers at the beginning of 2008, nearly 75% were GSM subscribers.

With such rapid growth, the market shares of mobile companies in the Indian market have changed drastically over the past five years. Although there are currently twelve mobile operators in India, the leading five have a total market share of about 83%. The seven other operators share the remaining 17% of the market. Although an 83% share seems concentrated, when the Indian market is compared with other markets in the Asia-Pacific region, there is clearly room for consolidation. In the other markets, the top three operators have a combined market share of more than 95%, says Kobita Desai, analyst at Gartner Research.

The leading players in the Indian mobile market are Bharti Airtel, Reliance Communications, BSNL, and Vodafone Essar. Bharti Airtel is India's largest mobile operator, with about 60 million subscribers and a 24% market share in early 2008. Reliance Communications ranks second, with a market share of about 17.5%. Vodafone Essar, which was created in 2007 when Vodafone acquired Hutchinson Essar, is next, with a market share of 17%. BSNL is the government-owned telecom company and currently the fourth-largest mobile service provider in India, with a 15.5% market share.

BSNL started mobile services in 2000 and has been aggressively rolling out networks across the country since then. Aggressive pricing, cross-selling mobile subscriptions to its fixed-line customers, and access to rural markets has helped it become a top player. As a government entity, BSNL has the responsibility to take mobile coverage to all parts of India and help increase teledensity. With several large companies currently dominating the market, and with price competition already at an all-time high, it is very unlikely that a new operator will be able to enter the market in a significant manner, especially across India, although niche players may still be able to enter the market.

The Continuing Battle for Market Share

When telecom licenses were initially awarded, the market that resulted was highly fragmented—an environment intended to prevent monopolies and ensure opportunity for many players. Initial regulations specified that no one company could have more than 66% of the business in any one area. However, in true Darwinian form, the field has been consolidated significantly over the past ten years through a number of mergers and acquisitions. Mobile operators have fought to increase their stake and market share through aggressive pricing. Ongoing regulatory changes as well as those in the offing are likely to intensify the battle for market share, particularly for the large operators. So, continued downward pressure on tariffs for the industry as a whole can be expected, at least in the near term.

Although the introduction of unified licensing was crucial to increasing penetration, providers still needed to obtain a unified license in each area where they sought to provide services (India is divided into twenty-three operation areas). To promote the most efficient market conditions and ensure growth, a pan-India license is now available that will give license holders the right to provide all forms of telecom service throughout India with one license. This is a major step for the larger providers, which have been plagued by red tape just to maintain their current businesses. On the other hand, this change puts the smaller providers at a competitive disadvantage, because they do not have the scale to take advantage of a pan-India licensing scheme.

The larger providers also have a competitive growth advantage, because they can guarantee connections to more people than the smaller providers can, as connecting to users across company networks can still be a cumbersome process. According to India's cell phone protocol, users do not pay for a received call unless they are roaming outside the local area when the call is received. Moreover, there are currently about three countrywide providers and nine more-localized players, so determining how revenue is divided when calls go across networks becomes a major task. Historically, many providers were stingy about providing interconnections with other firms because of revenue issues—a condition that restrained the growth of the market by limiting the potential of the network effect. According to Desai, regulators recognized this barrier to growth and began requiring providers to give a certain number of interconnections per year, starting in 2006. This directive has benefited smaller providers by allowing their customers to make calls to other networks more easily, reducing the competitive advantage of larger providers. In 2007, the government recommended letting providers offer multiple technologies and eliminating the cap on the number of providers in a defined area of operation. In most areas, there are already six or seven providers, which puts further pressure on tariffs. For instance, Reliance, with the launch of its pan-India GSM services, is expected to affect the market share of current GSM providers significantly and to provide formidable competition for other new entrants.

Another recent policy change, introduced in 2007, is mobile number portability (MNP). Previously, India did not have a system that enabled number portability; rather, the phone numbers belonged to the providers, and switching providers involved switching numbers. MNP places the ownership of phone numbers in the hands of subscribers, enabling them to switch easily from one provider to another, and thus further increasing competition. Initially, MNP will be launched in four metros—Delhi, Mumbai, Kolkata, and Chennai—by the end of 2008; it is expected to expand to all regions by 2009. Implementation of MNP entails high expenditure by all operators to upgrade their networks to comply with the MNP regime. This might increase the cost of subscriber acquisition along with retention. Larger operators, such as Bharti, Reliance, and Vodafone, are therefore better positioned than smaller operators and will continue to gain market share at the expense of the smaller operators. This situation may lead to industry consolidation in the long run.

Because of all these policy changes, competition is likely to increase as individual operators try to capture market share. Additionally, the easing of restrictions on the subscriber base came at a time when the number of subscribers was increasing rapidly while operators were facing a "spectrum crunch." Simply stated, the government had not given India's mobile operators enough space on the radio spectrum to carry the additional call volume crisply and reliably. Providers argued that the 2G (second-generation) bandwidth (900–1800 MHz) was almost full, and plans for expansion or reallocation were constrained by insufficient additional bandwidth. However, new norms for subscriber-linked spectrum allocation have eased restrictions on subscriber thresholds, and the new criteria are significantly more positive for GSM operators such as Bharti.

The next place for expansion is in the 3G (third-generation) bandwidth (1900–2100 MHz), and this expansion is essential for the sustained growth of India's mobile telecom market. Compared with traditional GSM and CDMA technologies, 3G technology is widely considered to be technically superior. For instance, 3G base stations can accommodate greater network traffic in a given amount of spectrum than its predecessors can. Consequently, fewer base stations can support the same number of subscribers per area that a 2G network can. In addition, 3G technology will enable network providers to offer value-added services via cell phones, including Internet and video. According to a senior manager at Motorola, the adoption of 3G technology is crucial for both handset manufacturers and network operators, because it will enable firms using this bandwidth "to retain customers in urban centers while providing a more efficient way to penetrate the rural market." Regulators are still debating how to allocate the bandwidth. The Indian military and the space program control some of the 3G spectrum, but operators are pushing hard to gain access to a portion of this bandwidth. The government has earmarked part of the spectrum for 3G networks. However, it has not decided when to release this bandwidth, nor has it fixed a base price for auctioning the licenses. Depending on who acquires the rights to the 3G bandwidth first, it will be a key driver to market growth. Large operators such as Bharti Airtel and Reliance are likely to benefit while smaller operators will likely be in a weaker competitive position.

Clearly, these policy changes favor larger network operators over smaller ones, but regulations such as those providing interconnections and number portability level the playing field to some extent. Number portability, it has been argued, could lead to even less consumer loyalty in the mobile market than currently exists. These changes are likely to produce continued downward pressure on tariffs, even as mobile operators focus on improvements in quality and customer service to retain customers. Still, as tariffs continue to fall, subscriber growth needs to occur. The question, then, is where?

The Promise of the Rural Market

Many experts agree that a large portion of mobile subscriber growth will come from rural India. As growth in the urban areas and commercial segments begins to plateau, mobile operators are eyeing the vast rural areas, where 70% of India's population lives and the teledensity is 4% to 6%. Rural mobile telecom subscribers, estimated at 42 million in 2008, are expected to increase to 167 million in 2010 and to make up 50% of all new subscribers.

To develop the rural market's potential fully, domestic telecom providers will need to invest heavily in expanding coverage to the sprawling countryside. Traditionally, operators have incurred the capital expenditures of constructing base stations, power generators, and backhaul networks. In urban centers, operators can expect to recover their base station investments after one year of operation. Originally, industry analysts believed that the capital expense incurred in developing the rural markets was too high to see a reasonable return on investment within three years.

The Costs of Infrastructure

Many of India's largest mobile operators are looking for funds to build out India's vast mobile infrastructure. The acquisition of Hutchinson Essar by Vodafone increased the valuation of all Indian service providers. That helped them to attract private equity and other investments, bringing in much-needed capital for rural market expansion. Given the challenges of this expansion, one distinct trend among mobile telecom operators in India has been to divest their engineering and construction operations into new companies. Bharti Airtel is employing this tactic by divesting their tower business into an independent company, Bharti Infratel, in which it would ultimately have a minority stake. Bharti Infratel will focus exclusively on building the infrastructure and operations business, which includes doubling the number of towers in Bharti's network from 40,000 to 80,000 by the end of 2008. As a fully independent company, Bharti Infratel can enter into comprehensive sharing agreements with other companies. It has already collaborated with Vodafone Essar and Idea Cellular to form Indus Towers.[1] According to Akhil Gupta, joint managing director at Bharti Airtel, "Indus Towers will be an independently managed and operated company, offering services to all telecom operators and other wireless services providers such as broadcasters and broadband services providers." Given Bharti's focus on increasing capital productivity while reducing operating expenses, the divestment of its tower business appears to be in line with its go-to-market strategy for rural areas.

"Pursuing a rural strategy," says Gupta, "is part of selling more. minutes, which is part of the Bharti business model for driving revenue growth."

Other business divestitures include Reliance Infratel, a partially divested business of Reliance Communications. Through this business, Reliance hopes to build out its network of towers to a total of forty thousand around the country. Tata Teleservices provides yet another example of tower divestitures: it is looking to divest up to a 49% stake into a new company, Wireless TT Info Services. Through this company, it can accelerate the construction of towers, ten thousand of which are to be added by early 2010.

This passive infrastructure-sharing model, in which operators no longer rely solely upon internal resources to construct and develop their mobile network infrastructure, may very well be the future of infrastructure development for the rural market. In a setting where reducing costs is critical to survival, operators are becoming increasingly aware that tower sharing may be one way to reduce costs as they market services to a consumer base with low average revenues per user.

The Problem of Power

Along with the installation of towers and base stations goes the need for access to reliable power. Power outages are common in rural India. Although the electricity network covers most of the country, another twenty years will likely pass before electricity will be a fact in some villages. Even villages now covered by the network suffer blackouts regularly.

Such power issues imply that long battery life would be an especially valuable feature of a cell phone in rural areas (although base stations may be affected by power cuts). Nevertheless, the batteries need to be recharged, and for villages without any power supply at all, this is a problem. Some solar cell power stations are already in use, but these are a costly alternative to conventional power stations. Innovative solutions to the power problem include bicycling for extended periods to generate enough electricity to charge a phone, and using biogas to generate energy. Another solution is a charger that is driven by hand with a crank. It is a relatively slow way of charging a phone, but it might have great potential if developed.

The Affordability Issue

In addition to infrastructure and power supply issues, pricing expectations of handsets and services distinguish the rural segment greatly from the urban segment. The challenge of the rural segment lies in building a sustainable business model customized for consumers who are significantly more price sensitive. With the majority of the rural population living on less than $2 a day, buyer power as a whole is limited. Additionally, not only is there a large divide between rural and urban segments, but the rural one is not homogeneous either. Operators need to differentiate services and tailor them to the specific needs of both the rural wealthy, who lead adoption, as well as the tier 2 adopters, who constitute the lower- to middle-income segment employed in agriculture, services, and trade. It is the latter group who will drive rural consumption of mobile communications technology.

According to industry analysts, the main challenge in the rural market remains ensuring affordability for low-income consumers. Subscribers who want to limit their monthly mobile budget to Rs 200 ($4) can hardly be expected to purchase an Rs 4,000 ($87) handset. Indeed, how to put a low-cost handset into a low-income subscriber's pocket is the challenge for both service providers and handset manufacturers.

According to the GSM Association, the single largest barrier to affordability of cell phone service in emerging markets is the initial cost of the handset. This is certainly true in India, but the sizable growth in subscribers there is driving down the price of handsets. Bharti strategists explain that falling handset prices create a secondary market for used handsets at incredibly low prices, thus giving many more consumers the opportunity to obtain a phone and significantly increasing penetration rates.

In India, regulations regarding revenue sharing make it difficult for network operators to sell handsets, so a completely parallel
market exists for handset sales. In the GSM space, consumers go to
handset manufacturers to buy handsets and then to network operators to get network services. Most global handset manufacturers are
present in India. For instance, Nokia, the market leader, had a share
of 70% in 2007, driven by strong demand for its mid- and low-tier
models (although its mid-tier and high-end devices generate 25% of
its sales revenues). Many of these handsets are specially designed for
emerging markets through consolidation and elimination of unnecessary features and functions. However, the design of handsets has
also become much more multifunctional, because value for money
is an important attribute for rural consumers. Rural consumers see
their cell phones as something of a status symbol and demand all
the "bells and whistles" of a fully functional cell phone. Even in
poorer areas, cell phone purchasers want to ensure that they are
getting the most for their money and are demanding value-added
features such as FM radio or a flashlight attachment.[2]

According to Pankaj Mohindroo, president of the Indian
Cellular Association, "There's an insatiable hunger for mobile
phones permeating all layers of society." Different low-cost versions
are an attempt by handset manufacturers to segment and capture
this growing demand. Motorola, for instance, splits the handsets they sell into three types: the entry-level segment, which is
booming, with a target price of $30; the niche business segment,
which includes Research in Motion's BlackBerry; and the growing
youth segment, which demands phones that can handle rich entertainment content. Reliance also offers three variants of its handsets:
from an Rs 777 (US$19) model aimed at first-time buyers; to an
Rs 1,234 (US$31) model aimed at repeat buyers who are upgrading
their handset; and finally an Rs 1,888 (US$47) model aimed at
the young, with an FM radio and access to Reliance's R World (a
gateway to data applications). Reliance's low-cost Classic handset
brand has become the second-largest-selling handset brand in India,
having sold more than ten million handsets within five months
of its launch. Reliance is also planning to launch new low-cost
models with camera and MP3 capabilities. Its prospective entry

into the GSM market will continue to focus on providing afford-able handsets, thereby helping to differentiate itself from other new players.

A Bundling Strategy

Handset prices are likely to continue to fall as the market for wireless subscribers increases. As the prices fall, margins for handset manufacturers are shrinking, and all the stakeholders in the supply chain now realize that a joint market strategy is the way to address the low-cost segment. A collaborative strategy between handset manufacturer and mobile operator would help penetrate the rural market, and operators have begun bundling the low-cost handset with additional services. For instance, Vodafone has launched its ultralow-cost bundled handset, the Magic Box, which consists of the Vodafone 125 or 225 plus a connection available at Rs 1,199 (approx US$30) and Rs 1,599 (approx US$40), that includes free talk time and a cheap tariff rate. Bharti Airtel has met Vodaphone's challenge with its own low-cost strategy. It has teamed up with Nokia to offer bundled phones at partly subsidized rates to get a bigger share of the rural Indian market. Nokia was one of the first handset manufacturers to realize that utilitarian handsets were not appealing to resource-limited rural consumers, so it reintroduced inexpensive models that provided a greater value proposition for this segment by including fashionable designs and integrated media features, such as FM radio.

The Rural Market: The Next Battleground

For network operators that see strong growth potential in the rural market, that market will be the next battleground. To continue to make inroads, operators will need to be more attuned to the distinct needs and challenges of the rural market, and manufacturers and operators will have to continue to find ways to keep costs down, differentiate their phones and services on features other than price, and maximize margins through value-added services for niche segments.

The diverse linguistic, cultural, and socioeconomic landscape of rural India is also a key challenge. The high illiteracy rate in rural India, and the lack of an alphabet for many rural languages, means that operators must come up with creative solutions like simplifying product access and offering customer-centered solutions like songs, music, and popular hello tunes. Innovative phone features, like a voice-enabled or symbol-based caller, must cater to the illiterate segment. However, value-added services that drive growth in urban India are expected to be key in drawing subscribers in the rural segment as well.

In fact, during many of our interviews, the one service that was brought up immediately and repeatedly was access to sports updates, especially cricket scores. One of the most popular and profitable cell phone services in India today is SMS cricket score updates, and entertainment services like Bollywood news would also likely be highly valued by cell phone users. While cricket and Bollywood updates seem to be the minimum that telecom providers will have to deliver to fuel growth, the challenges of expanding into rural India cannot be underestimated.

Meeting the Challenge of Declining ARPUs

Clearly, pricing strategies have been at the forefront of the revolution that has allowed customers access to cell phones. In addition to connectivity costs, handset costs have been falling throughout the industry, and with disposable incomes on the rise, more Indians can now afford basic cell phone technology. Price-cutting competition has driven rates down to rock bottom, and the tariffs for Indian cell phones are among the lowest in the world. From a peak rate of around $0.50 per minute in 2003, tariffs have decreased to about $0.02 per minute. Subsequently subscriber growth has come at the cost of declining average revenue per user (ARPU). India, in fact, generates the lowest ARPU among the major world markets.

The use of prepaid services also leads to low ARPUs. Prepaid cards entice users to try mobile services at minimal cost and maximal flexibility. Cards serve as the most cost-effective option for operators, because they make little to no demand on billing and client management resources. In addition, plans and tariff structures allow Indian consumers to minimize monthly expenditure and choose plans that let them switch easily since they shop on price. Because receiving calls in India is free, very often consumers will only receive calls on their phones. Thus, revenue per prepaid user is low—about $5.60 per month. While the average postpaid user spends much more—about $19 per month—postpaid users compose only a small segment of the market in India. As operators expand into rural areas, they are expected to see their annual ARPU fall from $82.10 in 2007 to $59.50 by 2011. Successful operators will make up for the falling ARPU through economies of scale.

Growing Revenues Through Value-Added Services

As operators continue to expand their customer base, they will have to develop alternate strategies, such as charging a switching fee, to discourage subscribers from constantly switching cell phone services solely to get the lowest price. They will need to focus on quality of service, which will ultimately benefit the subscribers. Most importantly, operators will need to look at value-added services to increase differentiation, customer loyalty, and ARPUs.

Market potential and low prices ensure that revenues from the voice market will drive growth for the next few years. While the revenues will continue to grow, profits from voice services will continue to shrink. This problem is compounded by users' lack of operator loyalty. In a 2006 study of Indian cell phone usage, 30% of users said that they would likely switch mobile providers despite being content with their current level of service. In the face of this problem, operators may look to increase their value-added services (VAS), ranging from basic text messaging to ringtones and gaming, to enhance profitability. In this context, VAS is important because it could drive profitability in niche segments, especially as voice services become more commoditized. VAS includes everything from receiving stock market information, downloading cricket highlights, streaming Bollywood trailers, and reading e-mail on the go. Services can be broadly classified as information, entertainment, or communication.

Forms of VAS

The most basic VAS is short-message service (SMS), or as it is commonly referred to, text messaging. Operators hope that the value proposition of such services improves to the point that rural customers want additional services. For example, operators offer services that allow users to request data by SMS and receive results in the same format. Thus, users can request cricket scores, stock prices, or movie listings and get an SMS response. Often, such services are run by mobile operators. When they are not, revenue is split between the operator (who gets the message revenue) and the content provider (if there is a charge for the content). The content comes from content owners, such as movie studios and sports leagues. This content is aggregated and then sold to operators. In this class of service, revenue is split among several parties. Westbridge Capital's Sumir Chadha estimates that the revenue sharing split is 40% operator, 30% aggregator, and 30% content owner. Thus, the operator gets a significant part of the value created by the VAS. As the revenue from voice traffic continues to decline, operators will rely increasingly on this revenue.

While SMS is the most basic VAS, ringtone downloads are by far the most popular. Other entertainment content includes data streaming, mobile music downloads, and mobile gaming. Similar to wallpaper and ringtones, these services involve content providers, middlemen, and mobile operators. However, these services require higher-quality phones and more network bandwidth than is typical today. Thus, it will probably take longer for these services to roll out in the Indian market than elsewhere, and when they do roll out, operators will demand a larger percentage of revenues. Similarly, e-commerce, mobile wallet applications, and productivity enhancement services form a small but very profitable niche of the overall market. In this context, the value chain consists mostly of the consumer and the merchant, with the operator just charging for use of the network.

By rolling out services such as mobile banking and field sales automation, telecom operators are trying to offer clients utility for their existing mobile connections. Additionally, a number of creative uses have been developed in specific industries. The most heralded of these uses by far is the use of text messaging by fishermen and farmers to track real-time prices for their products across various local markets. An even more creative program has been implemented by Indian Oil Corporation. This program calls for using cell phone SIM cards along with GPS technology to track oil tanker locations as well as oil theft and adulteration. Such uses make up but a small portion of VAS with specific industry uses.

Potential VAS Users in India

While VAS has the potential to add to margins, increase loyalty, and grow the consumer base for wireless services, the ability of VAS to increase ARPU is still unclear. One key challenge in providing VAS is the current economic makeup of the Indian population. With close to 25% of the population still living below the poverty line, the Indian markets are in their infancy and so too are the needs of average Indian buyers. This is not to say that India does not have its fair share of sophisticated users, but these users constitute the small percentage of the population at the top of the economic pyramid. Since most clients are first-time users of cell phones, another challenge is explaining to the clients how to use the phones, especially the nonvoice functions. Educating the market is critical in pushing adoption. Tata Teleservices, for instance, addresses this issue by employing peer-group education, counting on early users to explain how to use the phones to later users.

As previously mentioned, mobile operators are offering VAS for free, hoping that customers will like the service enough to continue using it when the operators start charging money for it. However,

Desai of Gartner Research believes that operators could still optimize prices for VAS to encourage return users. Comparing the evolution of VAS in Europe, Singapore, and Malaysia with that in India, she predicts, "By 2010, 25% of the wireless companies' revenues in India will come from data services, compared to 35% currently in Japan. Most of these revenues will be from consumer applications."

Currently the most successful VAS in India is messaging applications, which make up 71% of VAS revenue. This percentage, per Gartner's predictions, will go as low as 37% by 2011, replaced by revenue from entertainment applications, such as ringback tones and games. Contributing to this change is the increasing popularity of entertainment applications among Indian youth. This population is helping drive the increase in demand for VAS. Youths are more tech-savvy than their elders and thus more open to additional services for their cell phones. Furthermore, as this segment becomes wealthier, it will have more means to spend on entertainment services. Finally, because this segment sees VAS as status symbols, there is large scope for peer-to-peer adoption.

Typically, relatively well-off urban consumers trade up to more feature-laden phones. Indeed, there is a big replacement and upgrading market moving toward more-sophisticated phones. Most handset manufacturers have taken strides to move consumers up to better, feature-rich phones, which in turn promise higher profit margins to the manufacturers. These phones have greater VAS capability, so they may affect demand for VAS.

Another potential VAS driver is the professional segment. The business market in India has been relatively slow to adopt wireless data services to improve productivity. "Awareness of enterprise solutions remains low," says Zubin Dubhash at Tata Teleservices. "We still have to create a need and teach businesses how to use the services," asserts Abdul Khan, vice president of marketing at Tata. Still, as more businesses search for ways to improve productivity, and as they become familiar with technology and overcome fears regarding security and robustness, business VAS will increase. For instance, some companies have adopted Research in Motion's BlackBerry device to facilitate mobile e-mail. Thus, while VAS to businesses will clearly increase ROI for service providers, educating business users and integrating with their systems to ensure security and reliability remain key hurdles.

Challenges to Providing VAS

Although VAS is an increasing segment of the overall mobile services sector, it still makes only a small percentage of overall telecom revenues. The smallness of the percentage is partly attributable to the challenge VAS entails. For instance, since VAS depends highly on the user interface, India's many languages and its illiteracy problem pose a challenge to providing VAS. India has eighteen official languages and a 60% to 70% literacy rate, so consumers may be limited in their ability to use VAS involving "word typing." Moreover, the handsets themselves usually support only Hindi and English, further limiting many consumers' ability to use VAS. To address the language and literacy challenge, the Indian market employs a unique solution: the voice portal. The voice portal is a multilingual voice-recognition application that users dial to access. It then allows them to speak their native language to access services such as activating ringtone downloads. For example, Vodafone's current voice portal supports five languages. Instead of surfing with the phone's browser or typing a message to request a service, the user dials into the voice portal and follows the oral instructions to complete the request. "For 15 cents a minute, even first-time users get access to sport, entertainment by calling in to our number without worrying about learning to send an SMS," asserts Khan. The benefit to new users is significant. Almost all operators now have an interactive voice portal offering multiple services with multilingual recognition. Examples include Vodafone's 123, Airtel's 646 Simply Talk, and Tata's Do More service.

In India, GSM network operators normally do not control the types of handsets that are sold in the market and thus need to ensure that their delivered content is compatible across all makes and models. "When we roll out a new service, we have to ensure compatibility with over sixty different types of handsets in the market," says Vodafone's Shailesh Varudkar. "This is compared to just ten in developed markets with operator subsidies." In addition, to drive adoption of premium services, operators depend on the handset manufacturers to reduce handset prices. Services independent of handsets are thus easier for operators to handle and can help grow the pool of services and the size of the market that would see value. For instance, use of ringback tones, which do not depend on the phone one has, is growing at a phenomenal rate. Companies such as Motorola have been investing in software that could be run on any handset or network VAS (VAS that runs on the network and not on the handset), rather than in offerings that require a sophisticated handset.

While reducing the price of VAS dramatically increases the number of clients using that service, industry experts strongly believe that VAS is not truly a unique offering, and hence a means to reduce churn, since it is easily imitated. With more than 70% of the market prepaid, network operators are suffering from high churn and clients are choosing a network mainly on the basis of price. Indeed, voice service remains the primary driver of volume growth within the sector and will continue to be that for some time. "The Indian wireless market is and will remain a voice market for the near future," claims TRAI chairman Pradip Baijal. Consequently, VAS is not thought to be a major competitive advantage. Tata Teleservices believes that operators can only use VAS as an advantage for a short time before competitors copy the VAS and compete away the benefits. An operator always has to innovate (both in content and in form of VAS) if it wants to play the VAS game. So for now, the potential for VAS may be limited to a small segment of the market, and VAS may not affect ARPUs significantly.

Indian mobile telecom operators will have to focus more on the volume of subscribers to drive growth than on VAS for profitability. However, operators cannot ignore the potential for entertainment VAS (when offered through bundled services) to help penetrate a large linguistically and culturally diverse rural market.

Conclusion

The Indian mobile telecom market has experienced astonishing growth over the past decade. After China, India is the largest market in the Asia-Pacific region in terms of subscribers. Furthermore, industry estimates indicate that the Indian market will top five hundred million subscribers in the next few years. A large portion of that growth will come from rural India, presenting a huge untapped market opportunity. Against this backdrop, network providers are working hard to acquire and retain new customers. They are building capacity in rural areas, marketing to lower-income subscribers, and reducing costs and prices as fast as possible to win this figurative and literal "land grab." This pursuit, however, comes with a price: reduced profitability. One opportunity to attract and retain customers while also increasing margins is to develop VAS. These services—including information services, entertainment offerings, and business applications—could change the way consumers use cell phones while also changing the way operators, content owners, and content aggregators make money. Consumers, urban and rural, are likely to be the beneficiaries as major players, both existing and emerging, continue to battle for market share.

Notes

1. TMC Net, 2008.
2. Chris Monastersiki, "Race to the Bottom: Cell Phones in India, *Private Sector Development Blog,* May 27, 2007, http://psdblog.worldbank.org.

Bibliography

Ablett, Jonathan, Aadarsh Baijal, Eric Beinhocker, Anupam Bose, Diana Farrell, Ulrich Gersch, Ezra Greenberg, Shishir Gupta, and Sumit Gupta. 2007. "The 'Bird of Gold': The Rise of India's Consumer Market." McKinsey Global Institute 79 (May). http://www.mckinsey.com/mgi/reports/pdfs/india_consumer_market/MGI_india_consumer_full_report.pdf.

Abraham, James, David Dean, and Arvind Subramanian. 2007. "Ringing in the Next Billion Mobile Consumers: A Road Map for Accelerating Telecom Growth in India." Boston Consulting Group 13 (December). http://www.bcg.com/impact_expertise/publications/files/Next_Billion_Mobile_Consumers_Dec_2007.pdf.

Answers.com. 2008. "Demographics of India." http://www.answers.com/topic/demographics-of-india.

Baijal, Pradip. 2006. Personal interview, March.

Bharadwaj, V. T., Gautam M. Swaroop, and Ireena Vittal. 2005. "Winning the Indian Consumer."*McKinsey Quarterly* (September). http://www.mckinseyquarterly.com/.

Bharti Enterprises. 2008. www.bharti.com.

Briones, Elena, Aarti Kumar, Alvin Leung, Sang'ona Oriedo, and Andrew Pinzler. 2008. "Mobile Telephony in Rural India: Consumer Trends and Growth Strategies." GIM-India (April).

BusinessWeek. 2007. "India Attracts 30 Firms Vying for Mobile American-Style Licenses," October 4. http://www.businessweek.com/globalbiz/content/oct2007/.

———. 2007. "Nokia's Big Plans for India," August 31. http://www.businessweek.com/globalbiz/content/aug2007/.

Cellular Operators Association of India. 2008. "About Us." http://coai.in/aboutus-history.htm.

Centre for Monitoring Indian Economy. 2008. *Monthly Review of the Indian Economy*, April.

Chadha, Sumir. 2006. Personal interview, March.

Desai, Kobita. 2005. "India's Emerging Mobile Market Offers Big Opportunities." Gartner Research, March 30.

———. 2005. Personal interview, March.

Economic Times of India. 2005. "Some Call the Shots, Others Left Holding On," April 1.

Economist. 2007. "Full-Spectrum Dominance: India's Fast-Growing Mobile-Phone Operators Vie for Capacity on the Airwaves," November 29. http://www.economist.com/business/.

Financial Express. 2007. "India Best Bet for Mobile Users," March 30. www.financialexpress.com/.

Frontline Magazine. 2005. "The Reliance Tussle," January 1.

———. 2004. "Special Feature: BSNL," October 23.

Gartner, Inc. 2007. "Gartner Says Indian Cellular Services Market to Exceed US$25 Billion by 2011," July 18. http://www.gartner.com/it.

GSM Association. 2008. "Emerging Market Handset Programme." *GSM World*. www.gsmworld.com/emh/index.html.

Gupta, Rahul, 2007. "Low Cost Handset: Connecting Bharat with India." *iGovernment.com*, November 6. http://www.igovernment.in/.

Hindustan Times. 2005. "Is India Ready for 3G Rush?" February 4.

————. 2005. "Telecom FDI Hike to Set Off Equity Recast, Major IPO's," January 15.

IDC India. 2007. "IDC India Mobile Handset Usage and Satisfaction Study," October 16. http://www.idcindia.com/press/oct16.html.

————. 2006. "India Mobile Service Usage and Satisfaction Survey." July 15. http://www.idcindia.com/research/idc_india_research.htm.>

India-Cellular.com. 2008. "Cellular Phone Subscribers in India," March 31. http://www.india-cellular.com/Cellular-Subscribers.html.

Jain, S. K. 2006. Personal interview, March.

Khan, Abdul. 2006. Personal interview, March.

Khanna, Tarun, Krishna Palepu, and Ingrid Vargas. 2004. "Bharti Tele-Ventures." *Harvard Business School—Case No. 9-704-426,* March 12 (Revised).

Lakshman, Nandini. 2006. "The Explosive Mobile Growth in Rural India." *BusinessWeek,* August 6. http://inhome.rediff.com/money/2006/aug/08mobile.htm.

Majumder, Shubham. 2008. "Indian Telecom Sector." Macquarie Research, May.

Monasterski, Chris. 2007. "Race to the Bottom: Cell Phones in India." *Private Sector Development Blog,* May 27. http://psdblog.worldbank.org.

Pasricha, Anjana. 2006. "India's Massive Mobile Phone Market Expands to Rural Areas." *VOA News,* August 20. http://www.voanews.com/.

RelianceCommunications.http://www.rcom.co.in/webapp/Communications/rcom/index.jsp (accessed 2008).

Singh, Shalini. 2007. "Indians Talk Too Much on Mobile." *Economic Times,* June 13. http://economictimes.indiatimes.com/articleshow.

Tata Indicom. http://www.tataindicom.com (accessed 2008).

Telecom Regulatory Authority of India. 2008. www.trai.gov.in.

TeleGeography. 2007. "Indian GSM Subscriber Base Almost Doubles; CDMA Triples." *PriMetrica,* January 17. http://www.telegeography.com/cu.

Thomson Reuters. 2008. "Regulator for Mobile Number Portability in India," April 11. http://www.reuters.com/article.

Varudkar, Shailesh. 2006. Personal interview, March.

Willing, Nicole. 2008. "Indian Mobile Carriers Add 8.4M Subs." *United Business Media,* March 19. http://www.unstrung.com.

Chapter 5

INDIA'S AIRLINE INDUSTRY: FAIR SKIES AHEAD?

Ann Aguero, Albert Lin, Ryan Lisiak, Deidre Stoken

Long reserved for the wealthy, air travel in India is becoming common among the growing middle class, resulting in an astonishing overall market potential. With twelve major carriers in aggressive competition, the domestic aviation market is expected to grow at 16% per year over the next three to five years. Passenger traffic is expected to grow at the rate of 25% to 30% a year to reach sixty million by 2010, up from forty-eight million in 2006. Longer-term estimates see two hundred million passengers per year by 2020.[1] Moreover, according to Praful Patel, India's minister for civil aviation, investment in this sector is expected to grow by about $120 billion over the next ten years, creating at least three million jobs.

This surge in traffic and volume is a direct result of a robust economy, rising consumer wealth, and the emergence of low-fare carriers. The entry of such carriers in India, pioneered by G. R. Gopinath of Air Deccan in 2003, has caused an influx of first-time fliers, for whom air travel had previously been unaffordable. Currently, more than sixteen million Indians travel by train every day. Of these, approximately three million are traveling by first or second class and can easily fly if airfares are brought down to be near par with train fares. Compared with train service in Europe, service between large cities in India is neither comfortable nor reliable. And many Indians traveling by train are headed to smaller towns and cities. It is feasible for them to travel part of the journey by air and the rest by road, if airfares allow. Thus, a significant percentage of all passengers of low-cost air carriers are former or current train travelers that have made the switch from trains to planes because of lower fares. Gopinath claims that up to 30% of his passengers were flying for the first time. Ajay Singh, director of the competing low-frills airline SpiceJet, which started flying in 2005, estimates that more than half of all his passengers are first-time fliers.

Low-cost airlines have emphasized that, with only about 2% of the Indian population traveling by air, the growth potential lies in attracting first-time fliers from the vast pool of train and bus travelers rather than in competing directly with the full-service airlines. By adopting this strategy, India's low-cost carriers (LCCs) have effectively created a whole new market with attractive growth dynamics. In fact, these airlines have for the first time seen an increase in corporate interest from several groups looking for financial investments. The Tata Group recently invested in a 7.5% stake in SpiceJet (estimated to be $17.2 million), and the Reliance Vision Fund, a mutual fund scheme under the Reliance Mutual Fund umbrella, acquired a 3.5% stake in Air Deccan. Such corporate investments are being viewed as a very positive development for the sector. According to Vijay Mallya, chairman of Kingfisher Airlines, "The fact that institutional investors are beginning to see the potential in the business is a healthy sign."[2]

Meanwhile, the Indian airline industry's growth has also been augmented by increasing international traffic, which has opened up opportunities in the feeder segment. In response to this traffic into India, the government created an "open sky" policy, which increased the number and frequency of international flights into India. The policy allows foreign airlines to deploy additional capacity during the peak travel season (i.e., offer more seats by means of extra flights and larger aircraft). Because of high passenger demand, foreign airlines have been expanding their India operations and reaching an occupancy rate of more than 80% on their flights during the peak season. With several international operators traveling to a greater number of Indian cities, opportunities have opened up in the feeder segment. When international passengers disembark in major cities, they can now connect to smaller towns and cities through feeder airlines.

To meet the high demand for air travel in India, the two largest aircraft manufacturers in the world, Airbus and Boeing, are vying to ramp up their investments in fleet expansion, pilot training schools, and maintenance/engineering units. Boeing estimates that India will need 856 aircraft at an estimated cost of $72 billion over the next twenty years. According to John Leahy, chief commercial officer at Airbus, "India is one of the world's most promising markets."[3] Indian carriers have collectively ordered approximately 480 aircraft through 2012 against their current fleet of 280. In the last two years alone, 135 aircraft were added.

Despite the promising outlook, however, there are serious obstacles to the future growth of the airline industry in India. First, although the industry as a whole has been growing, most airlines have been plagued with losses, raising the question as to whether the LCC business model is viable and sustainable for India over the long term. Moreover, there are severe infrastructure constraints. Airports are congested, underdeveloped, and outdated, and they have limited reach. There are currently about 454 airports, fewer than 100 of which have more than one daily service. There is also a growing shortage of airline personnel at all positions, and lastly, government regulations could still limit growth despite the progress made at the start of the century. These issues suggest that, although strong growth is forecast for the industry, Indian airline operators need to overcome significant barriers to profitably satisfy the growing demand of the market. In this chapter, we give an overview of the Indian aviation industry, consider the rise of LCCs and their outlook, and discuss the challenges facing the industry and their implications.

Major Domestic Carriers

The civil aviation industry in India emerged in the early twentieth century. In the absence of government regulation, entrepreneurs from many different backgrounds entered the market to try their luck. In 1953 the Indian government reined in the chaos that had developed and nationalized the entire industry. Modeled after the

British system, two national airlines were created: Indian Airlines for domestic and regional service, and Air India for international flights.

In 1992, during the first wave of economic liberalization, the Indian government declared an "open skies" policy, which allowed private operators to reenter the aviation market. Numerous private airlines were founded as a result. Many of them were started with a spirit of innovation, a customer service orientation, and the desire to develop and grow the aviation market beyond its present limits—qualities largely missing from the state-owned airlines after decades of monopoly position and job security for its managers and employees. However, despite good intentions and grand visions, many of the newly founded airlines failed within a few years—most spectacularly East-West Airlines in 1995, the fastest-growing private operator at the time, when its CEO was shot dead in his office for what was rumored to be failure to pay back loans from India's criminal underworld.

A third wave of entrants joined the market in the mid-2000s, during India's unprecedented economic boom, and contributed to the most rapid growth of the industry in its history. We will profile the largest three Indian aviation groups, who together dominate 85% of the market, and briefly discuss some of the smaller players operating today.

Air India and Indian Airlines

The beginnings of Air India go back to the earliest hours of commercial aviation. In 1932, J. R. D. Tata founded the aviation department of his company Tata Sons Ltd., and personally operated the first flight from Karachi to Bombay. During its first full year of operation Tata Airlines carried 155 passengers and eleven tons of mail. Tata Airlines became a public limited company in 1946 under the name Air India. In 1948, after the independence of India, the Indian government acquired 49% of the company, with an option to purchase an additional 2%, and granted the airline the status to operate international services in return. In 1953, when the aviation industry was nationalized, the government exercised its purchase option and became the majority shareholder. Air India International Limited was born, and J. R. D. Tata was appointed chairman of the new entity, which was to provide international passenger service. In the following decades Air India significantly expanded its worldwide network of passenger and cargo service, adding terminals and hubs in Asia, Europe, and North America. The airline also extended and modernized its fleet, becoming the world's first all-jet airline in 1962.

Indian Airlines, the other airline emerging from the 1953 nationalization of the industry, had to integrate the operations of eight domestic players and inherited a diverse fleet of more than ninety aircraft. This legacy slowed Indian Airlines' modernization; in fact, it added the first jet plane to its fleet only in 1964, two years after Air India has already converted its entire fleet. When the deregulation allowed private operators into the market again in 1992, Indian Airlines' monopoly on domestic air transport ended, and it had to face tough competition from Jet Airways and other private carriers. With the emergence of LCCs during the mid-2000s, the airline lost market share year after year, and had one of the lowest load factors (airline performance as measured by the percentage of available seats filled with passengers) among domestic carriers. In 2005, the airline embarked on a major rebranding effort to improve its image and prepare itself for an IPO.

However, given the financial hardships both Indian Airlines and Air India were going through in 2005 and 2006, the government shelved the privatization plans and decided to merge the two companies in 2007. The merged entity, the National Aviation Company of India Ltd. (NACIL), created one of the largest airlines in Asia and integrated both companies' operations into a single airline under the Air India brand.

At this writing, the new Air India is attempting to complete its postmerger integration efforts. Its market share of domestic passenger service sank to less than 15% in 2008. To stanch its losses, the company is trying to realize operational synergies, standardize its IT systems, and scale back its aggressive fleet expansion plans. As a state-owned enterprise, however, Air India is not as agile as some of its competitors. For example, in 2008, when private operators reduced or cancelled passenger services on less profitable routes because of weak demand, Air India had to maintain its service because it is required to deploy aircraft to remote areas of the country. An official from the airline explained: "We are thinly spread across 60 airports in the country while other carriers deploy bare minimum capacity and achieve optimum commercial deployment of capacity."[4]

Jet Airways Group

Jet Airways was founded in 1992 by Naresh Goyal. Goyal, who still serves as the public company's chairman and owns 80% of its stock, had previously provided sales and marketing for foreign airlines in India. Jet Airways was positioned as a full-service airline that would compete primarily on service quality. The company deliberately stayed away from the "irrational" pricing of many of its competitors and instead invested heavily in its fleet and terminals. The airline offers luxurious first-class cabins—the result of a two-year design effort personally overseen by Goyal—and large private LCD touch screens with on-demand programming for all its passengers. It also introduced a number of check-in convenience options for its passengers—such as inner-city check-in facilities, self-service computers, and single check-in for same-day return flights—and it invested substantially in advertising. These efforts earned the airline a place as one of India's top ten marketers in 2007 in *Business Today* (one of India's leading business journals), a number of international awards, and high rankings on international travelers' surveys. Importantly, it also made the airline one of the few profitable enterprises in the industry.

Since 2004 the airline has expanded its international routes to New York, Toronto, and San Francisco, and to important Gulf destinations, such as Abu Dhabi, Bahrain, Muscat, Doha, and Kuwait. In 2007, Jet Airways purchased its competitor Air Sahara for $354 million and spent a significant amount of money to overhaul the carrier. Rebranding its new subsidiary JetLite, the company introduced a new menu of buy-on-board meals, and launched other initiatives such as scratch cards to win gifts. The acquisition has turned the Jet Airways Group into India's largest airline (as measured by passengers carried). It now operates a fleet of eighty-five aircraft, with an average fleet age of 4.45 years, one of the youngest fleets in the world.

Kingfisher and Deccan Airlines

Vijay Mallya, 52, who has been dubbed "India's Richard Branson," was one of the last high-profile entrants to India's airline industry. Having made his fortune with his liquor empire, Mallya announced the launch of Kingfisher Airlines, named after his Kingfisher beer, in 2005. Known for his flamboyance and colorful public persona, Mallya orchestrated a major publicity blitz, promising passengers a unique experience. He called his glamorous flight attendants "flying models" and announced plans to hold in-flight beauty pageants. Mallya also announced that his airline would break even in a year.[5]

Starting with only four leased Airbus aircraft for domestic routes, the airline grew quickly, most notably through the acquisition of its rival Air Deccan in 2007. Air Deccan, now renamed Kingfisher Red, had been India's first LCC. Launched in 2003 by G. R. Gopinath, the carrier shook up the competition by offering ticket prices 50% lower than those of all other carriers at the time.

Today, Kingfisher Airlines is competing with Jet Airways for the spot of India's largest airline (in February 2009 Kingfisher led the domestic market for the first time). In 2008 it started international routes and, like Jet Airways, it seeks to woo passengers with its service quality. Mallya declared the airline the "Harrods of the Sky" when he commenced service to Heathrow.[6]

However, for all its glamour and explosive growth, Kingfisher's revenues are lower than its operating expenses.[7] As part of the effort to reduce its losses, Kingfisher announced a comprehensive alliance with Jet Airways in October 2008. The alliance involves joint fuel management, joint ground handling, network rationalization, and crew sharing, and it might help reduce the payroll of nearly 19,000 employees that both companies have. The agreement is estimated to save the carriers a combined $307 million.

Other Players

The other players in India's aviation market are significantly smaller than the three leading groups: IndiGo Airlines, SpiceJet, and Paramount together have fewer than twenty planes; however, some small players prosper at the margins of the market while the major players suffer. Chennai-based carrier Paramount Airways, started in 2005 by textile company Paramount Group, has been getting some media attention, particularly for the shrewd business tactics of its thirty-two-year-old chairman M. Thiagarajan. When all the new players bought Airbus and Boeing aircraft, for example, Thiagarajan opted for lighter and more fuel-efficient seventy- or seventy-five-seat Brazilian Embraer jets. Since these jets weigh less than 88,185 pounds, Paramount pays significantly lower taxes on fuel and does not have to pay any landing or parking charges at major airports. Furthermore, instead of launching service all over India, Thiagarajan focused his five-aircraft fleet on southern India and targeted business travelers exclusively.[8] So far, his airline's growth ambitions have remained largely rhetoric and carefully constructed public relations; since 2007 the company has repeatedly announced plans to acquire another twenty to thirty new Embraer jets and another airline, but as of early 2009 these expansion plans remain unrealized. Industry observers suggest that a tie-up is probably crucial for Paramount if it hopes to realize its goal to be a major national player.[9] In the meantime, Thiagarajan has taken more pragmatic steps, such as re-allocating more of his fleet's capacity for door-to-door cargo service.

Industry Challenges

The Rise of Low-Cost Carriers: Growth at the Expense of Profitability

Before deregulation, India's airline industry was a state-owned monopoly and earned small but steady profits. The two state-owned airlines, Air India and Indian Airlines, serviced the bulk of India's international and domestic passengers, and India's passenger traffic increased by less than 1% per annum through the 1980s. In 1989, in an effort to boost domestic capacity (especially on tourist routes), the Indian government allowed private airlines to operate as "air taxis," running what were essentially privately chartered flights. However, fare prices remained regulated, and air taxi operators were required to operate an equal number of flights on routes of less than and greater than 435 miles. These stringent policies led to the failure of many of the new airlines.

In light of these failed attempts to spur growth, the government finally deregulated the industry and opened the floodgates for competition in 2004. Since deregulation, barriers to entry into India's airline industry have been relatively low. The required investment level for new entrants was only $6.8 million (Rs 30 crore), and the minimum fleet size was only five, though these rules have since changed. While some airlines have focused on providing a no-frills experience, others have sought to offer a unique brand of service. Nearly 44% of the increase in passenger traffic in the three-year period following deregulation, however, can be attributed to the LCCs, who now account for 16% of the total market share.

By adding capacity at a frantic pace and fighting a bruising price war, LCCs such as Air Deccan (now Kingfisher Red), Sahara Airlines (now JetLite), and SpiceJet have succeeded in grabbing market share from full-service legacy carriers such as Indian Airlines and Jet Airways. Unfortunately, however, they have done so at the expense of profitability. Using low fares as a strategy to generate strong demand and achieve high load factors has caught LCCs in a vicious cycle. To remain financially viable, such carriers depend on high load factors to break even. With intensifying competition, achieving such load factors became increasingly difficult, forcing many players to offer lower and lower fares to increase their load factors. The resulting gap between actual fares and load factors and viable fares and load factors has threatened long-term profitability for individual carriers as well as for the industry as a whole.

While the average fare and load factor for LCCs is Rs 2,800 to 3,000 ($61 to $65) and 72% to 74%, the fare and load factor required to be viable would be Rs 3,300 to 3,400 ($71 to $74) and 83% to 85%. For full-service carriers, the average fare and load factor is Rs 3,500 to 3,800 ($76 to $82) and 62% to 67%, whereas a viable fare and load factor would be Rs 4,200 to 4,400 ($91 to $95) and 72% to 75%. The full-service carriers need to raise average fares by around Rs 400 to Rs 700 ($9 to $15) per seat to break even or turn a small profit; the LCCs need to raise fares by around Rs 500 ($11) per seat. Load factors for the LCCs should be in the mid- to high 80s, and for the full-service carriers, in the low to mid-70s. In 2004, Jet Airways exceeded the break-even load factor and was the only airline to achieve profitability in India. Consequently, while competition from and among LCCs has clearly fueled demand, it has not yet produced a sustainable business model to service this demand.

The Struggle to Survive Losses and High Input Costs

India's airline industry as a whole is struggling to cope with losses. According to estimates, private airlines lost $250 million in 2005 and about $300 million in 2006. In 2008, when price wars and rising fuel costs took a strong toll and demand temporarily soft-ened, the situation worsened: the Federation of Indian Airlines estimated that the country's airline industry would post total losses of more than $2 billion for the year.[10] Most airlines have committed huge funds to acquire aircraft and are not in a position to pull back. According to Kapil Kaul, CEO at the Centre for Asia Pacific Aviation (CAPA), "The Indian market is the fastest growing, and yet no one is making money."[11] Kaul thinks that this situation is likely to continue for the next year. Yet even as they experience losses, LCCs have been severely constrained in their efforts to lower operational costs.

A big factor preventing LCCs from having any operational cost advantages is the decentralized nature of Indian air travel. The network of traffic consists primarily of point-to-point routes that directly connect two cities. This model differs from that of countries like the United States, which is dominated by a hub-and-spoke model. In this model, major cities like Atlanta, Chicago, Philadelphia, and New York serve as hubs for traffic to and from secondary cities. The hub-and-spoke model allows for airport dominance, which in turn allows for higher fares, premium parking spots, and lower airport handling charges. The decentralized nature of Indian air travel is a more efficient and cost-effective means of servicing demand, similar to the model used by LCCs in other regions. On the other hand, it minimizes the operational cost differential between traditional legacy carriers and new LCCs in India. This environment differs drastically from that in the United States and Europe, where some LCCs can have significant cost advantages over network carriers. For example, in the United States, one of the major cost advantages of LCCs comes from the use of secondary airports. These airports offer lower landing fees and allow for higher gate turnaround times since they are less congested than primary airports. In India, 80% of an airline's operating costs are the same, regardless of its business model, given the near-term infrastructure. Since most Indian LCCs operate from the same airports as the traditional legacy carriers, they are unlikely to enjoy significant cost benefits, if any. In addition, the major Indian cities have no separate terminals from which LCCs can operate.

According to Sunil Chopra, professor of operations management at Northwestern University, some key drivers that explain the operational cost differential between LCCs and traditional legacy carriers in the United States are employee costs. These costs are affected by the number of employees necessary for each departure and available seat mile (ASM). LCCs overseas operate with a lower number of employees per ASM than full-service or legacy carriers. The lower number of employees per ASM is not that of in-flight personnel, but that of ground personnel. In India, however, carriers have to deal with rising labor costs resulting from a shortage of skilled personnel. Consequently, cutting labor costs is not an option. Besides such variable cost factors, another relevant factor is block hour utilization of assets—that is, the average number of hours per day that planes are used. This factor captures a carrier's ability to use its primary fixed asset to amortize cost over a greater number of revenue-generating flights. In India, though, this factor may not be much of a differentiator. While airport charges in India are higher than those in other countries, aircraft use and turnaround times in India are lower than they are elsewhere because of poor infrastructure (e.g., few runways and hangars) at Indian airports. Also, many Indian carriers are buying or leasing new-generation aircraft at high prices.

Another major cost factor is fuel prices. While all airlines worldwide have to cope with fluctuating fuel prices, in India excise and customs duties and a sales tax on aircraft turbine fuel (ATF) increase the prices above international levels. Kingfisher's Mallya describes the problem: "The industry is overtaxed. If you see Hyderabad, the fuel price, after a 4% sales tax, is Rs 35,662 [$773] (per kiloliter), while the same in Bangalore costs Rs 41,285 [$894] after a 28% tax. You tax any industry at 25% to 30%, and figure out for yourself whether that industry has any chance of survival. To me, it is like a guillotine."[12]

Seeking a bailout from their financial predicament, the airlines have appealed to the government to bring India's ATF prices into line with international prices by eliminating the excise duty of 8.24% and the customs duty of 5.14% on ATF, and by categorizing ATF as declared goods and thus limiting the state sales tax at 4%. The government met the request partway by reducing the customs duty on ATF to 5% in June 2008.[13]

Reducing Costs and Generating Revenues

Because of India's infrastructure limitations, Indian air carriers have had to reduce costs through other means and discover innovative methods to increase asset use and generate additional revenue. They have increased asset use by increasing the number of seats per plane. They have generated additional revenue by using onboard advertising. Furthermore, they have reduced costs by outsourcing long-term aircraft maintenance checks and engine repair. Food and personnel expenses have been cut to the bare minimum, although salaries remain high because of the shortage of pilots and support staff at all levels. Despite the low prices, many customers want to see improvement in customer service.

For foreign LCCs, Internet penetration is the main ticketing medium. Web sites make purchasing tickets convenient for the customer and cheap for the airline, because they allow operators to shave agent and distribution margins. In India, LCCs are trying to lower distribution costs by selling tickets through various retail formats, trying to bring about a shift in passenger purchasing behavior. But unlike foreign airlines, India's airlines rely heavily on travel agents to source demand. Still, direct online purchases (including those made through online travel agents) have increased from 35% in 2006 to 2007 to 50% in 2007 to 2008. Portals such as MakeMyTrip.com and Ghumo.com maintain a list of fares offered by various airlines and allow consumers to pinpoint the lowest fares. Despite the growth of ticket Web sites, only a small portion of all Indian consumers use them. Consequently, distribution costs are still high, so airlines are making large investments in technology to keep recurring distribution costs low through call centers and the Internet.

These strategies have not yet ensured profitability for any of the LCCs. SpiceJet, for instance, is the most efficient LCC in the industry. This company, which has a market share of about 8% and a passenger load factor of about 77%, has an identical fleet configuration, which helps reduce its operational costs. Because the planes are the same, spares are common, seat configurations are identical, and training is uniform. The airline offers only an economy class configuration, pushing in more seats (189 instead of 145 to 150). The absence of food on board helps the airline achieve a better turnaround. Furthermore, SpiceJet has started focusing on additional ways to boost revenue. These include onboard food and beverage sales, in-flight retail, and travel insurance. The share of ancillary revenue is expected to increase from 7.5% of total revenue in 2006 to 2007 to about 10% in the next couple of years. As the industry moves away from price wars, SpiceJet hopes to achieve profitability in 2009.

Jet Airways, in a creative move to stimulate demand, sponsored screenings of the Oscar-winning movie *Slumdog Millionaire* for travel agents around Asia to promote India. A representative explained in a recent interview, "We find there is an increase in interest in India. The screening of the movie as well as the number of Oscars it has won have been a godsend."[14]

Since October 2008, fares have come down significantly, and domestic carriers have started competing with one another despite their poor financial health and the global economic meltdown. Competitive fares and a number of discount schemes, such as special advance purchase prices and free companion travel in business class, which were put on hold for a while, have been reintroduced.

The Outlook for Low-Cost Carriers

Global numbers indicate at least five failures for every successful low-cost airline, and the case for India's LCCs may be no different. Continued entrance of new, well-capitalized carriers will benefit the consumer in the form of lower fares and more flight options. In addition to expanding into new markets, new carriers will serve to replace failed start-ups. Despite the challenges, and given the fare wars and the trend toward price commoditization, many believe that low-cost air travel is the future.

According to Kaul, "By 2010, the [low-cost] market share will be 50%, up from 16% today." He contends that on parameters like fuel prices and airport charges, India will be on par with international levels then. Coupled with labor cost advantages and high-quality IT infrastructure (at low prices), India will be one of the lowest-cost aviation markets by 2010. Industry veteran A. N. K. Kaimal agrees. He envisions a significant number of LCCs surviving in the marketplace as they carve out differentiating niches. Professor N. Viswanadham of the India School of Business also believes that a significant number of LCCs will survive because of new airports and an expanding market, despite the inevitable consolidation resulting from fare pressures.

Industry Trends: A Bumpy Ride

Industry Consolidation

India's aviation sector has witnessed significant M&A activity in 2007. With fare wars wreaking havoc on profitability, consolidation was inevitable. The top three players now have a market share of about 85%, compared with 71% before consolidation. The merger wave was kicked off in March 2007, when the government announced the merger of its two state-run airlines—Air India and Indian Airlines—to better tackle intensifying competition.

With the merger of Air India and Indian Airlines, the new Air India has become colossal, carrying more than thirteen million passengers annually and securing a market share of 30%. The merged entity ranks among the largest airlines in Asia and in the top twenty globally in number of planes. The carrier now has a combined fleet of 122 aircraft, and it plans to add 111 more. Most of the new planes, though, are expected to replace aging planes in the fleet. The combined staffs of the merged airlines number about 33,500, but Air India has no plans to cut personnel. The merger should help the airlines gain lost market share, although since the merger, the airlines has faced all sorts of problems, including strikes by ground staff. The synergies resulting from the merger were expected to pay off in about a year, but this assessment may have been overoptimistic. After eighteen months of postmerger integration efforts, Air India was still struggling to turn its business around.

In a long-drawn-out deal, Jet Airways, the airline preferred by India's business travelers, acquired Air Sahara in April 2007 and renamed it JetLite. It then cut more than half the staff. This acquisition created the largest fleet of aircraft in the domestic market, gave Jet Airways a 22.5% market share at the time, and positioned the carrier well in terms of scarce resources such as pilots, engineers, hangars, parking slots, and routes. Jet Airways gained 50% of parking bays at Mumbai airports and a 50% market share on the popular Mumbai–Delhi route—a key revenue- and profit-generating sector. To lower costs, Jet Airways has separated certain aspects of its business, such as marketing and customer care, while tapping synergies in back-office operations, frequent-flyer programs, and purchasing. Like other carriers, Jet Airways has also lowered costs by outsourcing maintenance, baggage handling, cargo loading, cleaning, catering, and flight reservations.

In June 2007, a month and a half after Jet Airways acquired Air Sahara, its private-sector rival Kingfisher Airlines took a 26% share in the LCC Air Deccan, raised its share in 2008, and then merged with the LCC. The Kingfisher–Air Deccan merger resulted in an operating fleet of seventy-five aircraft with a domestic market share of around 30% at the time—placing Kingfisher ahead of the Jet Airways–JetLite combine and Air India. The merger also allowed Kingfisher to start its international operations to the United States and Great Britain in 2008, as Deccan Aviation by then had completed the required five years of service to be eligible for an international license (see below). Kingfisher's Mallya expects combined operations to lead to significant cost savings. Synergies are expected to arise in the areas of ground staff, aircraft, operation and maintenance, ground and baggage handling, increased connectivity, feeder services, and distribution penetration. Mallya indicated that the airlines could achieve further savings by sharing reservation services, service stations, spares, pilots and other crew, and parking bays at airports. Also, both Kingfisher and Deccan operate identical aircraft (the Airbus A-320 family and ATR-72-500), which is expected to help both airlines save on engineering and maintenance costs.

Civil aviation experts argue that consolidation gives market power to players to indulge in predatory pricing and create entry barriers unhealthy for the growth of a competitive airlines market. However, many analysts agree that the shakeout will lead to more-rational pricing, improving the health of the industry. Fare wars have led to profitless growth, and with consolidation, the dynamics of the industry may shift from market share to profitability. The fallout from consolidation has already begun. Most airlines increased their fares in the fall of 2007, in the form of fuel surcharges. Periodic fare hikes in 2008 were also more pronounced and more coordinated. In 2009, India's antitrust body and aviation regulators launched an investigation into domestic airlines' pricing decisions and warned them against cartelization.[15] At about the time of the investigation, however, the airlines had already flung themselves into another round of price reductions and discounts.

With Jet Airways' acquisition of Air Sahara and Kingfisher's merger with Air Deccan, both groups' business model is now a mix of an LCC plus a full service carrier—a mix that could work well in a growing economy like India's. With their LCCs, the two private groups can target the price-sensitive middle class, and with both domestic and international passenger traffic growing, Jet Airways and Kingfisher can effectively and flexibly address short-haul and long-haul routes and be strong players in both segments.

The recent Jet Airways–Kingfisher alliance, announced in October 2008, may point toward an alternative to mergers and acquisitions in the industry. Some observers suggest that alliances would help the industry to stabilize and would allow smaller players to form alliances or join the existing ones to cut costs and enable them to survive the competition.[16]

The Rise of the Cargo Market

India's airlines purchase and lease aircraft depending on the airlines' level of capital commitment, and while the airlines are rushing to purchase enough aircraft to meet Indians' growing demand for air travel, purchases increase the fixed costs of operation, which tends to intensify rivalry. Players are diversifying into carrying air freight, which reduces rivalry and makes them less reliant on passenger ticket sales.

Currently, most of India's airlines earn about 10% of their revenue from the cargo business. The Indian air freight market accounts for less than 5% of the global air freight market. Consequently, the airlines see a tremendous growth opportunity here, especially as the cargo business generates greater revenue than passenger traffic relative to costs. LCCs have been entering the cargo market and offering attractive prices to companies seeking to transport a variety of goods. For instance, the lack of refrigerated trucks and warehouses in India forces exporters of perishable goods to use aircraft. A growing number of other industries have also opted for air transport. Both domestic and international cargo operations are likely to lead to increased revenues for India's airlines in the next few years.

Expanding Domestic and International Route Networks

India's domestic air traffic is increasing with the number of key regional destinations. Passenger growth has been fastest in new airports (e.g., Amritsar and Srinagar), because there were few flights to these locations previously. Smaller cities such as Chandigarh, Rajkot, Calicut, and Mangalore are being connected. In the northeast, many cities now get flights from Kolkata. This system of regional connections has led to a large growth in domestic aircraft movement. In the south, new airports in Bangalore and Hyderabad opened in 2008. Work on Chennai's new airport is under way, and Cochin has a new international airport. The development of this infrastructure in the south is giving aviation there a massive boost. Indeed, the south has become the most sought-after location for regional airlines, and at least four small start-ups in the south are planning services. According to Kapil Kaul, CEO of the Centre for Asia Pacific Aviation, the rise of regional hubs is critical for the future of the Indian aviation industry: "Aviation in India has always been Delhi-Mumbai–centric. But in order to grow as an industry, aviation will have to go to tier 2 and 3 cities. You cannot just operate in only metros any longer. Regional connectivity is critical in the long run, and it is good to see that airlines are connecting a lot of smaller destinations."[17] The biggest advantage the regional airlines have is freedom from route dispersal guidelines that stipulate how many flights must be operated on which routes. These guidelines, for example, stipulate that all scheduled airlines operate at least 10% of their flights on trunk routes (lanes between two major airports) like Delhi–Mumbai, Jammu and Kashmir, Andaman and Nicobar Islands, and Lakshadweep. One way to ensure the industry's sustainability is to examine the viability of these routes to feed passengers into mainstream hubs. The guidelines therefore need to be reexamined.

During the economic downturn in 2008, many of India's airlines slowed their network expansion efforts and even started to cancel routes or flights. Given the industry, and especially LCCs' reliance on maximum asset use, carriers keep a close watch on demand levels for individual routes. To increase demand for some routes, SpiceJet has started offering heavy discounts on return tickets. "We are trying to attract fliers. If there is no increase in demand, then we will have to stop operations during the off-season," a SpiceJet representative said.[18] A spokesperson for Kingfisher Airlines explained that even during the better times, routes often took six to ten months to stabilize. "Right now it would take much longer, maybe even two years, and it is far too expensive to deploy aircraft on loss-making routes," he says.[19]

International Expansion

In 2007, India's airlines handled just 15% of the country's international air traffic. Even today, national carriers are underdeployed; they have fewer departures than foreign airlines instead of an equal share, as mandated in bilateral agreements. Until Jet Airways' entry in 2007, Air India (with Indian Airlines on some Gulf routes) was the only Indian carrier serving international passenger traffic. Because of the inadequate size of its fleet, Air India could not deploy the maximum number of seats permitted under various bilateral agreements. Jet Airways has significantly ramped up its international operations: nearly a third of its revenues are now from international routes, and it hopes to increase this share to half.

Under current regulations, there is a minimum five-year waiting period after an airline incorporates in India before it is allowed to fly internationally, although this rule may change. Jet Airways could take advantage of this situation when in 2004 it became India's first private airline to operate international flights. Kingfisher commenced international service in 2007 and has aggressive international expansion plans as well. A number of India's smaller airlines have also announced their intention to apply for international licenses.

According to Civil Aviation Minister Praful Patel, the ability to fly international routes should be a function of the size of an airline rather than the number of years in operation. Furthermore, he believes that "at least 50% of all traffic in and out of India should be carried by Indian carriers. This is the case with most countries, that their home-grown carriers do at least 50% if not more. So we want Indian carriers to have an opportunity to grow, to scale up, and be able to participate in this great growth which is taking place from India."[20]

Limits to Growth and Profitability

In addition to mergers and acquisitions, fare hikes, the expansion of international routes, and the rise of domestic feeder routes, other factors are important to sustained profitability—particularly infrastructure, industry regulation, and labor costs. We turn now to the potential impact of these on profitability.

Inadequate Airport Infrastructure

Wolfgang Prock-Schauer, CEO of Jet Airways, noted that "with the Indian aviation market growing faster than India's GDP, the current growth rate is not sustainable given the existing infrastructure." Airports that were meant to handle two hundred flights a day are now handling eight hundred flights a day. Many of India's airports have exceeded their intended capacity. Delhi's airport handled 20.5 million passengers in 2006, against a capacity of 12 million. Similarly, Mumbai handled 22 million passengers against a capacity of 14 million. Gaurang Shetty of Jet Airways argues, "Airport size is the single largest inhibitor to growth in India's airline industry. Even as new airlines add several hundred flights, they depend on the same number of runways, leading to delays during peak hours. Airports have single runways, which limits the volume of flights, and therefore the frequency of business and leisure travel."

With traffic exceeding capacity comes congestion. For instance, it is not unusual for passenger planes to spend an hour circling above an airport, waiting for a landing slot. This practice drives up fuel consumption, adding an estimated 10% to flight costs.[21] In addition, at New Delhi's and Mumbai's airports, about a third of all planes must wait fifteen to twenty minutes after landing before gaining approval to head to a terminal. Infrastructure issues are not limited to physical facilities on the ground. Airlines complain about the lack of airspace—35% of which is controlled by the Ministry of Defence— which prevents straight flight paths, particularly on routes between the north and the west. In addition, India's air traffic control system needs additional controllers and technology upgrades.

Delays due to bottlenecks in the air traffic control system cost airlines money, inconvenience passengers, and seriously limit expansion of airline traffic. Current airport facilities lack the technology to accommodate large modern aircraft and to cover baggage handling and check-in procedures to minimize the waiting time of both airlines and passengers. Mumbai's airport desperately needs more slots for night parking of aircraft. India's poor aviation infrastructure accounted for an estimated 16% of airline industry losses in 2006 to 2007.

Ironically, while some Indian airports are bursting at their seams, many others—including some with full infrastructure— handle only one or two daily flights, according to the Airports Authority of India (AAI). The AAI manages 127 airports in the country, including fourteen international airports, seventy-nine domestic airports, eight customs airports, and twenty-four civil enclaves of which 80% are loss making. Despite the vast network available for use, domestic airports are for the most part underused; 51% of air traffic flows through the airports in Mumbai and Delhi. The top twenty airports account for more than 91% of the volume of air traffic in India. Only sixty-one of the airports are now used for airlines, and only six airports can accommodate international traffic. Despite the inadequate infrastructure, airport user charges are higher than international norms.

Along with increasing the capacity of major airports, the development of India's secondary airports needs to be encouraged. The development of secondary, less-congested airports would especially benefit Indian LCCs. The lower usage fees and faster turnaround times of such airports would reduce the carriers' operating costs. Additional secondary airports could be built close to existing airports. For instance, in the United States and Great Britain, multiple airports service the same area. London has five airports within the Greater City area, and New York City has three airports all servicing Manhattan. Development of secondary airports in India would also allow new carriers to expand the market from the more crowded trunk routes that have become highly competitive and aggressively priced.

Recognizing the long-overdue need for improvement in India's aviation infrastructure, the government has taken measures to privatize and modernize the country's airports. The move toward privatization is a late but much-needed step toward expanding the capacity of Indian airports. Many changes resulting from privatization and modernization should start becoming apparent in the next two years. India's two most popular airports, Delhi's and Mumbai's, are already privately contracted expansion projects and are now being privately run. A second airport will be built in Mumbai, and one is under consideration for Delhi. Bangalore and Hyderabad were bid out to develop replacement greenfield airports, which opened in 2008. Work on Chennai's new airport is under way, and Cochin International Airport, India's first private airport, has seen the city become a small hub of sorts. With the development of these southern airports, air connectivity among southern cities is likely to grow exponentially.

Other greenfield airports are being planned in different parts of the country. The government plans to develop three hundred currently unused airstrips across the country over the next few years, and there are suggestions to upgrade or build new airports in key regional centers. In addition, plans are under way to upgrade nearly thirty-five nonmetro airports in other parts of the country at an estimated cost of $800 million. These much-needed improvements will reduce congestion at existing airports, reducing operational costs of carriers (because of lower fuel consumption) and shortening their turnaround times.

To facilitate airport development, the Indian government is allowing 100% foreign direct investment (FDI) in existing airports as well as greenfield airports, and it is offering a 100% tax exemption for airport projects for ten years. The government has allowed private-sector participation in airport infrastructure management, passenger and cargo handling, and related services. However, the new airport managements are raising the price of all services, including airport handling charges, which will affect the profit-ability of the airlines. The government is considering quadrupling the investment allocation in aviation infrastructure for the coming five-year period, with most of these outlays being met by the internal resources of organizations connected with the country's aviation infrastructure. It is also considering increasing FDI in domestic carriers to 74% from the current 49%. The increase in the cap on foreign funding will help these airlines raise capital to expand their fleets. With large-airport modernization under way, Indian aviation can be poised for a leap forward. But delays in the development of these airports would add to the existing pressures on profitability.

Labor Shortage

One major obstacle to the growth of India's airline industry is the acute shortage of pilots. When Kingfisher commenced flying opera-tions, its established rivals, Air Sahara and Jet Airways, had to prune back their flight schedules because of lack of cockpit personnel. Air Sahara alone lost ten pilots to Kingfisher and SpiceJet. "There is a real pilot bottleneck in India,"[22] says Jet Airways chief operating officer Peter Luethi, who is also having difficulty manning the new intercontinental services. For many nations, air force retirees serve as the primary source of commercial pilots. However, unlike the situation in the United States, the need for pilots in India cannot be filled primarily by air force retirees, because of the surge in the airline industry's growth. Industry analysts estimate that India will require eight hundred more pilots every year until 2010, making for a shortage of two thousand pilots in the next two to three years. According to Indian aviation expert A. N. K. Kaimal, this labor shortage has driven up salaries of India's airline pilots to levels seen at many international carriers.

To alleviate the labor shortfall in the near term, the Indian government has relaxed regulations on aviation personnel. Foreign pilots are now allowed to operate Indian planes so long as there is an Indian copilot. In addition, the retirement age of pilots has been extended from sixty to sixty-five. Lastly, the government introduced a rule requiring commercial pilots to give at least six months' notice before resigning, which has resulted in lower turnover. While these efforts have increased the supply of pilots for now, they are not a long-term solution. There are about six hundred foreign pilots operating in India right now, four hundred in training in India, and about two thousand training overseas. The training to become a pilot is long and costly, involving up to three stages, substantial capital investment, and a fourteen-month completion period, so the situation is likely to change only over the next few years.

As a longer-term solution, many major Indian carriers have created alternative training facilities to supplement government facilities and help increase the supply of pilots. For instance, Air India has established a joint venture with its major supplier, Boeing, to train pilots as well as maintenance personnel and cabin crew. Leaving aside pilots, the airline industry is labor intensive, and staffing costs are substantial. There is a shortage of cabin crew, aircraft maintenance engineers, and an even larger number of support staff, all of which affect operations, performance, and profitability.

Reeling under the cost pressures of 2008, and running out of other options to reduce their costs, a number of airlines have started to cut staff. While in the last couple of years about four thousand pilots were hired by India's airlines, including nearly nine hundred expatriates, at least sixty pilots were asked to leave or did not have their contracts renewed in 2008. In addition, Jet Airways is considering a pay cut of up to 10% for employees earning more than Rs 500,000 ($10,800) per month and 5% for those earning Rs 75,000 to Rs 500,000 ($1,600 to $10,800) per month.[23]

Conclusion

Change of government regulations and company strategies, though ongoing, has not kept pace with the growth and dynamism of India's airline market. Still, the aviation industry is beginning to see the benefits of privatization of infrastructure, other regulatory adjustments, and the strategic reorientation of the major players. More of these changes are likely over the next few years. Substantial government reforms are under way—relating to airports, ground service, maintenance, and repairs—to make the industry more resilient. Given the low penetration of airline services in the country and the tremendous scope for growth, massive additions in capacity could surpass demand in the short run, leading to overcapacity and another round of price wars and consolidation. To help maintain competitive pricing, the government should support efforts by new carriers to enter the market. And to reduce the possibility of market commoditization, established carriers should focus on increasing efficiency to free up funds to innovate and differentiate their services from competitors' services. The relative success of Jet Airways, Kingfisher, and Paramount shows that the Indian aviation market is demanding but, if addressed properly, can be very profitable.

Even as the industry as a whole is aggressively expanding network operations to offset losses, launching cargo operations, anticipating great synergies through consolidations, and receiving strong foreign and domestic corporate backing, turbulent times are still ahead. CEOs are extremely optimistic about the industry's growth, but some believe that the strongest threat to the health of the industry is its current state of overcapacity and its mounting burden of debt. By some estimates, 15% of the industry's capacity needs to disappear before airlines begin to improve their profitability. Most major carriers have started to address the issue. Capacity additions are slowing down or have been postponed; some excess capacity is being deployed to nonmetro, far-flung routes for a price premium or leased to foreign airlines. The development of secondary airports will allow new entrants better access to untouched consumer segments, further spur the growth of the industry, and use available capacity while reducing congestion around the few major airports that now exist. Servicing these new facilities will require significant growth in the supply of both pilots and technical staff, but as more people complete their training and come on stream, labor cost pressures should start to ease up.

The recent spate of consolidations suggests that the industry might be experiencing a paradigm shift—one that results in a focus on top-line *and* bottom-line growth and prevents cutthroat competition from endangering the survival of the major players. Even as mergers and acquisitions become more commonplace in the industry, investor interest will undoubtedly remain alive, keeping in mind the lucrative long-term prospects. And undoubtedly India will eventually become a one-thousand-aircraft market. What remains to be seen are whose aircraft they will be and which airlines will have weathered the storm.

Notes

1. Nandini Lakshman, "Merger Mania Reshapes Indian Airlines," *BusinessWeek,* June 11, 2007, http://www.businessweek.com/globalbiz/content/jun2007/gb20070609_067193.htm (accessed April 5, 2009).

2. Siddharth Srivastava, "India's Airlines Look to Fly High," *Asia Times,* January 4, 2007, http://www.atimes.com/South_Asia/IA04Df01.html.

3. Tom Allett, "Asia Pacific—The Booming Market," *Airports International,* November 1, 2005, http://goliath.ecnext.com/coms2/gi0199-4997962/Asia-Pacific-the-booming-market.html.

4. *Hindustan Times,* "Air India Flies Least Passengers per Plane," June 23, 2008.

5. F. K. R. Balasubramanyam and Kushan Mitra, "Fighting the Bad Times," *Business Today,* November 27, 2008.

6. *Evening Standard,* "Harrods in the Sky Lands at Heathrow," September 2, 2008.

7. Balasubramanyam and Mitra, "Fighting the Bad Times."

8. N. Madhavan, "High Flier," *Business Today,* November 13, 2008, http://businesstoday.intoday.in.

9. Madhavan, "High Flier."

10. *Times of India,* "Crisis Hits India: Airlines Seek $1Bn Bailout," October 13, 2008.

11. Anjuli Bhargava, "Toughest Business to Be In," *Businessworld,* January 29, 2007, http://www.businessworld.in/index.php/Toughest-Business.html.

12. Balasubramanyam and Mitra, "Fighting the Bad Times."

13. *Economic Times,* "Airlines Fly High on 5% Cut on ATF Custom Duty," June 6, 2008.

14. Sandy Hendry, "Jet Airways' Koh Says Discounts, Slumdog, Rupee Filling Seats," *Bloomberg News,* March 16, 2009, http://www.bloomberg.com.

15. *Hindustan Times,* "Anti-Trust Body, Regulator Ask Airlines to Explain Fare Hikes," February 12, 2009.

16. *Statesman,* "Airlines Merger May Push Fares," October 15, 2008.

17. Raghvendra Rao, "Now Calling at All Towns," *Indian Express,* November 4, 2006, http://www.indianexpress.com.

18. Arpit Basu, "Low-Cost Carriers Fly Away from City," *Times of India,* March 29, 2008.

19. "Hitting an Air Pocket," *Business Today,* April 2, 2009.

20. Nicholas Ionides, "Praful Patel: Overseeing Change in India," *Airline Business,* November 16, 2007.

21. Lakshman, "Merger Mania."

22. Andreas Spaeth, "Air Transport Booms in India," *Flug Revue,* August 2005, http://www.flug-revue.rotor.com/FRheft/FRHeft05/FRH0508/FR0508b.htm.

23. *Hindustan Times,* "Despite Government Plea, Airlines Clip Pilots' Wings," November 24, 2008.

Bibliography

Balasubramanyam, F. K. R., and Kushan Mitra. 2008. "Fighting the Bad Times." *Business Today,* November 27.

Bangkok Post. 2006. "India's Busy Skies: Merger of the Two Big Carriers Could Intensify Dogfight," November 11.

Basu, Arpit. 2008. "Low-Cost Carriers Fly Away from City." *Times of India,* March 29.

BBC News. 2006. "India Airport Contracts Announced," January 31. http://news.bbc.co.uk.

Bellman, Eric, and Bruce Stanley. 2006. "Infrastructure Prized in India Air Deal; Jet Airways' Sahara Buyout Would Yield Scarce Workers and Key Airport Logistics." *Wall Street Journal,* January 16: A13.

Bhargava, Anjuli. 2007. "Toughest Business to Be In: The Indian Aviation Industry Is Losing Money Hand over Fist. 2006 Was Bad, but 2007 Could Actually Get Worse." *Businessworld,* January 29. http://www.businessworld.in/bw/.

Bhattacharya, A. K. 2006. "Who's Afraid of the Jet-Sahara Deal?" *Rediff.com*, January 18. http://in.rediff.com/money/2006/jan/18guest.htm.

Biswas, Soutik. 2005. "India Worried over Air Fare Wars." *BBC News,* June 29. http://news.bbc.co.uk/.

Cuckoo, Paul, and Sudipto Dey. 2007. "Regional Airlines Look for a Slice of the Sky." *Economic Times,* August 14.

Das Gupta, Surajeet. 2005. "Scramble in the Sky for Re 1 Fares." *Rediff.com,* May 7. http://us.rediff.com/money/2005/may/07spec.htm.

Datamonitor. 2007. "Airlines in India: Industry Profile." November. http://www.datamonitor.com/.

Economic Times. 2008. "Airlines Fly High on 5% Cut on ATF Custom Duty," June 6.

Evening Standard. 2008. "Harrods' in the Sky Lands at Heathrow," September 2.

Financial Times. 2006. "Steady Rise in Airline Passenger Traffic," April 29.

———. 2005. "Air Cargo Biz Attracts Airlines, but Faces Infrastructure Hurdles," December 11.

Goyal, Malini. 2004. "Flying Middle Class." *India Today,* September 6. http://www.india-today.com/.

Hendry, Sandy. 2009."Jet Airways' Koh Says Discounts, Slumdog, Rupee Filling Seats." *Bloomberg News,* March 16. http://www.bloomberg.com.

Hindustan Times. 2009. "Anti-Trust Body, Regulator Ask Airlines to Explain Fare Hikes," February 12.

———. 2008. "Air India Flies Least Passengers per Plane," June 23.

———. 2008. "Despite Government Plea, Airlines Clip Pilots' Wings," November 24.

ICMR Case Studies and Management Resources. 2007. "Kingfisher Airlines Acquires a Stake in Air Deccan: The Indian Aviation Sector Moves Toward Consolidation," August 22. http://www.icmrindia.org/business/.

Ionides, Nicholas. 2007. "Reforming India's Skies." *Airline Business* 12 (December 23): 34–37.

Iyer, Bharat, and Jamshed Dadabhoy. 2005. "Airlines—Low Cost Airlines—Battling for a Piece of the Pie." Citigroup Research Report, October 17.

Jain, Satish, and Deepak Gupta. 2005. "Key Takeaways from India Aviation Day in New York." Morgan Stanley Research Report, September 19.

John, Jacob. 2005. "Bangalore Airport: Real Estate or Runway?" *India Together,* January 5. http://www.indiatogether.org/2005/jan/.

Kaimal, A. N. K. 2006. Personal interview, March 16.

Kripalani, Manjeet. 2005. "Dogfight over India." *BusinessWeek,* May 2. http://www.businessweek.com/magazine/.

Krishnan, Aarati. 2005. "Bargain Airfares: Spoilt for Choice." *Hindu Business Line,* October 16. http://www.thehindubusinessline.com/iw/2005/10/16/stories/.

Lakshman, Nandini. 2007. "Merger Mania Reshapes Indian Airlines." *BusinessWeek,* June 11. http://www.businessweek.com/globalbiz/content/jun2007/ (accessed April 5, 2009).

Madhavan, N. 2008. "High Flier." *Business Today,* November 13. http://businesstoday.intoday.in/.

Manju, V. 2006. "No Night Parking for New Airlines." *Times of India,* January 11.

Mehra, Puja, and Sandeep Unnithan. 2005. "Airborne Indians." *India Today,* July 11. http://www.india-today.com/itoday/.

Merchant, Khozem. 2006. "Jet Flies into a Storm of Criticism—Rival Carriers Want a Fairer Distribution by the Government of Airport Infrastructure." *Financial Times,* January 25.

Meredith, Robyn. 2008. "Beyond Airlines, Beyond India." *Forbes,* April 7. http://www.forbes.com/business/global/2008/0407/016.html.

Mitra, Kushan. 2007. "Wanted: Better Infrastructure." *Business Today,* September 9. http://businesstoday.digitaltoday.in/.

Mitra, Kushan, and T. V. Mahalingam. 2007. "Wind Under Their Wings." *Business Today,* August 29. http://businesstoday.digitaltoday.in/.

Phadnis, Ashwini. 2007. "A Year of Airline Consolidations." *Hindu Business Line,* December 28. http://www.thehindubusinessline.com/2007/12/29/stories/.

Press Trust of India. 2006. "Civil Aviation Likely to Get Rs 3045 cr in 06–07," January 2.

Prock-Schauer, Wolfgang. 2006. Personal interview, March 16.

Roy, Abhijit. 2006. Personal interview, March 22.

Sabarad, Mahantesh, and Aniket Mhatre. 2007. "India Aviation: Blue Side Up." Prabhudas Lilladher, December.

Sanjai, P. R. 2006. "A-I, Indian Merger to Create Behemoth." *Business Standard,* November 28.

Sharma, Rajesh. 2006. Personal interview, March 16.

Srivastava, Siddharth. 2007. "India's Airlines Look to Fly High." *Asia Times,* January 4. http://www.atimes.com/.

Statesman. 2008. "Airlines Merger May Push Fares," October 15.

Subramaniam, G., and Sudipto Dey. 2005. "Big Airlines Seek Entry Barriers Against Low-Cost Rivals." *Economic Times,* July 6. http:// economictimes.indiatimes.com/.

Subramanian, K. 2006. Personal interview, March 16.

Times of India. 2008. "Crisis Hits India: Airlines Seek $1Bn Bailout," October 13.

———. 2006. "No Job Cuts After AI, IA Merger," November 24.

Timmons, Heather. 2007. "India's Airline Industry Runs into Turbulence." *International Herald Tribune,* May 6. http://www.iht.com/articles/ 2007/05/06/business/.

Tribune India. 2005. "Pilot Project," June 22. http://www.tribuneindia .com/2005/20050622/jobs/main1.htm.

Viswanadham, N. 2006. Personal interview, March 22.

Yadav, Kiran. 2006. Personal interview, March 16.

Chapter 6

INDIA'S CHANGING HOSPITALITY INDUSTRY

Francis Abeling, Mario Rivera, Brian Schneider

India's historical propensity to shy away from tourism has impeded the growth of its hospitality industry. For many foreign tourists, travel to India is not a preferred option. This is surprising given that India offers one of the most diverse ranges of tourism in the world: twenty-six world heritage sites, twenty-five specific biogeographic zones, more than 3,700 miles of coastline, and several word-class beaches. Unfortunately, demand has been discouraged by inadequate infrastructure, uncompetitive hotel and airline rates, and a general lack of hygiene. Consequently, compared with tourism in other countries, tourism in India represents a much smaller portion of the country's GDP and employment base. Of the fifty most visited countries in 2006, according to a survey by the World Tourism Organization, India ranked near the bottom (42nd). And in terms of tourism's overall contribution to the economy, it ranked 146th out of 176 countries studied by the World Travel and Tourism Council (WTTC).

Despite India's shortcomings, the WTTC has identified it as one of the world's foremost tourism growth centers. The organization estimates that India will be the third-fastest-growing tourism destination over the next decade, with an annual growth rate of about 8%, which will create about four million new jobs. Indeed, recent numbers support this prediction. Foreign tourist arrivals rose to 4.4 million in 2006 from 3.9 million in 2005, which is an increase of about 14%. The year 2007 was not only a record year for India's inbound tourism, but was the fifth consecutive year showing a double-digit increase in foreign tourist arrivals. Tourism contributed about 7% of the GDP and provided employment to more than forty-one million people, about 9% of total employment in the country. With the rise in tourism has come a rise in India's foreign exchange earnings from this sector. Indeed, tourism is the third-largest generator of such earnings.

Much of the growth in tourism has resulted from India's growing economy. And while a large part of this growth is ascribed to international business travelers who frequent the high-end hotels, domestic tourism has been growing sharply as well. Both domestic leisure and domestic business travelers now constitute a very important segment of India's tourism market, and since domestic travelers largely prefer budget and value hotels, the domestic midmarket and budget segment has emerged as a compelling business opportunity. How has the changing composition of tourists affected India's hospitality industry? Are the biggest players in the industry expanding and diversifying their services to capture the midmarket segment? Is the time right for foreign investors and other domestic players to meet the demand, seize the opportunity, and enter an industry that has historically targeted the very wealthy traveler? In this chapter we discuss the current state of demand-supply mismatch in India's hospitality industry, the need for increasing market segmentation, and the competitive challenges faced by the established hospitality firms as they redefine their strategic goals in response to growing interest by foreign investors and tourists.

The Effects of Rising and Excess Demand

Since the recent growth in tourism has been driven mostly by an increase in international business travelers, who prefer higher-end hotels, the primary beneficiaries of this segment's growth are such hotels in business centers like Delhi, Mumbai, Hyderabad, and Bangalore. Moreover, since this demand is business rather than tourism driven, seasonality is less important.

High-end hotels are also benefiting from a deregulated airline industry, which has contributed to a substantial demand for luxury hotels by airline crews, who also have a strong preference for this category. Gaurang Shetty, vice president of marketing at Jet Airways, said that in other countries, the airline industry grows at a rate of 1.0 to 1.1 times the GDP. In India, however, the airline industry has grown at 1.25 times the GDP because of tax reductions and airline deregulation.

The lower cost of travel following the liberalization of the airline industry has also opened up travel opportunities for the domestic tourist. While the foreign segment has shown faster growth than the domestic segment, domestic guests accounted for 75% of all guests in 2005 to 2006. According to industry estimates, domestic tourism grew by 40% annually in the three-year period ending in 2006 and is now estimated at 230 million travelers. Midlevel domestic business travelers constitute a key target market for most luxury hotels in commercial destinations, and the segment exhibits comparatively high average length-of-stay patterns.

However, the sudden rise in demand has also resulted in a severe shortage of hotel rooms. While the estimated number of required hotel rooms is around 240,000, the current availability is just 90,000, leaving a shortfall of 150,000 rooms (other studies estimate the shortfall to be 200,000 rooms). According to some estimates, closing this gap would require an estimated investment of up to US$20 billion.

Because of this massive gap between demand and supply, occupancy ratios have increased and room rates have soared. Occupancy ratios indicate the percentage of available hotel rooms that are full throughout the year and are the clearest measure of hotel demand. In India, occupancy ratios are around 75%, while the average increase in room rates has been around 18% to 22% annually in recent years. There have been particularly sharp increases in average room rates in Delhi, Hyderabad, Bangalore, Mumbai, Pune, Goa, and Kolkata. Bangalore had the highest average room rate across all categories, with Delhi in second place. Industry analysts believe that as the Indian economy expands, the extreme shortage of rooms will be particularly felt in Delhi, Mumbai, Bangalore, and Goa—the hubs of tourist traffic.

This growth of domestic and international tourism, unaccompanied by an adequate increase in hotel rooms, has suddenly made India among the most expensive hotel markets in the region. The predominant concern is that if the acute shortage of rooms and the rise in room rates continue for the next few years, companies are likely to find midlevel domestic business travel prohibitively expensive, forcing them to search for more cost-effective alternatives. Major IT companies such as Infosys and Wipro are already considering the development of guesthouses at their campuses in Bangalore.

Likewise, while growing disposable incomes in India have led to a higher expectation of domestic leisure travel, the exorbitantly high hotel rates across key leisure destinations in India have made it more economical for the domestic traveler to visit many Far East destinations than to travel on domestic circuits.

The Tight Hospitality Market Will Continue

With New Delhi hosting the 2010 Commonwealth Games, the government has approved 300 hotel projects, nearly half of which are in the luxury range. Most of these projects are in various stages of development and will likely be completed in the next three years. In 2006, hotel construction boomed and 35 five-star hotels began operations during the year; 155 more hotels are under construction. Some 112 new projects, which are expected to open up about 3,500 rooms, were sanctioned in India's southern cities that are at the forefront of the IT and IT-enabled services boom. In Bangalore, construction has started on 27 hotels and service apartment developments.

When these projects come on stream, room capacity will increase by about 75,000, but the shortfall will continue. This fact implies that high rates and low availability will continue for some time and will worsen for key events, like the Commonwealth Games in 2010 and the cricket World Cup in 2011. Consequently, Indian cities are likely to see further increases in average room rates. However, the growing supply of new hotel rooms means that rates will

probably start correcting over the next two to three years. "Over
the next few years, most of these cities . . . will have sufficient supply coming into the market across most of the categories and this
is likely to lead to a correction," says Akshay Kulkarni, director for
South Asia at Cushman & Wakefield Hospitality, an international
hospitality consultancy firm.[1] Meanwhile, the rise in room rates is
already slowing. According to Rajiv Kaul, senior vice president of
the Leela Group hotels and resorts company, tariff hikes are more
likely to be 8% to 10% rather than the 18% to 20% that has been
typical in recent years.

Targeting the Affluent Segment Then and Now

India's hospitality market continues to be heavily skewed toward
the higher-end segment. In fact, in the last five or six years, India
has morphed into a chief player in the global luxury hotel market.
The recent hotel projects approved by the government to meet the
shortfall also seem to prioritize this space. The three major home-
grown players in India's hospitality industry—IHCL (Indian Hotels
Company), ITC Hotels, and Oberoi Hotels & Resorts—primarily
target the very exclusive and upscale luxury leisure and business
segments.

Much of the growth in India's hospitality market has taken
place in five-star and heritage hotels—converted forts and palaces
of the royal families of India that qualify for tax holidays—followed
by three-star hotels. At the three-star level and above, there are
slightly more than 55,000 hotel rooms in all of India. To put this
number in perspective, consider that the sixteen largest hotels in Las
Vegas have 56,825 rooms, although India has only three million
visitors annually compared with more than thirty-five million for
Las Vegas. India's number of rooms is about the same as New York
City's and stands below the 130,000 rooms offered in Shanghai.
Nearly all the Indian hotels rated four stars and above are registered
with the Federation of Hotel and Restaurant Associations of India
(FHRAI). According to FHRAI, rooms rated three stars or higher
account for most of the hotel rooms in the country.

In 2006 the demand by domestic and foreign travelers for five-star hotels and five-star deluxe hotels in India was 14% and 36% of total occupancy, respectively. At the four- and three-star levels, however, these numbers change dramatically, to 38% and 18%. The domestic tourism segment is one of the most significant demand sources for hotels rated four stars or less, as domestic travelers are generally more price sensitive than foreign travelers. Hotels that can provide clean accommodations at a reasonable price will capture this domestic segment, as infrastructure such as roads and airline capacity improves.

India's Budget Hotel Shortage

Because of high demand from the domestic segment, India's hotel room shortage is most acute in the budget segment. Hotels in the price range of Rs 3000 ($65) per night vary highly in quality, cleanliness, safety, and service. Until recently, there were no brands or hotel chains in this segment. Midrange hotels are particularly lacking in places like Mumbai, Bangalore, and New Delhi.

Given India's rising room rates, budget and midmarket hotels are likely to flourish, although luxury hotels will also see high growth over the medium term. Consequently, an investor hoping to capitalize on growth in the domestic business travel segment in Delhi would much prefer a three- or four-star hotel to a five-star or five-star deluxe hotel. Indeed, industry experts believe that, with a growing middle class and the rise of domestic tourism and business travel, the potential of the midmarket segment is huge. The size of the midprice hotel market is estimated at Rs 800 crore (Rs 8 billion or $173.7 million), of which the branded segment is roughly over Rs 400 crore (Rs 4 billion or more than $86.8 million). According to Mandeep Lamba, president of Fortune Park Hotels (ITC's budget/midmarket brand), the midmarket segment will double every four to five years, as 80% of its business is driven by the domestic sector. A budget hotel offering comfortable accommodations and satisfactory food and beverages at affordable prices has much to gain from the domestic travel market. A focus on the domestic segment decreases the volatility of portfolio cash flow by reducing dependence on highly cyclical international tourism. Moreover, changes in the international tourist segment are more difficult to predict than changes in other demand segments. Hotels in locations better known for tourism than business, such as Agra and Goa, have a less diversified customer base than hotels in cities with active business centers. Consequently, such hotels are extremely dependent on the international tourist trade.

Investing in India's Hospitality Industry

The appeal of India to hospitality companies is obvious: India is fast growing yet underserved; it boasts wide topographical diversity; and it has a large population. All of these characteristics make India's hospitality industry ripe for investment. Steve Rushmore, founder and president of hotel industry consulting firm HVS International, noted that India has had insignificant foreign direct investment (FDI) in the hospitality sector, as all the leading foreign hotel chains have been there on management or franchisee contracts. Foreign hotel operators, however, are now eager to invest, helped by recent changes in Indian law that allow full foreign ownership of hotels in the country. Around forty international hotel brands have entered India, including chains like Hilton, Accor, Marriott International, Berggruen Hotels, Best Western's Cabana Hotels, Premier Inn, InterContinental Hotels, and Hampshire. Furthermore, new brands are planning to enter through joint ventures with domestic hotels. Simultaneously, international hotel asset management companies are also entering India. Already, U.S.-based HVS International has firmed up plans to enter India, and others like Ashford Hospitality Trust and IFA Hotels & Resorts have followed suit.

Before India's hotel supply squeeze, real estate companies had focused on developing residential and commercial buildings, and international hotel companies had been investing in individual hotel projects. Now, major real estate developers—such as DLF, Emaar MGF, and Unitech—have been trying to cash in on India's hospitality industry, in partnership with major hotel chains. For instance, DLF has announced a joint venture company in India with Hilton Hotels to develop and own seventy-five hotels and service apartment buildings over the next seven years. While DLF will hold a 74% stake in the joint venture, Hilton will hold the remaining minority stake. Over the next five to seven years, Hilton will invest in hotels in several key locations, including Chandigarh, Chennai, and Kolkata. Unitech is planning to develop more than thirty hotels. It has already started partnerships with international players—such as Marriott, Ritz Carlton, and Country Inn—who will manage its hotels.

Soaring urban land prices in India are making it expensive for hotel chains to expand, and when they do, they are building pricier hotels. Compared with more-developed Asian and Western real estate markets, the Indian market has less good space available, typically smaller parcels, and higher prices. Urban land supply is largely controlled by state-owned development bodies like the Delhi Development Authority (DDA), resulting in a dearth of free developable space. And public auction prices for land set by the DDA may be far above the appropriate market price. Land prices as a percentage of total project costs present another predicament for developers in India. Internationally, land cost is 15% to 20% of the total project cost, whereas land cost in India is 40% to 50% of the total project cost. The unavailability of quality sites for hotel development has forced international brands to become more flexible about their product specifications. Many of them are entering the midmarket and budget segments.

Rising Foreign Investment in the Midmarket and Budget Segments

One example of how international hotel companies are capitalizing on the India opportunity is a joint venture agreement signed in March 2005 between InterGlobe Enterprises, India's leading travel and technology company, and Accor, a French-based owner of four thousand hotels worldwide. This venture aims to develop a network of twenty-five economy ibis hotels in India over the next ten to twenty years. This India-wide, internationally branded network hopes to redefine the economy hotel sector in India. The pan-India ibis hotel development plan represents one of the most significant financial commitments to this sector by an international hotel chain. The challenge for hospitality firms undertaking this strategy would be finding reasonably priced land suitable for developing an asset that generates less revenue than luxury hotels. Consequently, development opportunities are more likely to exist in tier 2 and 3 cities than in prime locations in downtown business districts. There are now ten ibis hotels in various stages of development across India, adding up to 1,850 rooms in tier 1 and 2 cities, and several other sites are under negotiation. Ibis hotels in India, priced at less than half the rates of upscale hotels, will cater to the burgeoning business and leisure travel segments in India. According to Michael Issenberg, managing director of Accor Asia Pacific, the objective of the ibis hotels is to capture the growing demand for budget chain hotels across India's emerging cities. In addition to the leisure traveler, ibis hotels want to capture the increasing business activity in many Indian cities—and the resulting demand for value-driven accommodations by international and intraregional business travelers.

At the end of 2006, Accor announced expansion plans for its Indian operations covering the full spectrum of the market, including budget hotelF1 hotels, economy ibis hotels, midmarket Novotel hotels, and luxury Sofitel hotels. The company signed agreements to develop 100 hotelF1 hotels in India with its Dubai-based partner Emaar Properties. Owned by the Accor Group, hotelF1 is an international chain of "super low budget" hotels (there are currently more than 380 of them in thirteen countries worldwide). The total development will add ten thousand hotel rooms to India's economy sector. These hotels will be located in city locations and will feature a minimum of eighty rooms. Sites for these hotels are being finalized, and ten hotels are scheduled to open in the next two years.

Dubai-based Istithmar Hotels proposes to establish eight budget easyHotels in India, using an on-site building concept called "stack, connect, and stick." The units are stacked atop one another, then connected with prefabricated corridors and lift units, and finally "stuck" onto a concrete platform. A typical 200-room easy-Hotel can be readied in about five months if the platform is in place. According to Peter Gowers, chief executive of InterContinental Hotels Group (IHG) Asia Pacific, "In the Indian hotel business, the greatest opportunity for growth is in the midscale segment, in which Holiday Inn has a leading position."[2] Indeed, IHG, one of the world's largest hotel groups by number of rooms, is enjoying robust growth in India, with fourteen new-look Holiday Inn hotels in various stages of development across the country. Accounting for more than 3,700 rooms, these hotels are scheduled to open over the next three years in eleven cities nationwide. In the 2007 *BDRC Asia Pacific Business Hotel Guest Survey,* Holiday Inn was the top midmarket hotel choice among business travelers in India and across the Asia-Pacific region.

In addition to hotel and real estate companies, investment firms and private equity companies are establishing a foothold in the midmarket hotel sector in India. For instance, Berggruen Holdings India, a subsidiary of New York–based investment company Berggruen Holdings, is seed-funding a nonluxury hotel chain in India. Private equity firm Warburg Pincus has also invested in a 27% stake in a midmarket hotel chain, Lemon Tree, for $60.2 million.

With all these new players—established international hotels, private equity firms, real estate developers, and domestic companies—making substantial entries into the midmarket segment, the question is, Are the major domestic hospitality players also seizing the opportunity to enter this market? Yes, they are, albeit cautiously.

Strategic Directions of Domestic Hospitality Players

IHCL (Taj) Hotels

Under the umbrella of the Tata Group, IHCL, the company commonly known as Taj Hotels, Resorts, and Palaces has grown to become the largest hotel chain in India. It owns and operates eighty-three properties under the Taj brand in India and abroad. The company's biggest strength is the spread of its properties across tier 1 and 2 cities in India as well as sixteen hotels outside the country.

Although IHCL claims to span the entire gamut of the hotel market, including properties of different brands in various price segments, the firm focuses primarily on upscale Taj-branded lodging facilities. Taj properties are grouped into luxury, leisure, and business segments to provide consistency across different hotels of the same brand and to standardize product and service. IHCL caters to a wide cross section of travelers with its luxury, business, and leisure hotels, including beach resorts, garden retreats, and palace hotels. The group as a whole is marketed as providing world-class, personalized service to guests, and claims to retain old-world charm by upholding the traditions and heritage of India

In a dramatic departure from IHCL's historical focus on upscale luxury lodging, the Taj Group recently unveiled its indiOne line of hotels, which was subsequently renamed Ginger Hotels. This brand, which had a national rollout in March 2006, already has its presence in six locations. Raymond Bickson, managing director of IHCL, points out that in the last few years the dynamics of the entire Indian hotel industry has changed, with the economy hotels emerging as a compelling business opportunity. According to Bickson, "Significant demand exists in the metros, secondary, and tertiary cities across the country." The economy segment is considered to be far less prone to demand fluctuations than the luxury and upscale segments are. Ginger Hotels aims to establish twenty-five hotels throughout India, having already established hotels in Bangalore, Bhubaneswar, Hardwar, Mysore, and Tiruvananthapuram. However, to maintain the Taj image as a luxury brand, Ginger properties are not associated with the Taj name.

Besides expanding into a lower price point hotel offering, IHCL is leveraging its reputation for luxury and service and expanding its presence in the full-service, extended-stay apartment rental business. In 2004 it opened the eighty-unit Taj Wellington Mews Luxury Residences in South Mumbai. Including this property,

IHCL now manages three full-service apartment properties and plans to continue exploring opportunities in this segment in the future.

ITC Hotels

After IHCL, ITC is the second-largest hotel chain in India. Its properties include superdeluxe and five-star hotels, heritage palaces, *havelis* (old personal residences that have been refurbished), resorts, and full-service budget hotels. Like its major competitors, ITC focuses largely on giving guests superior service, but it does so across a broader range of price segments and product types than its major competitors do.

The group operates primarily under four closely linked brands. ITC Welcomgroup Hotels are superdeluxe and premium hotels in strategic business destinations. WelcomHotel properties provide five-star hospitality for the upscale business and leisure traveler, and WelcomHeritage is the umbrella brand for all of ITC's palaces, forts, *havelis,* and resorts, which offer guests a unique lodging experience.

ITC's entry into the budget class has been through its Fortune Park Hotels, which offer full-service accommodations all over India, including smaller towns and cities, primarily for the budget traveler. Under its Fortune Park Hotels brand, ITC owns or manages an inventory of 1,600 rooms. With the company's stated strategy to expand into the three- and four-star segment, however, the number of rooms marketed under the brand is expected to increase to 4,200 by 2010.

Oberoi Hotels & Resorts

Oberoi Hotels & Resorts is the third-largest hotel chain in India. Its parent company, the Oberoi Group, owns and manages thirty hotels and five luxury cruisers across six countries under the Oberoi and Trident brands. In addition to a strong presence in the metros, the chain also has leisure hotels in Jaipur, Agra, Udaipur, Shimla, and Ranthambhore. The activities of the Oberoi Group include airline catering, management of restaurants and airport bars, travel and tour services, car rental, project management, and corporate air charters.

Like the properties of the Taj Group, Oberoi Hotels & Resorts properties are marketed as providing the right blend of service, luxury, and quiet efficiency. Oberoi is the most successful purveyor of luxury hospitality in the country. The group pioneered the shift into ultraluxury properties in nonmetro cities with its very upscale "vilās" properties in Jaipur, Udaipur, and more recently Agra. These resorts are incredibly expensive by local standards, but they have caught on with the affluent international traveler. In fact, Oberoi Hotels & Resorts has been internationally recognized for all-round excellence and superior levels of service, and its new resorts have particularly strengthened the chain's reputation for the highest levels of luxury among resort hotels around the world. Nine Oberoi hotels are members of the Leading Small Hotels of the World, a select association of international luxury hotels chosen for their extraordinary levels of guest comfort and service. Additionally, seven Oberoi hotels are members of Small Luxury Hotels of the World, a collection of exclusive hotels carefully selected for their style, sophistication, and the highest standards of service.

Trident Hotels, Oberoi's other primary brand, are superior first-class international hotels with contemporary facilities but with more of a focus on quality and value than their Oberoi-branded counterparts have. Friendly and efficient service in a warm and relaxed atmosphere makes these properties a likely choice for business and leisure travelers. The Oberoi Group opened its first Trident Hotel in Chennai in 1988. Trident Hotels have since opened in India at Agra, Udaipur, Cochin, Jaipur, Bhubaneswar, Chennai, and recently in Gurgaon. The group also operates Trident Hotels in the Saudi Arabian cities of Jeddah and Khamis Mashayt.

Overall, the Oberoi Group does not appear to be exploring a downstream move into the value segments or budget offerings. One risk for the group, therefore, is the lack of revenue diversification, with its two metros contributing 70% of revenues and no presence in budget hotels.

It is clear, however, from the various strategic initiatives of IHCL, ITC, and the Oberoi Group that even as these firms begin to expand into lower-priced segments to take advantage of growing demand, their primary focus and trajectory for growth will remain the luxury segment.

Faced with growing competition and the expansion of international chains into India, the three major Indian firms are solidifying their premier positions through a host of innovative strategies— namely, strengthening their brand image, diversifying into luxury segments that leverage India's natural resources and cultural heritage in response to changing leisure trends, forging marketing alliances with large international operators, expanding internationally into gateway cities, and generating alternative revenue streams from the food and beverage business.

Strengthening Brand Image

To preserve their brand image and their top position in the market, IHCL, ITC, and the Oberoi Group will continue to expand into domestic properties consistent with their existing portfolios. According to IHCL's Bickson, some of the properties inherited from earlier years pose a challenge to the consistency of the company's portfolio and are being reviewed in light of its brand equity. IHCL's focus is to continue positioning the Taj brand strongly in the high-end luxury and five-star segments. Similarly, ITC has focused on establishing and upgrading its ITC Welcomgroup brand across what it perceives to be the six major business hubs in India: Delhi, Mumbai, Kolkata, Hyderabad, Chennai, and Bangalore. With its Trident brand, the Oberoi Group also remains active in the relatively upscale business segment. The group has focused primarily on the development of new high-end luxury resorts both in India and overseas in the last few years.

Almost all major hotel groups in India are now looking at management contracts to free up their balance sheet and improve their return on equity. This asset-light strategy helps them use capital for expansion and increase their portfolio of properties, hence preserving brand dominance. This dominance will become more important as foreign firms increasingly make inroads into the Indian market and challenge domestic players.

The Taj Group chooses to leverage the growth in its business by holding minimal equity interest in its hotel properties when possible. This strategy enables IHCL to partner with other hotel owners to diversify real estate risk and to reduce capital investment in fixed assets. This is a fairly common approach in the hotel industry, and it benefits IHCL's joint venture partners by simultaneously providing them with the benefit of professional management by a well-recognized brand with deep local expertise. IHCL benefits from this arrangement in a couple of ways. First, its capital outlay in this ownership structure is much less than would be expected in a 100% IHCL ownership structure—resulting in a much more flexible and financially nimble organization. IHCL can leverage its capital into a greater number of new projects, which yields a high return on investment, lucrative management contracts, and portfolio diversification. Second, this structure allows the Taj Group to grow its brand rapidly by reaching a greater number of hotels. This is also a strategy pursued by ITC and the Oberoi Group.

Capitalizing on Changing Leisure Trends

Given India's growing importance as a travel destination, and given changing leisure trends, each of India's three largest hotel groups is considering diversification into segments leveraging India's natural resources and cultural heritage. These segments include ecotourism, adventure tourism, and spa resorts—all of which seem to be a natural fit for India. To maintain service quality and provide best-in-class offerings that capitalize on demand, these firms are using alliances with well-established providers.

To capitalize on these trends, two initiatives are already under way in the industry. One of these initiatives is the integration of full-fledged spas on luxury hotel premises, originally a mainstay of resort properties. Because India is a business destination, international travelers are on the lookout for recreational activities, thus encouraging hotels in India to offer a wide range of services—from cosmetic and antiaging treatments to wellness therapies. In fact, two Indian spas were ranked by London-based travel and tourism magazine *Condé Nast Traveller* among top-destination spas worldwide in 2006 and 2007.

These rankings underscore the fact that India is a growing market for spas. At many of its hotels, IHCL has placed spas that are positioned as the first uniquely "Indian spas." The objective is to leverage IHCL's reputation for luxury and service, cater to a growing customer demand, and increase nonroom revenue per guest at each of the Taj properties. To provide the highest-quality spa offerings, which are increasingly demanded by guests, Oberoi has partnered with Banyan Tree Spa, an experienced operator of upscale spas and resorts. Under the brand name Oberoi Spas by Banyan Tree, all new resorts and many existing Oberoi Hotels now feature full-service spas managed by the group.

In addition to offering spa services, Indian companies are also leveraging India's natural resources and capitalizing on the growing trend of wildlife tourism. In late 2004, IHCL entered into a joint venture with Conservation Corporation Africa and Cigen Corporation, part of the Chaudhary Group, to provide wildlife enthusiasts, circuit tourists, and high-end domestic travelers with "wildlife experiences" in an ecologically sustainable model. IHCL's Bickson said, "With the immense global interest generated about India in the recent past, we believe there is tremendous opportunity in a planned, aggressive thrust to promote the abundant wildlife offerings in this country. . . . [We] will make a concentrated effort on improving the quality of safari management in India and taking it to international standards, while promoting wildlife tourism within the country." In conjunction with its high-end resort focus, the Oberoi Group has already begun to leverage trends in the tourism industry and move into the luxury wildlife tourism segment. In 2001, it opened the Oberoi Vanyavilás in Ranthambhore, adjacent to the world-famous Ranthambhore Tiger Reserve.

Marketing Alliances and Cobranding

Given the expected increase in international tourism and busi
ness travel, joint venture agreements, cobranding agreements, and
marketing alliances with large international operators that have
strong brand equity, name recognition, and quality association
allow Indian hotel companies to tap into an existing loyal international customer base effectively. Such collaboration allows these
companies to leverage already established sales and marketing
channels overseas. Compared with other established international
tourism destinations, India is still perceived by many travelers to be
quite foreign and often intimidating. Consequently, close association with a familiar brand and sales network may help ease traveler
concerns and provide a competitive advantage for the Indian operator wise enough to partner with a well-known international chain.
Over time, as India's hospitality brand names become more broadly
known overseas, these cobranding agreements could be phased out.
The risk, of course, is that a close association with another hospitality brand might dilute or confuse the brand message of both
partners. As Indian companies position themselves to expand
in India and abroad, the role of alliances has been reconsidered,
because of potential conflict of interest between the players and the
risk of brand confusion.

ITC has traditionally placed significant emphasis on a partnering and cobranding strategy. It has had a long-standing
relationship with Sheraton, which is part of United States–based
Starwood Hotels & Resorts Worldwide. Several of the firm's
upscale ITC Welcomgroup Hotels were marketed worldwide by
Sheraton. This strategy allowed ITC to leverage Sheraton's international marketing expertise, sales force, and brand, and help draw
international customers to ITC properties. However, both ITC and
Starwood have aggressive expansion plans: ITC looks to expand
in India and overseas, and Starwood looks to expand within Asia.
Starwood has several top-end brands in its portfolio that it plans to
bring to India. In fact, in association with another Indian group, it
has already brought the Westin brand to India. While ITC wanted
exclusivity in their agreement with Starwood, the latter wanted to

partner with different groups and introduce its brands in India. This conflict of interest strained the long-standing relationship, and under a new franchisee and marketing agreement, Starwood will introduce the Luxury Collection brand in India through ITC. Several of ITC's properties will form part of the Luxury Collection brand, and ITC will no longer have exclusive rights on the Sheraton brand in India.

Similar to ITC, Oberoi terminated a long-standing strategic alliance with Hilton for marketing and cobranding its Trident brand of hotels. Again, both groups were in expansion mode; Hilton entered into a joint venture with DLF for both the Hilton and the Hilton Garden Inn (lower-end) hotels, which led to concerns about brand confusion and led to termination of the alliance.

Given the size of its portfolio and its aggressive international expansion plans, IHCL chose not to pursue a cobranding strategy. Taj is betting that it can be successful without a partner, but it has formed marketing alliances in the international market, for cross-exposure and promotion of its services, with Shilla Hotels & Resorts in Korea, Raffles Hotels & Resorts in Singapore, and Silversea Cruises in Monaco. In addition to this marketing alliance and others that Taj might be exploring, the firm has a strong direct sales and marketing network. It also increased the international reach of its group by opening international sales offices. The goal is to increase media visibility in these countries and to help complement the firm's international expansion strategy.

International Expansion into Gateway Cities

International expansion is another important strategy that will allow overseas guests to become more familiar with India's hotel brands, and thus help Indian hotels capture increasing business from Indians traveling abroad. While Indian firms without at least a few properties in strategic markets overseas will risk losing clientele to those that have such assets, expansion of the portfolio beyond India will help reduce volatility of the cash flow stream and reliance on the health of India's hospitality industry. Both IHCL and Oberoi are undertaking aggressive international expansions. In the international market, IHCL is building luxury hotels in Cape Town and Johannesburg, as well as a high-end resort in Phuket, Thailand. It has also entered into management contracts for a high-end resort on one of the Palm Islands in Dubai and a golf resort in Doha, Qatar. IHCL's management believes that by providing a consistent and luxurious Taj product to new overseas customers, it can build positive brand awareness, and ultimately brand loyalty, on an international scale. Currently, foreign acquisitions make up 20% of IHCL's revenues, but the company is aiming for global operations to account for a third of revenues. Specifically, it is considering investment options regarding what its management calls "key gateway cities" or "feeder markets." Commenting on the implementation of this strategy in Dubai, Bickson said, "This is part of IHCL's strategy of expanding into the key gateway cities of the world as Dubai today is fast emerging as a commercial hub of the region."

While ITC may rely on its cobranding agreement with Sheraton to draw international travelers familiar with the Sheraton name, and thus partially capitalize on international growth, this agreement does little to capture the growing business from Indians traveling abroad. Nor does it help diversify cash flow sources beyond India's borders. ITC Hotels is now planning to invest in the hotel sector in Britain.

Food and Beverage Revenue

As competition increases, hotels are under tremendous pressure to generate new, alternative lines of revenue with creative approaches. The food and beverage (F&B) business is one extremely critical revenue and profit driver. In addition to drawing hotel guests, a well-known, international-quality restaurant draws nonguest tourists, business visitors, and affluent local residents, thereby increasing the prestige and reputation of the hotel brand. At the same time, unique cuisine offerings allow luxury operators to differentiate their product from the competition, helping to maintain high price points and healthy margins.

ITC has perhaps been the most successful in this area. It was the first major Indian hotel chain to brand its cuisine. Bukhara, Dakshin, and Dum Pukht are today powerful cuisine brands, which continue to attract customers to restaurants in several ITC Welcomgroup Hotels. Other well-known brands include Dublin, West View, and the Pan Asian. Expectedly, ITC continues to pursue branded cuisine opportunities and expand its restaurant offerings across its portfolio. The Taj Group also remains particularly focused on upgrading and branding F&B offerings at its properties. Over the next few years, IHCL intends to open a number of F&B outlets by celebrity chefs featuring international cuisine. Like the Taj Group and ITC, the Oberoi Group seems to realize the value of branded upscale international food offerings in their hotel properties. It launched an upscale Italian restaurant at the Oberoi, New Delhi, and shortly thereafter partnered with Hotel Hassler, Rome, to further push fine Italian offerings in its hotel portfolios.

Overcoming Hurdles and Looking Ahead

Despite the successes of both domestic and foreign players, the Indian hospitality industry still faces many challenges. It has struggled with low investment levels, from both public and private sources, because of the absence of a national consensus on the role of tourism, a low priority given to tourism due to unappreciated potential, and a lack of a centralized vision for the industry. These low investment levels have contributed to a weak and variable hospitality product offering, which has prevented India from capitalizing on the positive economic benefits of a potentially vibrant hospitality industry. Furthermore, poor infrastructure, a complex tax system, and restrictive land policies have significantly deterred new and established players from entering or expanding into other market segments.

Without doubt the overriding factor restricting the growth of the Indian hospitality industry has been poor infrastructure. Accessibility to tourist areas is a major driver of both demand and supply in this sector. India, for example, has only 2.6 million miles of railroad tracks, as opposed to 14.5 million miles in China. The inefficiency of the Indian train network has impeded the construction of infrastructure needed for the development of the hospitality industry. Similarly, Indian roads are poor. Currently, only 50% of all roads are paved, and of these, only 20% are in good condition, according to government estimates. Construction activity is hampered significantly and truck access is extremely limited by the abominable state of India's roads. Capacity constraints in the major airports also pose a huge challenge to satisfying travel demand.

Shift in Government Policy

A shift in Indian government policy toward tourism is beginning to improve the operating environment. The most visible indication of the shift is the "Incredible India" campaign mounted in December 2002 by the Ministry of Tourism to promote India as a tourist destination. This highly successful multimillion-dollar campaign represents the first time the Ministry of Tourism has mounted a focused and centralized effort to increase tourist inflow. The campaign initially focused on promoting ayurveda (India's traditional system of medicine), yoga, meditation, and other spiritual practices to an international audience. Despite yoga's Indian origins, hotels in other countries had used yoga retreats as a tourist draw. Hotels in India, meanwhile, were not capitalizing on India's centuries-long development of these practices. Partly because of the campaign, this situation is now beginning to change.

Because the Incredible India campaign focused largely on destination, the Ministry of Tourism decided to launch a related campaign that focused on improving Indian hospitality. Called *Atithi Devo Bhava,* which means "Guest is God" in Sanskrit, the campaign aims to create an "awareness about the effects of tourism and sensitizing people about preservation of [India's] rich heritage and culture, cleanliness, and warm hospitality. It also re-instills a sense of responsibility toward tourists and re-enforces the confidence of foreign tourists toward India as a preferred holiday destination." The campaign tries to achieve its objectives through a seven-point program that ends with a certification for professionals working in the tourist trade.

The government has also declared the hotel and tourism industry to be a high-priority sector, allowing for 100% FDI. The primary shapers of policy at the local level have been state governments. But most of these governments have failed to recognize the potential for hospitality to be a catalyst for growth within their borders. This attitude is beginning to change, however, as evidenced by incentives state authorities such as Rajasthan have provided for developing and converting property into heritage hotels.

Investments in Infrastructure

Substantial investments in tourism infrastructure are also helping the Indian hotel industry to achieve its potential. The opening up of the aviation industry in India has important implications for the hotel industry, as hoteliers rely on airlines to transport 80% of international arrivals. Changes in Indian aviation policy that have stimulated demand for air travel include the abolition of the inland air travel tax of 15%, the reduction in the excise duty on aviation turbine fuel to 8%, and the removal of several restrictions on outbound chartered flights, including restrictions on the frequency and size of aircraft. The government's decision to upgrade twenty-eight regional airports in smaller towns substantially and to privatize and expand Delhi's and Mumbai's airports will also improve the business prospects of the hotel industry.

Upgrading national highways connecting various parts of India has opened up new opportunities for the development of budget hotels in India. The government's recent decision to treat convention centers as part of core infrastructure, and to provide critical funding for the large capital investment that may be required, has also fueled the demand for hotel rooms. While these limiting policies have definitely improved, they still pose problems for both local and international investors alike. For instance, the bureaucratic costs of current land policies discourage private investment in the construction and operation of hotels. As the government notes,

activities such as "mining, unauthorized construction, encroach-
ments, and haphazard development around tourist resorts must be
prevented through appropriate legislation and public support."

Despite the government's favorable policy shifts, there remains
a key government perception of the hotel industry as a luxury service
provider catering specifically to the wealthy. This view results in the
imposition of numerous high taxes that lower demand. According
to Bickson of IHCL, the government's view of the hotel industry as
a luxury good is rather antiquated, since 80% of the occupancy at
Taj Hotels is business related and therefore should not be taxed at
the luxury rate of 25% to 30%. Similar taxes levied by neighboring
countries are much lower. In fact, the license fees for an entire hotel
in the United Arab Emirates, Singapore, and Nepal were lower than
those imposed for a single bar in Delhi.

Geopolitical Uncertainties

The terrorist attacks on the famous Taj Mahal Palace and Oberoi
Trident hotels in Mumbai on November 26, 2008, led to loss
of human life and also to some concerns regarding significant
economic fallout. A number of Western news media ran cover
stories highlighting concerns for the safety of foreign travelers and
corporations in India. Analysts warned of harm to India's financial
markets, decreasing foreign investment, a decline in key industries
such as outsourcing, and a general weakening of confidence in the
Indian economy due to the attacks. They also expected pronounced
negative effects on the hospitality industry.

However, few of these effects materialized. While foreign
tourist arrivals and room rates did decrease after the attacks, by
February 2009 they had begun to rise again.[3] Financial markets
witnessed an inflow of capital rather than an outflow: between
November 28 and mid-December 2008, they injected close to
$700 million into India's debt and equity markets. Economists
interpreted this reaction as a signal that the long-term India story
remained unchanged. Terrorism is part of that story, and the risks
are familiar and well understood by foreign and Indian investors.[4]

Some foreign companies in Mumbai are looking for new premises within the city, and some have beefed up security, but they have not abandoned the city. Real estate developers and hospitality companies, too, appear to remain optimistic about Mumbai and hospitality in India generally. Both Ratan Tata, CEO of the Tata Group, and Biki Oberoi, CEO of the Oberoi Group, have vowed to quickly rebuild their Mumbai hotels, which were ravaged in the attacks. In addition, the Hilton Group, Hampshire Hotels & Resorts, West Pioneer Properties (India), and Mumbai-based real estate developer Hiranandani Group have all announced significant investments and property developments in Mumbai and other Indian cities in the next two to three years. These announcements make clear that, despite the Mumbai attacks, domestic and foreign investors firmly believe in the growth of the Indian hospitality market and continue to see it as a highly attractive investment opportunity.

Conclusion

While India has historically ignored the hospitality industry, recent factors have increased travel both to and within the country. With demand for hotels in India at an all-time high, and barriers to growth in the hospitality industry rapidly disappearing, both foreign and domestic hotel firms find themselves in an incredibly favorable business environment. Rising room rates mean that budget and midmarket hotels are likely to flourish, while luxury hotels will also see considerable growth over the medium term. The service apartment sector, convention business, adventure tourism, and amusement park tourism are all ripe for development.

Still, to be successful, firms must carefully define and execute specific strategies, especially concerning the market segments they plan to target. The dominant players will continue to expand and innovate to secure their position in the luxury market—a segment in which they have excelled. Meanwhile, new government policies have opened up opportunities for both international and domestic players to collaborate and target the high-end and midmarket segments, responding to a pent-up demand for value-driven accommodations.

The government's recent prioritizing of tourism and infrastructure development could well be the stimulus India's hospitality industry needs in order to take advantage of changing tourism trends and cause an infusion of more investment. Such investment, both public and private, into a diversified market could signal the promise of a more consistent, vibrant industry, whose profits depend less and less on cyclical international tourism.

Notes

1. *Indian Realty News,* "Hospitality Sector Sees Addition of Rooms Bringing Tariffs Down," April 19, 2008, http://www.indianrealtynews.com/real-estate-india/hospitality-sector-sees-addition-of-rooms-bringing-tariffs-down.html.

2. IGH (press release), "IHG Enjoys Robust Growth in India with Fourteen New-Look Holiday Inn Hotels Under Development," April 1, 2008, http://www.chinanewswire.com/pr/20080401095501254.

3. *Livemint.com,* "Sharekhan Maintains Buy on Indian Hotels," March 17, 2009, http://www.livemint.com/.

4. Swaminathan S. Anklesaria Aiyar, "Investors Swoop in After Mumbai Attacks," *Forbes,* January 2, 2009, http://www.forbes.com/2009/01/02/.

Bibliography

Aiyar, Swaminathan S. Anklesaria. 2009. "Investors Swoop in After Mumbai Attacks," *Forbes,* January 2. http://www.forbes.com/2009/01/02/.

Australia India Business Council. 2006. "Accor Announces Significant Hotel Expansion in India," November 27. http://www.livemint.com/.

Baxi, Sachin. 2007. "Food and Beverage Revenues Rise for Hotels." *Economic Times,* January 4.

Bickson, Raymond. 2005. Personal interview, March 30.

Bindra, Anupma. 2007. "India's Mid-Market Sector Has Room for HK Investment." Hong Kong Trade Development Council, July 31. http://info.hktdc.com/.

Booker, Nick. 2008. "Recent Indian Hotel Rate Rises Set to Reverse." *in2perspective.com,* April 14. http://www.in2perspective.com/.

Business Standard. 2004. "ITC Upgrades Hotel Brand," December 15.

Chisholm, Charlyn Keating. 2005. "The 20 Largest Hotels in the World." *About.com,* April 24. http://hotels.about.com/.

Dasgupta, Somnath. 2004. "Room for Fresh View." *Financial Express,* August 21.

Dey, Sudipto. 2007. "Starwood and ITC to Stay Together." *Economic Times,* April 5. http://economictimes.indiatimes.com/.

Economic Times. 2008. "Destination India: Foreign Tourist Arrivals Up 13%," February 10. http://economictimes.indiatimes.com/.

———. 2007. "Realtors Check into New Hotels in India," March 1.

———. 2006. "Hospitality Sector Sees Salaries Zoom as Talent Pool Dries Up," October 30.

Economist. 2005. "India's IT and Outsourcing Industries: The Bangalore Paradox," April 21.

Express Hospitality. 2007. "India on a Fast Track," January. http://www.expresshospitality.com/.

Federation of Hotel and Restaurant Associations of India. 2004. *Indian Hotel Industry Survey.* http://www.fhrai.com/Publication/IndianHotel Survey4.html.

Financial Times. 2007. "Unitech Ties Up with Global Hotel Chains," March 30.

———. 2006. "Hotel Boom Fires Up Salaries (The Hotel Industry Needs Around 1 Lakh Trained Manpower by 2011)," December 13.

———. 2006. "Hotel Occupancy, Rates Up for 3rd Straight Yr.," October 28.

———. 2006. "India Taj Hotels Resorts and Palaces Continues Expansion Drive," December 6.

Hotel Report. 2006. "HHC to Develop 75 Hotels in India," December.

HVS International. 2007. "Indian Hotel Industry Survey 2005–06." *Hospitality Net,* February 9. http://www.hospitalitynet.org/news/.

India Ministry of Tourism. 2005. "Incredible India." April 27. http://www.incredibleindia.org/atithidevobhava.htm.

InterContinental Hotels Group. 2008. "IHG Enjoys Robust Growth in India with 14 New-Look Holiday Inn Hotels Under Development," March 31. http://www.ihgplc.com/.

Jayaswall, Rajeev. 2004. "ITC to Ramp Up Hotel Business." *Financial Express,* August 18.

Jhaveri, Bhavika. 2006. "That Healthy Feeling." *Express Hospitality,* November. http://www.expresshospitality.com/.

Livemint.com. 2009. "Sharekhan Maintains Buy on Indian Hotels," March 17. http://www.livemint.com/.

Nichani, Meena. 2005. "Global Funds Keen to Invest in Local Hospitality Sector." *Times News,* April 6.

Oberoi Group. 2004. "EIH and Hilton Launch Strategic Alliance: Eight Hotels in India Rebranded Today," April 2.

Philip, Lijee. 2007. "Hotel Chains to Pump in Rs 4,500 Crore in 2 Years." *Economic Times,* March 30.

———. 2006. "Global Hotel Chains Seek More Room in India." *Economic Times,* November 9.

Rao, Girish. 2005. "B'lore to Get 4,000 More Rooms in 3 Years." *Economic Times,* March 8. http://economictimes.indiatimes.com/.

Rediff.com. 2007. "Indian Hotels Set to Woo the World," April 9. http://www.rediff.com/money/2007/apr/09spec.htm.

Sahu, Ram. 2008. "No Vacancy." *Business Standard,* May 12. http://www.business-standard.com/.

Shanker, S. 2007. "Istithmar Lines Up 8 easyHotels for India." *Business Line,* April 18. http://www.thehindubusinessline.com/2007/04/18/stories/.

Shetty, Gaurang. 2005. Personal interview, March 31.

Shyam Suri. 2005. "Strategies for Hotels." *Federation of Hotel & Restaurants Association of India,* January. http://www.fhrai.com/.

———. 2002. "FHRAI's Representation to the Excise Department Govt. of Delhi for Reduction of the High Bar License Fee Being Levied in the State." *Federation of Hotels & Restaurants Association of India,* February 26.

Thaker, Siddharth. 2005. "Demand-Supply Imbalance: Boon for Budget Brands in India." *Breaking Travel News,* February 15. http://www.breakingtravelnews.com/.

Thandani, Manav, and Deepika Malkani. 2004. "Hotels in India: Trends and Opportunity." *HVS International,* November 1.

Times News Network. 2005. " 'Incredible India': Set for a New Push," March 22. http://www.incredibleindia.org/newsite/.

USA Today. 2006. "India's Hotel Industry Isn't Keeping Up with Country's Hectic Growth," November 21. http://www.usatoday.com/travel/news/.

Vora, Shivani. 2007. "Splurge on India's Ultra Luxury Hotels." *MSNBC.com,* August 20. http://www.msnbc.msn.com/.

Wall Street Journal. 2007. "AAI Preparing Feasibility Studies for New Airports in NE," October 15. http://www.livemint.com/.

Chapter 7

India's Pharmaceutical Industry: A Shift in Strategy

*Caroline Berman, Dave Cavanaugh, Aayush Kabra,
Hadar Kramer, Josh Lawrence, Michael McNerney,
Kimberly Vender, Steve Waddell*

The beginning of 2005 signaled a new era in India's protection of intellectual property rights, particularly in the area of pharmaceuticals. The new regulations, in the works for more than a decade, fulfilled a commitment to adapt India's laws to global standards of patent protection established by the World Trade Organization (WTO) in 1995. Since the adoption of the new patent regulations, the Indian pharmaceutical industry has been undergoing a transformation—a fundamental change in the strategies of domestic pharmaceutical companies. The success of these strategies will determine future growth.

As the industry is evolving, it is creating opportunities both domestically and globally. The global generics market is opening up, growth opportunities such as contract research and manufacturing services are emerging, and prospects in the domestic market are improving. Indian pharma companies are trying to capture opportunities at every stage of the pharmaceutical chain—from drug discovery and clinical trials to commercialization. This evolution has led to increased capital investment in R&D as companies explore new avenues of drug development. While India's great strength is still manufacturing generic drugs, it is emerging as a global hub for contract research and manufacturing services (CRAMS).

Multinational corporations (MNCs) are seeking partnerships with domestic companies to handle drug discovery and clinical trials, or to serve in a contract manufacturing capacity. Indian pharma companies are scaling up their operations to capitalize on the growing demand by building their competencies in these domains. In this chapter, we examine each of these developments and their implications for Indian pharmaceutical companies.

India's Patent Protection History: Ensuring Drug Affordability

In the early 1970s, drug prices charged by a number of MNCs in India, such as Ciba, Sandoz, and Glaxo, were the highest in the world. These prices generated a public backlash and a hostile political environment that led the Indian government to abolish product patents. The primary result of "process-only" patent protection was that Indian pharmaceutical firms mushroomed and developed expertise in reverse engineering—taking pharmaceuticals invented by other manufacturers and devising their own methods of manufacturing them. Reverse engineering proved an effective means of providing low-cost drugs to the Indian population, but it frustrated global pharmaceutical companies, which received inadequate protection for their products. To help ensure affordability for Indian consumers, price controls have been another key feature of the Indian market. Price controls and multiple companies with their own version of the same product have created a commodity market and have contributed to making India's drug prices the lowest in the world.

With the focus on reverse engineering, most Indian firms did not invest significantly in creating new drugs. The trade-off between reverse engineering and original development was of little concern to most players in the industry, largely because India's status as a developing nation put a higher premium on providing a low-cost drug supply than on innovating in the global pharmaceutical industry. As India began to participate more actively in global trade, the country faced increasing pressure to tighten patent protection.

In 1995, facing concerns about intellectual property in many sectors, India accepted the WTO rules known as Trade-Related Aspects of Intellectual Property Rights (TRIPS). Although India made preliminary changes in trademark and copyright law soon after adopting TRIPS, it was not until March 2005 that the country entered the era of product patents. Under the 2005 amendment to the Patents Act, patents now protect products, not just processes. In the pharmaceutical context, this means that a specific drug, like Lipitor, can now receive more complete patent protection, and Indian firms cannot legally sell a reverse-engineered formulation of a protected product.

In addition, a 1999 amendment to India's patent law created a "mailbox," a temporary holding cell for patent applications for pharmaceuticals and agricultural chemicals. All patent applications for drugs discovered in 1995 to 2005 by Indian or international companies were to be deposited; the mailbox was opened in January 2005, and the applications within were referred to examiners for assessment under the provisions of the new patent regime, which now included pharmaceutical products as patentable subject matter. The provisions also ruled that companies already manufacturing the products whose mailbox applications were granted patents would be allowed to continue doing so after paying a reasonable royalty to the patent holder. Importantly, patent holders could not institute infringement proceedings against the generics manufacturers.

The process forced a shakeout in the domestic market, and led to the withdrawal of generic versions of drugs for which mailbox applications were submitted and granted a patent. If no generic formulations for a drug existed in the market, a patent granted later would also help to keep generics out of the market for the duration of the patent. For example, in December 2007 the Mumbai Patent Office granted a patent to Pfizer for the antiretroviral drug Selzentry, a second-line treatment for HIV. The patent was issued against Pfizer's mailbox application filed in December 1999. After the Indian patent was granted, to achieve true market exclusivity, Pfizer needed to overcome a one-year postgrant opposition period, during which any person could file an opposition and question the patent on grounds of nondisclosure, wrongful disclosure of important information, or nonfulfillment of patentability requirements (a popular opposition is to question the novelty or efficacy enhancement of the drug).

The Impact of India's New Patent Law

With the change in the market environment, Indian pharmaceutical firms have had to realign their business strategy to remain viable. These firms can no longer rely on a business model focused exclusively on reverse-engineered generic versions of drugs. They will need to increase R&D expenditures to compensate for lost opportunity so they can participate in the global market. To implement a successful R&D program, they will have to institute considerable quality control measures to ensure compliance with international standards.

Ajit Dangi, director general of the Organisation of Pharmaceutical Producers of India, claims that "unless Indian companies rapidly change their business model from imitation to innovation by 2010 there will be just five hundred to one thousand companies"—down from currently more than twenty thousand.[1] While several national players are well capitalized, Devinder Pal, director of Mumbai-based Catalyst Pharma Consulting, and Hasit Joshipura, president and managing director of Janssen-Cilag (Johnson & Johnson's Indian pharmaceutical division), both predict a continued shakeout of smaller Indian companies within the next three to five years. This shakeout is largely due to the cumulative effect of changes in intellectual property rights, supplier dependency among smaller players, and the change in Schedule M of the Indian government's Drugs and Cosmetics Rules, which requires investment and implementation of good manufacturing practice (GMP), including manufacturing procedure, validation, calibration, and documentation requirements.

With a stronger multinational presence and Indian companies having sufficient resources for R&D, barriers to entry into the Indian pharmaceutical market will increase. Indian companies that have already invested in R&D or have formed partnerships with

MNCs will be considerably better positioned than smaller, less pre-pared companies. Companies that were previously able to thrive because of the scale of reverse-engineering efforts or strong distribu-tion networks will now be forced to find areas of expertise where they offer a competitive advantage. Still, even though the number of firms may be reduced, the competition between the remain-ing firms is likely to increase. Many of these changes are indeed under way.

The Shift Toward Domestic R&D Centers and Contract Research

To achieve a sustainable long-term advantage, more and more Indian companies are embarking on R&D following the patent product regime. While smaller domestic companies may not be motivated or have the capital to amend current R&D practices, some domestic pharmas have initiated extensive R&D investment as they explore new avenues of drug development. For instance, large Indian drug firms such as Ranbaxy Laboratories and Dr. Reddy's are focusing on R&D in the hope of discovering their own blockbusters rather than simply making generic drugs. Ranbaxy has opened its third drug discovery research center in India and in 2006 spent about $100 million on R&D operations. Likewise, Piramal Healthcare has opened a $20 million R&D center in Mumbai. Overall, Indian firms' R&D spending has increased from 4% to 8% of total revenue since 2000. Inherent to the increased R&D spending is rapid devel-opment of IT resources.

These developments should allow Indian firms to bring prod-ucts to market faster as well as increase their ability to collaborate with MNCs. Following the introduction of product patents in India, the domestic industry has witnessed a spate of new product launches. Products launched since 2005 have accounted for 12% of overall market growth, but many Indian companies realize that later-stage clinical trials are too expensive to conduct independently, so research partnerships between Indian and Western drug firms will likely proliferate.

Drug Discovery Destination: Contract Research Outsourcing

For MNCs, the amendments to India's patent law make India a more attractive drug discovery destination. India is in fact emerging as a hub for contract research. With the high costs of drug discovery, pharmaceutical companies cannot sustain large R&D spending unless they can find ways to develop new drugs more cheaply. Drug discovery is a costly and lengthy process, taking anywhere from ten to twelve years and costing approximately $800 million to $1.2 billion from the laboratory to the market. The efficiency of pharmaceutical research in advanced countries is also under tremendous pressure, owing to spiraling costs (including manpower), falling productivity, and higher regulatory risk.

The economics of research in India looks appealing, as industry analysts estimate that R&D costs there are less than 40% of those in the United States. Despite challenges such as limited infrastructure, significant delays in obtaining clinical trial approvals, and strict rules regarding animal testing, the overall costs of R&D in India are more than ten times less than comparable costs in the United States. For example, $100 million to $150 million drug discovery projects in the United States would cost $10 million in India, and $300 million to $350 million clinical trials in the United States could be conducted in India for $20 million.

The main challenge facing contract research is the need to build trust in contractors. The global pharma companies need to be assured that contractors will safeguard intellectual property rights and that they can handle intricate chemical processes. Contractors that have established relationships with global pharma firms, strong manufacturing capabilities, and large portfolios of promising products are the best positioned to benefit from the contract research boom. Thus, Indian companies that do successfully invest in R&D should be able to capitalize on this advantage better than other domestic players. The cost advantages inherent in the market have positioned these Indian players to reap the benefits of increased willingness among MNCs to shift development opportunities to the previously unprotected market. A potential win-win approach, this partnership between domestic contractors and MNCs maximizes the intellectual and operational capabilities of both groups without pitting the two against each other.

With pressures on Indian companies to invest in R&D and incentives for MNCs to outsource their R&D, the strategies of domestic companies are shifting. Ranbaxy, for instance, is separating its R&D operations into a separate entity and starting a contract research organization (CRO) under the new research entity. This entity will include Ranbaxy's ongoing collaborative research programs with British drugmaker GlaxoSmithKline (GSK), but the company will also seek new contracts with global pharmaceutical companies, shifting the focus toward R&D. Many such collaborations are already under way, such as those between Dr. Reddy's and Novartis, Dr. Reddy's and Novo Nordisk, Torrent and Novartis, and Ranbaxy and Schwarz. As Indian firms shift their focus to R&D, their expenditures are beginning to show on the bottom line, affecting profitability. Such factors will combine to increase the already high internal rivalry in the Indian pharmaceutical market.

In addition to costs, the increasing number of products going off patent is expected to drive growth of the contract research segment. MNCs may enter into two kinds of collaborations: outsourcing and true collaborations. In the outsourcing model, the contracting company keeps the intellectual capital in-house and outsources discrete tasks or specific operations and processes to a contract firm or a strategic alliance partner. A growing number of MNCs have entered into more-collaborative ventures with Indian pharmaceutical companies and CROs, extending well beyond task-driven outsourcing. These transactions involve more-complex intellectual property considerations.

Biocon entered into a tie-up with Bristol-Myers Squibb for discovery and early drug development processes. Piramal and Eli Lilly have agreed to develop and commercialize a select group of Lilly's preclinical drug candidates that span multiple therapeutic areas. This alliance seeks to increase productivity in drug development by leveraging Piramal's low cost base and Lilly's expertise in discovering and launching medicines. The deal is unique in that risk and reward will be shared equitably. Ranbaxy Laboratories and GSK are expanding their existing R&D association. According to Ranbaxy, the new agreement could bring in an additional $100 million (Rs 440 crore) in "milestone payments" and higher royalties on worldwide net sales for a product developed and subsequently launched by GSK.

Globally in 2006, the CRO market was valued at $14 billion and is expected to reach $24 billion in 2010. In India that year, the CRO market was valued at about $265 million, with clinical trials contributing half of the revenues. In 2010, it is estimated to be worth $600 million. To harness this opportunity, companies are not only building expertise in research chemistry and biology, but also developing facilities for clinical trials.

Outsourcing Clinical Trials

Clinical research has long been a hallmark of pharmaceutical outsourcing. In the past, India's growth in this category was restrained by the lax intellectual property laws and Schedule Y of the government's Drugs and Cosmetics Rules, which noted that "clinical trials [in India] have to be one step behind other countries." However, the government modified the regulations in January 2005 so that India no longer has to be one phase behind worldwide trials. This change, along with the establishment of product patents, has increased MNC interest in Indian clinical outsourcing. Of the contract research outsourcing, 35% of business is in the area of drug discovery, and the remaining 65% is in the area of clinical trials.

Clinical trials in India cost up to a third less than they do in the United States or Europe, and they are cheaper than those conducted in China. India has a large pool of talented English-speaking personnel, fewer administrative barriers than China has, and faster patient recruitment times because of the many volunteers and "drug naive" patients (most Indians have had minimal exposure to pharmaceuticals). MNC interest in Indian clinical outsourcing is also driven by India's inherent advantages, such as a genetically diverse population as well as several hundred thousand

English-speaking physicians and millions of untreated patients. The time needed to recruit patients in India is less than half the time needed to recruit patients in the United States, data analysis times in India are reduced to six to ten weeks from four months in the United States, and cost savings are on the order of 50% to 60%. Furthermore, India's strength in information technology can help reduce clinical data management expenses, a significant cost driver of clinical trials. Therefore, the conditions for clinical research in India are ideal, and potential savings in both time and money are considerable. Inevitably, almost all the MNCs are either conducting their clinical trials in India or outsourcing their clinical data management.

Nevertheless, India's clinical trial industry is measured at $100 million a year, compared with a global industry of $50 billion. In September 2006, India accounted for 1% of the 763 clinical trials conducted around the world. Although India does not allow phase I clinical trials, because of patient safety concerns, it did start allowing phase II trials a couple of years ago. The Indian government also introduced a tax exemption for the sector in mid-2007, covering all services carried out by the contract research and clinical trials industry. Despite a shortage of specially trained workers, India's clinical trials sector could triple. With about seventy to eighty CROs in the country, industry analysts estimate that the domestic clinical trials market will touch $1.5 billion by 2010.

Pfizer, widely recognized for introducing clinical trials to India, established the Academy for Clinical Excellence in India to develop talent purely for conducting such trials. Reports state that Pfizer has twenty ongoing clinical trials in India, and the company has invested $13 million on clinical research there. Lilly shares Pfizer's aggressive approach to performing clinical research in India, with seventeen large and small clinical trials in the country's hospitals. GSK has started several simultaneous vaccine and pharma trials; the company expects that at least 25% to 30% of its global clinical trials will one day take place in Asia, with most occurring in India. Furthermore, along with Pfizer and Novartis, GSK has based one of its global hubs for clinical data management in India. Nevertheless, some companies, such as Abbott Laboratories, remain on the sidelines when it comes to performing or outsourcing clinical research in India, while others, such as Pfizer, have tempered their enthusiasm with caution.

The reason for caution is lingering legal uncertainties. Even after the passage of the third amendment to India's Patents Act in 2005, there are still questions regarding the exclusivity of the clinical data of the company sponsoring the research. Should the Indian government or legal system deem that such data belong in the public domain, the clinical research industry in India would likely stall as MNCs quickly shift to a more favorable intellectual property environment. As GSK's Limaye noted, the gray area in Indian law represents considerable risk, and MNCs will continue to be particularly discerning in the trials they route to India.

Moving Up the Value Chain: Outsourcing Manufacturing Services

Besides being a destination for contract research outsourcing, India has become an integral part of the manufacturing value chain for MNCs looking to maintain lean cost structures and combat intense competition in the global generics industry. In the past, the cost of manufacturing was less relevant for MNCs since this cost was quite low relative to R&D costs. However, pricing pressures around the world, especially in developed markets, are putting pressure on drug prices and thus on profits. The pressure to outsource manufacturing is growing as U.S. and European governments look for cheaper generics and lower-cost drugs to contain their health-care budgets. India currently accounts for a minimal share of the estimated $30 billion global outsourcing industry, but the country's advantages make it a launch pad for significant growth.

India has a large pool of trained chemists, the highest number of U.S. Food and Drug Administration–approved plants outside the United States, and a cost of manufacturing 30% to 40% lower than that in most Western countries. With MNCs beginning to look at low-cost manufacturing to bolster shrinking margins, India is one of the most preferred outsourcing destinations. In 2006, contract manufacturing outsourcing (CMO) accounted for approximately 70% of the global outsourcing market. While India still holds a very small share of this market (valued at $900 million), it is expected to reach $3.3 billion by 2010. Consequently, India's contribution to the pharmaceutical outsourcing market is expected to increase from 1.8% in 2006 to 4.4% in 2010.

Many Indian firms are indeed optimistic about the outsourcing potential. According to Pal of Catalyst Pharma Consulting, the new intellectual property regulations represent a "tremendous opportunity. . . . Hereon there may be situations when they see each other as potential collaborators." As Ajay Piramal, chairman of Indian drug giant Piramal Healthcare, explained, Piramal is pursuing a strategy focused on partnering rather than competition: "As an organization we do not want to compete with the global companies. We would like to collaborate with them." Piramal expects 50% of its estimated $1 billion of revenues to come from its global business by 2010, and much of that percentage is predicted to come from custom manufacturing (of generic drug intermediates) deals with major global pharmaceutical players.

Preparing for Contract Research and Manufacturing Services

Outsourcing of contract research and manufacturing services (CRAMS) is becoming one of the most promising opportunities for the Indian pharma industry. Frost & Sullivan, a global consulting firm, estimates that CRAMS will grow in India from about $900 million in 2007 to $6 billion in the next five to six years. To capitalize on the growing demand, Indian pharma companies are scaling up their operations by building their competencies in every area of the pharmaceutical value chain.

For instance, Indian companies are on the lookout for CRAMS opportunities through acquisitions overseas to build their custom manufacturing capacities. Piramal Healthcare acquired British-based Avecia, and Sun Pharmaceutical Industries acquired four companies in the United States. Dr. Reddy's Laboratories bought the German drugmaker betapharm to gain better access to the European market. Acquisitions determine which part of the value chain these firms will be addressing. While manufacturing of intermediates and active pharmaceutical ingredients (API) is done mostly in India, manufacturing of the finished form of the drug is mostly done overseas. CRAMS allows Indian pharma companies to move up the value chain and implies a more innovation-driven future in science and research.

Still a Market for Generics

While many industry analysts believe that the next wave of growth for the Indian pharma industry is in the drug discovery pipeline and in development outsourcing, India's strong competence is still in manufacturing generic drugs. Indian pharmaceutical companies have developed an unrivaled skill in chemistry and formulation. The flood of generic pharmaceuticals—and subsequent price erosion—forced Indian manufacturers to make their processes increasingly efficient. The result is that India is now the largest supplier of generic pharmaceuticals in the world. Expertise in reverse engineering and a history of quality production have positioned Indian drugmakers well to continue producing generic drugs, albeit on a more limited scale (only for drugs that have come off patent). Under most developed patent systems, firms that develop and patent a drug enjoy a certain number of years in which the firm maintains exclusive rights to manufacture and sell the formula. Once the drug comes off patent—typically twenty years after the patent application—the market is free to sell a reverse-engineered version of the drug under a different name.

Globally, the generics industry is estimated to be worth about $100 billion by 2010, and an additional $60 billion worth of drugs are going off patent by 2011. India now has only a 10% market share in this industry. As large-selling prescription drugs come off patent and governments across the world try to contain medical costs, generic drugs are becoming increasingly important. In established markets like the United States and Europe, the generics segment is expanding (in the United States, generics now account for 55% of written prescriptions). But, the generics segment is also expanding in emerging markets like Japan, Brazil, and China, where increasing health-care costs have become center-stage issues. Changing regulatory frameworks are promoting generic prescriptions, which are likely to be a primary driver of change in the global pharmaceutical market, expanding the generics segment in the United States and Europe. More and more countries are moving from branded generics to commodity generics in a bid to increase generic penetration and save on health-care costs.

Taking advantage of patent expirations, increasing focus on health-care cost containment in developed markets, and recognizing the need for collaboration, Indian companies have already entered into these markets through subsidiaries, tie-ups, and collaborations—and they are capitalizing on these opportunities. Ranbaxy, Sun Pharmaceutical, and Dr. Reddy's rank among the top five international generic players, and they are expected to address at least $24 billion (60%) of the U.S. generic product opportunity through first-to-file settlements. From being a traditional exporter to low-value, low-regulation markets, India is now expanding its presence in high-value, regulated markets such as the United States and Europe. For instance, India now has seventy-five plants approved to make drugs for the U.S. market—the most of any nation except the United States itself, and almost three times more than China has. India is also expanding into high-growth regions such as the Commonwealth of Independent States and South America. Some Indian pharmaceuticals are pursuing niche geographic markets in underdeveloped markets outside of India. For example, given the high brand value of the MADE IN INDIA label in the Middle East, Indian firms are well positioned to take advantage of this growing geographic niche.

Indian firms should be able to continue taking advantage of low-cost labor and manufacturing as well as finely tuned skills at engineering innovative drug manufacturing processes in order to remain an active player in the global generics market. Given that market's growth trend, and given frustration over high pharmaceutical pricing, Indian firms have been pursuing different global strategies, each with a different degree of risk. The least risky approach, typically undertaken by firms who plan to sell high-volume, low-margin products, is reverse engineering of simple drugs that are already off patent or that will come off patent over the next several years. For instance, Shasun Chemicals and Drugs currently produces 15% of U.S. ibuprofen supplies. Complex drugs, however, require difficult production procedures, even if they can be reverse engineered. For instance, injected drugs face more-stringent U.S. regulations and require more-sophisticated technology to reverse-engineer and produce in compliance with the regulations. This strategy is riskier because of the lower success rate of reverse engineering efforts, but Indian companies like Ranbaxy and Lupin believe that they have a significant leg up on the competition, which will face higher barriers to entry in this market. Thus, such companies should be able to reap greater rewards as more-complex drugs come off patent in the United States and Europe.

Developing and patenting new versions of off-patent drugs is risky because it usually requires convincing doctors to prescribe new versions of old drugs. Typically, marketing in foreign countries is not one of India's core competencies; thus, even though India may be able to satisfy the U.S. market by providing lower-cost versions of off-patent drugs, this strategy may not ultimately succeed unless Indian firms can partner with MNCs. However, a number of Indian firms have had some success with this strategy. Ranbaxy recently launched a liquid form of metformin, a diabetes drug that has traditionally been administered in pill form. The innovation—an example of success for Indian R&D—has given Ranbaxy twenty-year patent protection. Joshipura noted that Indian firm Glenmark Pharmaceuticals has already become a leader in phase I development for a new asthma formulation and is well positioned to capitalize on this specific segment of the market. Lupin is focusing much of its business on "the untouchables of the drug market" and has become a world leader in the treatment of tuberculosis. Some drugs launched by Indian firms are generics based on patented drugs. For example, Ceftriaxone, one of Lupin's drugs used to fight pneumonia and meningitis, is the generic version of Rocephin marketed by Hoffman-La Roche.

An even riskier approach is to directly challenge innovator patents in court. If the challenge is successful, the challenger is granted six months' exclusive rights to sell the generic version of the drug. The upside is huge: Ranbaxy successfully challenged Eli Lilly's patent on the blockbuster drug Prozac and reaped $60 million revenue in six months. The downside is costly legal battles that often leave the challenger with nothing but legal bills. With $20 million in outstanding patent challenges, Ranbaxy and Dr. Reddy's prove that the big Indian players still see patent challenges as a profitable strategy. But this situation could be changing: in the past year, Dr. Reddy's, Ranbaxy, and Sun Pharmaceutical settled patent litigation out of court.

Certification Issues

Independent of whether Indian pharmaceutical companies position themselves as an outsourcing partner or an exporting producer, they need to ensure that they comply with all relevant international quality and manufacturing standards. The recent U.S. Food and Drug Administration (FDA) probe against Ranbaxy is an instructive case in how important full regulatory compliance is for Indian pharmaceutical companies.

In 2006, the FDA started investigating Ranbaxy's plants in India. After months of discussion and what it regarded as inadequate responses from the company, the FDA issued two warning letters to the U.S. public in July 2008 that Ranbaxy's two factories in Dewas and Paonta Sahib did not meet safety and contamination standards for drug manufacturing set by U.S. GMP requirements.[2] In the following weeks, the FDA banned entry of the thirty drugs manufactured at those two factories and stopped sourcing Ranbaxy's three anti-HIV drugs. On the basis of its findings, the FDA dragged Ranbaxy to court and charged the company with selling substandard drugs in the United States, forging documents to get the drugs approved, and refusing to share documents. After further investigation, the FDA stated in February 2009 that while it did not find any health risks linked to Ranbaxy drugs, it did find that the company submitted "untrue statements of material fact in abbreviated and new drug applications filed with the Agency." The U.S. regulators also said that they planned to stop reviewing any new drugs made at Ranbaxy's Paonta Sahib site.

In response to the charges, Ranbaxy's share price plummeted. Questions were raised about whether the company had handled the investigation properly and whether it had informed its shareholders sufficiently about the resulting risks for the company. However, India's Ministry of Health and Family Welfare defended Ranbaxy and alleged that the FDA was being pressured by political and pharma lobbies to act against Ranbaxy. The drug controller general of India, Surinder Singh, pointed out that the FDA itself admitted that there was no problem with Ranbaxy's drug and that "even the deficiencies FDA has pointed out are small process violations."[3]

Ranbaxy proclaimed that it would address the FDA's findings "appropriately" and "in a timely manner." As one step in that direction, the company hired Rudolph Giuliani, former New York mayor and former U.S. attorney in Manhattan, as an advisor on compliance issues. The company also tried to clarify the scope of the charges. It claimed that they related only to one of the two factories and that the relevant factory's manufacturing practices had been approved by the drug regulatory authorities of Britain and Australia in a joint audit. Despite being under investigation, Ranbaxy received three final approvals from the FDA in February and March 2009 for several applications submitted by the company's Ohm Laboratories in New Jersey. However, reliance on Ohm's drug-making capabilities to replenish Ranbaxy's U.S. product portfolio could prove costly, because production in the United States does not have the same cost advantages as production in India.

While the outcome of the Ranbaxy case remains to be seen, some analysts are concerned that it could hurt Indian pharmaceutical companies in general. MNCs might become wary of buying Indian companies or giving work to Indian suppliers if their confidence in these companies' compliance is shaken.[4] One Indian industry insider warned that "people will be afraid to buy from you. . . . If they do, they will require additional checks and more detailed data than before."[5]

The Ranbaxy case should be seen as a learning opportunity for Indian pharmaceutical companies. It reveals that a key strength of the Indian entrepreneurial mind-set, the focus on outcomes, can become a handicap that can lead to negligence of process quality and compliance. This handicap is most evident in both Ranbaxy's and the health ministry's reaction to the FDA charges—namely, emphasizing the safety and quality of Ranbaxy products while dismissing the process issues as technicalities. But the United States and many European countries are more process focused; for them these issues are more than technicalities. To grow their business internationally, Indian pharmaceutical companies need to learn to combine their outcome orientation with more process orientation, by improving process design and reliability of execution.

The Changing Domestic Market

Owing to the weak patent regulations before 2005, the domestic Indian pharmaceutical market can be generally characterized as highly competitive, fragmented, and price sensitive. Because barriers to entry have been low (in comparison to countries where extensive R&D and expensive regulatory compliance is the norm), the Indian market is flooded with more than twenty thousand firms. The high availability of an educated workforce and the low cost of both input ingredients for drug manufacturing and labor have also contributed to the growth of the domestic industry. Although MNCs do play a considerable role in this booming market, domestic companies account for 8 of the top 10 pharmaceutical companies in the Indian market. The leading 250 pharmaceutical companies in India control 70% of the market, with the market leader holding nearly 7% of market share. The domestic market is focused almost exclusively on expert production of generic drugs. Consequently, price and access to distribution networks have been the points of differentiation among Indian firms.

With many local players building a global outlook and growing inorganically through mergers and acquisitions, there is increasing consolidation in the industry. The changing market dynamics are forcing larger companies to focus on Europe and the United States. With stronger product patent protection, additional MNCs have already begun to enter the crowded domestic Indian market, increasing competition among both domestic firms and established MNCs. After exiting the Indian market in 1986 because of excessive price control and inadequate patent protection, Bristol-Myers Squibb reentered the market. Merck purchased a 100% stake in its partially owned Indian subsidiary, and GSK looked to in-license products in other companies' global portfolios.

Higher barriers to entry and stronger brands will limit the number of new firms entering the market. Consequently, as the patent laws are enforced, supplier power should shrink, largely because of the concentration of the market. As the market concentrates and smaller firms exit or focus only on bulk drugs (input manufacturing), the largest manufacturers' purchasing power will grow significantly. Fewer and fewer large manufacturing firms will be seeking supply from more and more suppliers. Consequently, the scale of large firms will allow them to purchase commodity ingredients more efficiently. As firms grow or shrink, their input costs will change accordingly, giving the bigger firms even more of an advantage. Additionally, with the new regulations preventing reverse engineering, Indian bulk drug sellers will find it increasingly difficult to forward-integrate to produce the actual drugs. Thus, supplier power is expected to decrease.

The Entry of Patented Products

Since the introduction of the product patent regime in India, the domestic pharma industry has witnessed the launch of eleven patented products by MNCs. This number is expected to grow, as multinational pharmas are planning significant patented launches over the next few years. A range of MNCs we examined (e.g., Pfizer, Novartis, GSK, Lilly, and Abbott) now have a product portfolio distinct from their parents, with different reasons for its composition.

Contrary to the past, when new drugs were rarely introduced in India, the trend across MNCs is to release new, innovative products there as part of a global product launch. Pfizer's approach best represents the majority approach to product introductions. In India, brand equity has been of minimal importance, so commodity pricing has often been in play. Such conditions have discouraged Pfizer from bringing a mass-market product such as Lipitor, which faces upward of sixty generic equivalents, into the Indian market. Even after the product patent regime, if the net present value (NPV) does not justify a product launch, it will not occur. To accommodate such financial justifications, product launches will be limited to first-in-class drugs for which no therapeutic substitutes are easily available. Therefore, Pfizer plans to launch only selected high-science products such as Vfend, an antifungal specialty product that is well regarded by physicians. Pfizer will make more-frequent product launches in India only if the patent law is enforced effectively. This enforcement is particularly important to Pfizer, given the 373 mailbox applications it has filed—the largest by any single company.

However, the rationale behind product launches and portfolios differs among players. It is determined partly by the players' view of the market. As one of the largest pharmaceutical companies in India, GSK will launch products from its parent's portfolio regularly (at least one a year) even as it focuses on lifestyle indications—such as cardiovascular disease, diabetes, and central nervous system disorders—whose prevalence is increasing in India as Western lifestyles and the middle class grow. GSK's strategy seems to be to focus on building a franchise that stresses dominance in segments with high entry barriers, either through technology like vaccines or through its product brand or doctor image. GSK will focus on products that are not under price controls and thus help provide the margins.

Abbott India pursues a two-pronged approach to the Indian market, emphasizing its portfolio of mass-market and over-the-counter products as well as a selection of prescription drugs from its parent company (e.g., Hytrin [urology] and Forane, and Ultane [anesthesiology]). Eli Lilly's product strategy is representative of the likely strategies of the newer entrants to India, such as Merck and Bristol-Myers Squibb. While other companies consolidate around core therapeutic areas, Lilly India is picking products from its global portfolio for which it can demand premium pricing (or more appropriately, global pricing). Thus, it has omitted many of its neuroscience products because the Indian market has many therapeutic equivalents. In sum, the products such MNCs do introduce in India will be determined by market attractiveness and each company's therapeutic priorities. While many MNCs, such as Pfizer and Abbott, are taking a more cautious attitude, GSK and Lilly India are taking the more aggressive and distinctive approaches.

Marketing Approach

MNCs have followed classic pharmaceutical marketing strategies in India but have adapted them to the Indian environment. Thus, sales force detailing and distribution of free samples are important tactics, while direct-to-consumer (DTC) advertising is not, because it is prohibited by government regulations. Furthermore, pharmacies play an important role. They are not as strictly regulated in India as in the United States, so one can get a prescription drug without a doctor's prescription. Although targeting pharmacists is not a conventional marketing tactic in India, it is sometimes the most effective method of reaching patients. So while Lilly has been directly working with urologists to promote Cialis in India, it is growing market share mainly through over-the-counter means instead of direct prescriptions. That chronic and lifestyle drugs are primarily paid for out of pocket, instead of being paid for by third parties, adds another unique consideration to MNCs' marketing decisions.

Lilly has done much to market itself in India. For example, it has set up information hotlines that physicians can call to ask questions not just about Lilly's products but also about those of competitors. This tactic has helped Lilly enhance its brand image and raise awareness of the company, which is vital given Lilly's newness to the market. In addition, Lilly offers free syringes for diabetics, regularly brings in speakers, and sponsors visits of Indian physicians abroad to develop the Indian medical community's knowledge base.

As mentioned earlier, the sales force plays an important role in the Indian pharma industry's marketing strategies. Pfizer employs medical research teams to help solve physicians' problems and change the perception that MNCs are less innovative than domestic companies. Prompted by the product patent law, Pfizer is reorganizing its Indian sales force along therapeutic lines, thus synchronizing the company's practices in India with its global practices. Furthermore, MNCs are increasing their sales force to carry out the companies' planned expansion in education and product detailing.

Pricing

It is against the backdrop of this competitive, quasi-regulated market that MNCs are determining their pricing strategies. The common thread running through both our industry research and our meetings with senior executives was that pricing of drugs in the Indian market is constrained by the presence of many therapeutic equivalents. So, even if an MNC introduced a new statin whose patent was protected in India, the availability of hundreds of copies of same-class compounds such as Lipitor, Zocor, and Pravachol would prevent the MNC from pricing at a premium (i.e., the market would check any move toward U.S.-level prices). The price sensitivity of Indian consumers, their relatively weak spending power, and the likelihood that they must pay for drugs out of pocket (only 11% of Indians have health insurance) further constrain pricing.

GSK emphasized its strategy of remaining price competitive, as evidenced by its plan that its next product launch—of Vindia/Vindament (the diabetes drugs known as Avandia/Avandamet in the United States)—would not be at a price disadvantage. The outcome of Pfizer's experimental launch of several products at high prices in India during 2000 to 2004 must also be noted: domestic companies reacted with cutthroat pricing, reducing Pfizer's products to irrelevancy. While these products were not patent protected, Abbott believes the lessons from this case hold true even in the new intellectual property regime, preventing any shift toward a high-price environment.

Eli Lilly, however, did not go along with the prevailing MNC view on competitive pricing. It has based its strategy on a projection that India's pharmaceutical industry will evolve into two types of markets: a low-priced, off-patent market, accounting for 95% of sales, and a high-priced, patented drugs market, with 5% of sales. Consistent with its strategy of selectively introducing products from its global portfolio, Lilly affirms that the novelty and uniqueness of its drugs allow it to price at a premium sustainably and follow a global pricing strategy. It followed exactly this approach for Cialis, for which the Indian government granted Lilly now-contested exclusive marketing rights (EMR). Lilly believes that Cialis's relatively long duration will provide a strong enough differentiating edge against the numerous copies of sildenafil citrate, or generic Viagra. In India, Cialis is priced at Rs 425 a pill (approx. $9), whereas Viagra copies are available at Rs 5 to Rs 8 a pill (approx. $0.10 to $0.18). While Cialis achieved market leadership in eleven countries in 2006, it failed to qualify for a product patent in India after the basic constituent of the medicine was found to be a known substance, developed and patented by Indian scientists thirty-two years ago. Lilly has secured a process patent on Cialis in India, which means it can produce the same drug but through a different process. Without a product patent, though, Cialis must still compete against other, cheaper versions of the drug.

The Debate over Patent Protection

Despite the approval of a tougher patent law in India, the country's pharma market is at risk of losing foreign investment if it does not upgrade its intellectual property framework to international standards. The overall regulatory environment remains overshadowed by international pressure to implement reforms in areas such as market access, pricing, and patent legislation enforcement.

Are the newly product-patented drugs subject to government price regulation? They certainly meet the monopoly criteria, with the MNCs purportedly holding a 100% market share. At global prices, they are likely to have high margins. Given India's cost-plus pricing regime, prices may be brought significantly lower if controls are imposed. The government has indicated that it may cancel product patents and issue a compulsory license if the pricing puts products out of reach of Indian consumers. This action has been threatened for Gleevec, Novartis's groundbreaking treatment for myeloid leukemia, which was granted India's first-ever EMR in November 2003. Gleevec is now priced by the company at $2,769 per month—ten times higher than the generic copies available prior to the EMR grant. In what must certainly be a cautionary tale for other MNCs, Novartis is embroiled in litigation on this pricing issue and has been ordered by the courts to provide Gleevec free of charge to consumers earning less than $7,700 per year. Novartis has been fighting two battles in the Madras High Court—one in which it has challenged the overturn of its patent for Gleevec and the other in which it has petitioned the court to declare unconstitutional section 3d of the 2005 amendment to the Patents Act, which states that patents of a known molecule or any of its derivatives are the same unless they differ significantly in terms of usefulness.

Following Novartis's defeat in court in August 2007, after the local patent office decided to decline the patent for Gleevec, the company announced that it would reduce its investment in India in favor of China. If India's authorities continue to ignore the patent, Novartis and many of its peers might exit the country and invest elsewhere. The previously mentioned failure of Eli Lilly's Cialis to qualify for a product patent is another setback to big pharma in India. Lilly's attempt to secure both product and process patents for Cialis in the country was opposed by domestic drugmaker Ajanta Pharma, which held that the product was not a new invention.

The amendments to India's Patents Act, in fact, reflect a general suspicion of MNCs and the perceived risk that foreign firms would be allowed to patent discoveries of a new form of a known substance without proving increased efficacy of the substance. Many parties in India are also concerned that patent protection will restrict access to medicines to only the wealthiest Indians. In addition, Indians objected to the patent legislation on the grounds that it would be harmful to public health in underdeveloped countries outside of India, as India would no longer be able to manufacture and sell low-cost versions of patented drugs used in treating diseases such as HIV and AIDS.

As with existing intellectual property protection in the United States, the new restrictions in India retroactively afford drug companies monopoly rights for drugs they developed after 1995. This protection will make it easier for pharmaceutical companies worldwide to charge premium prices, as it reduces the threat of generic competitors. However, given the tremendous poverty throughout India and given that only 11% of the Indian populace has healthcare insurance, Indian consumers are likely to face a much more limited and more expensive pool of generic options for drugs still covered by a patent in the United States or in Europe.

Technically, only drugs that meet a certain minimum annual turnover threshold and have market dominance are subject to the cost-plus price controls. In 1979, price controls affected 90% of marketed products, but with the general deregulation of the Indian economy, the list of price-controlled drugs has been shrinking. Price controls provide disincentives for MNCs to introduce premium drugs into the national market. Moreover, the number of Indian consumers who can actually afford high-priced specialty drugs is limited. In fact, the government recently introduced proposals to include all essential medicines under the price control mechanism. While price controls may ensure affordability, they also encourage counterfeiting. Price controls and opaque pricing mechanisms are an object of long-standing criticism, and the industry has been lobbying for price liberalization.

As Indian pharmaceuticals increase R&D spending, they are exerting increasing pressure on the government to modify price control mechanisms so that domestic firms can charge Indians more for drugs. However, relaxed price controls coupled with domestic companies' refocus on both branded drugs and the international generics markets might further compromise the health of an already deprived segment of the Indian population. To offset this situation, domestic producers must have incentives for serving this constituency at a low cost. In addition, employer-sponsored health insurance plans are becoming increasingly common complements to limited public-service resources. This development, which suggests a growing ability of Indians to pay for health care, combined with the lower cost structure, may encourage Indian pharmaceutical companies to remain committed to R&D for treatments of common afflictions in India. Otherwise, India's consumers could become the true victims of the new patent legislation.

Conclusion

There is growing consolidation and competition in the Indian pharmaceuticals market, and barriers to entry are increasing. These barriers are increasing as large domestic firms invest in R&D, expand capacity domestically and overseas through acquisitions, and prepare to move up the value chain. Firms with R&D capabilities, scale presence, and relationships with established MNCs seem well positioned to benefit.

As more MNCs enter the Indian market, and as Indian firms consolidate, brand recognition is increasing. With MNCs planning to spend greater amounts on branding and physician education events, Indian firms will also have to spend much more on R&D and marketing efforts to build their brands. As the Indian middle class continues to grow, it will likely demand more-sophisticated drug choices. However, whether domestic and foreign firms will benefit from these new market opportunities will depend on the extent of price controls and on the Indian patent regime.

Notes

1. Manjeet Kripalani, "India: Bigger Pharma," *BusinessWeek*, April 18, 2005, http://www.businessweek.com/magazine/content/05_16/b3929068.htm.

2. Lisa LaMotta, "FDA: Ranbaxy Botched Manufacturing," *Forbes*, September 16, 2008, http://www.forbes.com/2008/09/16/.

3. Vikas Bhardwaj and Khomba Singh, "India: U.S. Pharma Behind Ranbaxy Ban?" *Business Week,* October 17, 2008, http://www.businessweek.com/print/globalbiz/content/oct2008/.

4. Ranbaxy itself was acquired on June 11, 2008—one month before the FDA's charges were made public. The Japanese pharmaceutical company Daiichi Sankyo—in what has been called a landmark deal for the Indian pharmaceutical industry—bought a controlling stake in the company for $4.6 billion. When the scope of the FDA's allegations against Ranbaxy broadened in the subsequent months, Daiichi Sankyo's share price suffered substantially and caused observers to wonder whether the Japanese firm was aware of the true extent of Ranbaxy's problems.

5. Kenji Hall, "More Pain for Ranbaxy, Daiichi Sankyo," *Business Week,* February 26, 2009, http://www.businessweek.com/print/globalbiz/content/feb2009/.

Bibliography

Ahmed, Rumman. 2007. "Indian Pharmaceutical Companies Bet on Outsourcing Services." *Dow Jones International News,* September 27.

Bell and Howell Information and Learning Company. 2006. "CRAMS: The Gateway to Indian Success." *Pharmaceutical Executive* 36 (9): S17.

Bhardwaj, Vikas, and Khomba Singh. 2008. "India: U.S. Pharma Behind Ranbaxy Ban?" *Business Week,* October 17. http://www.businessweek.com/print/globalbiz/content/oct2008/.

Bhatia, Kudrat. "India Geared Up to Tap $31 Billion Drug Outsourcing Market." *Economic Times,* November 2.

Bio Ventures for Global Health. 2004. "India Readies Its Biotech Industry to Capture Global Market Share," Summer. http://www.bvgh.org/news/report/2004/summer/india.asp.

Business Monitor International. 2007. *India Pharmaceutical and Healthcare Report, Q3.*

Business Standard. 2005. "Government Plugs Gaps in Patents Bill," March 22. http://www.business-standard.com/.

———. 2004. "Gujarat Pharma Majors Pop the Outsourcing Pill," November 29. http://www.business-standard.com/.

Chatterjee, Saibal. 2005. "Piracy Blocks India's Global Dreams." *Hindustan Times,* March 22. http://www.hindustantimes.com/news/.

Financial Express. 2007. "Ranbaxy to Complete Demerger of R&D Arm by 2008," October 31. http://www.financialexpress.com/news/.

First Global India. 2008. "Sector Research: Pharmaceuticals." (analyst report) April 7.

Go, Robert, and Ruth Given. 2005. "India Meets Doha." Paper presented at the Governors' Meeting for Health Care at the World Economic Forum's Annual Meeting, Davos, Switzerland, January 27. http://www.deloitte.com/dtt/cda/doc/content/India%20Meets%20Doha(1).pdf.

Hall, Kenji. 2009. "More Pain for Ranbaxy, Daiichi Sankyo." *BusinessWeek*, February 26. http://www.businessweek.com/print/globalbiz/content/feb2009/.

Hindu Business Line. 2007. "GlaxoSmithKline, Ranbaxy to Expand R&D Alliance," February 7. http://www.thehindubusinessline.com/2007/02/07/stories/.

Iloveindia.com. 2007. "Pharmaceutical Industry in India," July 21. http://www.iloveindia.com/economy-of-india/pharmaceutical-industry.html.

Jayakumar, P. B., and Joe Mathew. 2007. Eli Lilly Drug Patent Deflated on Indian Scientists' Claim." *Rediff.com,* December 14. http://www.rediff.com/money/2007/dec/14eli.htm.

Joshipura, Hasit. 2005. Personal interview, March 24.

Kamath, Gauri. 2004. "The Defence." *Businessworld,* November 1. http://www.businessworld.in/bw/.

———. 2004. "Is the Pharma Dream Run Over?" *Businessworld,* November 1. http://www.businessworld.in/bw/.

Kammili, Mrinal. 2006. "Get Ready for the R&D Revolution." *Hindu,* June 19. http://www.hindu.com/edu/2006/06/19/stories/.

Kripalani, Manjeet. 2005. "India: Bigger Pharma." *BusinessWeek,* April 18. www.businessweek.com/.

Kumar, Ashok Ram. 2004. "Impact of TRIPS on Indian Pharma." *Pharmabiz.com,* December 2. http://www.pharmabiz.com/.

Lall & Sethi. 2004. "Highlights of the Patent (Amendment) Ordinance." *Legal Summary from Lall & Sethi.*

LaMotta, Lisa. 2008. "FDA: Ranbaxy Botched Manufacturing." *Forbes,* September 16. http://www.forbes.com/2008/09/16/.

Limaye, Ravi. 2005. Personal interview, March 23.

Meredith, Robyn. 2004. "Lupin's Unsexy Bet." *Forbes,* December 13. http://www.forbes.com/business/free_forbes/2004/1213/168.html.

Murali, D., and C. Ramesh. 2007. "Pharma: Glowing with Growth." *Hindu Business Line,* June 17. http://www.thehindubusinessline.com/iw/2007/06/17/stories/.

Nath, Kamal. 2004. "Statement on the Ordinance Relating to Patents (Third) Amendment." *Press Information Bureau—Government of India,* December 27. http://pib.nic.in/release/press_rel.asp.

Pal, Devinder. 2005. Personal interview, April 18.

Panchal, Salil. 2005. "Patents Era: How Will Pharma Firms Cope?" *Rediff .com,* April 7. http://in.rediff.com.

Pharmaceutical and Drug Manufacturers. 2005. "Drugs Price Control Order (DCPO)," August 21. http://www.pharmaceutical-drug-manufacturers .com/pharmaceutical-policies/drugs-price-control-order.html.

Rediff.com. 2004. "Pharma: Through Porter's Eyes," August 27. http://www .rediff.com/money/2004/aug/27pharma.htm.

Sahad, P. V. 2004. "An Ideas Super Power." *iPolicy Networks,* January 18. http:// www.ipolicynetworks.com/news/articles/2004-0118-superpower.html.

Sappenfield, Mark. 2007. "Poised for Pharmaceutical Boom, India Is Revamping Its Drug Industry Hoping to Duplicate Success of IT Sector." *Christian Science Monitor,* January 2.

Sharma, Anand. 2007. "Destination: India-Drug Discovery and Development." *Mondaq Business Briefing,* September 17. http://www .thefreelibrary.com/.

Shetty, B. R. 2004. "Lucrative Middle East Beckons Indian Pharma Firms." *Pharmabix.com,* December 2. http://www.pharmabiz.com/article/.

Sikka, Harinder J. 2005. Personal interview, March 16.

Srinivasan, G. 2005. "Lok Sabha Passes Patents Bill with Left Support." *Hindu Business Line,* March 22. http://www.thehindubusinessline .com/2005/03/23/stories/.

Subbu, Ramnath. "Pharma Industry Well Positioned for Growth." *Hindu,* November 5. http://www.thehindu.com/2007/11/05/stories/.

Times of India. 2005. "Bristol-Myers to Enter India Again," April 25. http:// timesofindia.indiatimes.com/.

Chapter 8

SOCIAL ENTREPRENEURSHIP: EMPOWERING INDIA'S POOR

Nidhi Agarwal, Laurence Bass,
Benjamin Bove, Clifford Chen, Ashley DeMello,
Nathalie Gogue, Nancy Jo, Amyn Saleh

Despite tremendous economic growth in the last decade, India is still riddled by poverty. Nearly 260 million people in India live on less than one dollar a day, half of all the country's children are malnourished, and half of all homes have no access to electricity. According to the World Bank, the leading cause of poor living conditions in the country is the underperformance of India's government. In fact, only five governments in the world contribute less to public health than India's. Many regions of the country do not have access to piped water, and more than half of all children who receive education must do so by attending a private institution. While servicing the poorest rural segment of the Indian population is addressed in the annual government budget, this segment remains the most underdeveloped.

Some analysts argue that the lack of effective government policy can be blamed on India's political culture. For instance, the government's inability to implement sufficient public programs has been attributed to the "anti-incumbency factor," a term used in Indian politics to describe a forty-year pattern in which no party or coalition has won two consecutive terms. Many believe that this factor explains the bedeviled development of public-sector policy: one government's cherished project is abandoned by its successors, so no long-term policy is implemented. In addition, many of the programs are hampered by inept implementation with little of the intended funding reaching those it is meant for.

Still, while the constant churn of Indian government officials may not be resolved soon, social entrepreneurs in India have stepped in to meet public needs and improve education, health, access to jobs, and capital for India's poor—those at the bottom of the pyramid, living on less than two dollars per day. According to some estimates, there are 1.2 million social organizations operating in India.[1] Most of these organizations are very small and woefully ineffective in addressing the social grievances that they made it their mission to solve. However, there are also a number of initiatives that have had a transformative effect on India; they helped break the cycle of poverty and enabled India's poor to participate in and benefit from the country's rapid economic development.

Given the complexity of the social sector in India, we will focus most of our discussion in this chapter on two of the most important—and so far most successful—social initiatives: the microfinance movement, and public-private partnerships between large Indian companies and the government. We detail the development of these two models, discuss major players and critical challenges in both domains, and point toward the future development of social entrepreneurship in India.

Meeting the Challenge of Poverty Through Microfinance

Although India has a large banking network, almost 70% of the population has no access to a bank account. Institutions dedicated to eradicating poverty recognize microfinance as perhaps the most effective means to raise living standards in underdeveloped areas. Microfinance provides the extremely poor with a forum for collective action, training in a range of financial services, and access to credit. Since traditional banks were unwilling to take the risk of lending to the poor, and to incur the high transaction costs involved, the early focus of most microenterprise lending programs was on proving that the poor were creditworthy. The Grameen Bank of Bangladesh, often referred to as the pioneer of the new microenterprise lending movement, took the fundamental stance that credit is a human right and thus should be available to all people. It was not until the mid-1990s that the term "microenterprise lending" began to be replaced by a new term that included not only credit, but also savings and other financial services. "Microenterprise finance," or "microfinance," emerged as the term of choice to refer to a range of financial services to the poor. These services include not only credit, but also savings, insurance, and leasing.

According to the United Nations Capital Development Fund, India is home to one-third of the world's poor, with an estimated demand for microcredit of $30 billion. However, the supply is less than $4.5 billion. Vikram Akula, founder of SKS Microfinance, suggests that India's impoverished population can be segmented by income level, income source, and place of residence (rural or urban). The upper-poor segment comprises seventy million people with a consistent source of income, including small entrepreneurs and day laborers earning one to two dollars per day. The very poor segment comprises eighty million people earning less than one dollar a day, including day laborers with few or no income-generating assets and no consistent source of income. The ultrapoor segment comprises ten million people with no daily source of income.

Segments of the Indian Microfinance Sector

Currently, there are three main stakeholders in the Indian microfinance sector: self-help groups (SHGs), groups of about twenty persons engaging in peer lending; microfinance institutions (MFIs), which organize and train the SHGs; and banks, such as ICICI Bank and the State Bank of India, which provide the capital for loans.

In India, microcredit borrowers are individuals without access to traditional financial institutions. They tend to live in impoverished communities and need financing for small businesses. Typically, microcredit borrowers are organized into groups that are jointly responsible for repaying a loan. Of these SHGs, 90% are women's groups of twenty or fewer persons each, engaging in peer lending (groups greater than twenty must be registered as corporate entities). The SHGs receive a lump sum of money and then lend portions of the loan to individual members. After a few months of successful repayment on their loans, individuals of the group can borrow from MFIs or banks independent of the SHG. In India, the repayment rate for women is an astounding 99.6%.

Besides savings and credit activities, SHGs also serve as a forum for poor rural women to voice their opinions, interact with one another, share their experiences, exchange ideas, and initiate collective action on a wide range of social, personal, and economic issues. Only SHGs that have performed well in rotating internal savings in the form of small internal loans are assisted with external funds through linkages with banks and other financial intermediaries.

Even when successful, the formation of SHGs is time consuming and labor intensive. During the first six months after formation, the members of the SHG save a small amount of money, pool their savings, and deposit it in a bank. In the Tamil Nadu state, monthly savings are normally in the range of fifty cents to one dollar per member. SHGs also meet twice a month and receive training from an MFI staff member on how to organize their group meetings, start a bank account, calculate interest, and learn about women's rights and other general issues. During the second six months, group members begin to lend their savings to other group members. In this first year, SHG members become adept at handling money, understanding the implications of cooperating and pooling their savings, and recognizing the importance of repayment. At the end of one year, the group becomes eligible to receive credit from the bank. In Tamil Nadu, the average loan size is approximately $50 per member, but a loan may be as high as $200 to allow the individual borrower to undertake small business activities like raising a milk cow, setting up a tailoring shop, and producing food items. Repayment is made every month, and the group collects the amount and pays the bank. Under the Grameen model, repayments are made weekly, and loans have a duration of one year.

According to SKS's Akula, 73% of MFIs (2,321 institutions) serve fewer than 2,500 clients. Some 25% of all MFIs serve 2,500 to 100,000 clients, while only 2% (49 institutions) serve more than 100,000 clients. Traditional banks supply the microfinance industry by financing SHGs directly or by financing the setup of an MFI, a nongovernmental organization (NGO), or a nonbanking financial company (NBFC). Historically, because of infrastructure requirements and transaction costs, banks found it prohibitively expensive to provide credit to the rural poor. With the emergence of MFIs, which absorb the transaction costs and provide the necessary channels to the rural segment, banks can now use MFIs as an intermediary to provide capital to the rural poor. According to K. G. Karmakar, managing director of the National Bank for Agriculture and Rural Development (NABARD), going through an intermediary enables the banks to reduce the background check time and the transaction costs by an estimated 40%.

Over time, banks and the private sector have seen SHGs as a financially attractive segment. They discovered that lending small amounts to creditworthy poor people is both lucrative and socially responsible. Interest rates are around 25%, and the reimbursement rates are more than 95%. All Indian banks of significant size must take a small lending position in microfinance; the priority sector lending laws require banks to lend to priority industries and regions. Still, most microfinance institutions operate as NGOs and are very small. Currently, the most active banks in this sector are ICICI Bank and the State Bank of India. However, despite the fact that the SHG-bank linkage is more than 95%, according to a 2005 NABARD report, the share of microcredit in India is still just a drop in the ocean: only 1% of the total credit of the banking system.

Growth Barriers in Microfinance

Microfinance has proven to be very successful in India; established MFIs are continually expanding, and the number of MFIs is growing tremendously. Currently, there are more than one thousand MFIs in India, an increase of 30% from July 2004. Although the remarkable growth extends the reach of microfinance, demand still far outstrips supply. One of the greatest barriers to growth is lack of capital for the MFI, which is the channel for financial services to SHGs. This problem has several causes.

First, MFIs' access to funds is limited. Most MFIs have been started by philanthropic individuals with strong personal ties to a particular Indian banking institution, usually through a prior career. Consequently, the MFIs generally have a relationship with a single funding source and are therefore limited in growth because they lack additional funding sources. The cost of funds can eventually become a constraint on growth. Since funding sources base loans on personal relationships rather than on interest rates, MFIs cannot secure the lowest cost for their capital. In turn, the loans procured often have inflated interest rates—sometimes as high as 18% to 25%—despite extremely low default rates. Small to medium-sized rural banks cannot shoulder the increasing risk of infinitely growing shares of their capital tied up in microfinance schemes without being compensated with higher interest rates. Consequently, the cost of funds can hold up growth. Until recently, MFIs could accept local debt but not equity, making it hard for them to scale up their operations. Additionally, access to capital and to reasonable interest rates is hampered by the fact that most MFIs are NGOs, which have been unregulated. The MFIs have been able to penetrate the poverty-stricken segment because of their commitment to organize and educate borrowers and distribute funds, but this commitment makes it hard for them to access additional capital. Moreover, MFIs' lack of licenses hinders them from offering a full range of products. To address these issues, many MFIs are moving toward becoming NBFCs, thus allowing them to serve as a bank to the poor and offer a range of savings products.

Given the enormous potential demand, it is critical for microfinance to be both scalable and sustainable. Meeting those criteria depends largely on the availability and cost of funds. High rates of interest and repayment are drawing attention from institutional banks, capital markets, and private investors, resulting in an influx of capital that is forcing the current system to synthesize these new entrants. More and more private investment is entering the sector, which as we discuss later creates its own set of problems.

In addition to lack of capital, low capacity has prevented MFIs from increasing their market penetration and scalability. Changes in regulation would increase their access to capital, and thus enable them to grow. A key challenge to raising capacity is lack of access to talent. Microfinance is a transaction-heavy industry, and as MFIs scale up their operations, they need to hire and train a considerable number of junior staff. Because of the industry's history of socially responsible business practices and low compensation compared with that in the corporate sector, MFIs have trouble hiring qualified senior management. Moreover, as an MFI grows in borrowers, capital, and geographic reach, the management structure and institutional policies must be examined. During our meeting with ICICI Bank, the head of the rural lending department suggested that the main obstacle for growth is management leadership. ICICI Bank, which lends through approximately sixty MFIs in India, believes that most MFIs depend on a single dynamic leader. The bank is therefore urging MFIs to implement leadership succession plans by building robust management structures.

Largely because of state government regulations and cultural differences, the growth of microfinance activity in India has been uneven. Microfinance has gained the strongest foothold in western and southern India, particularly in the state of Andhra Pradesh. As the microfinance sectors continue to expand rapidly, it is increasingly difficult for governmental policy to keep pace. This situation is mostly due to the newness of microfinance and the lack of a common voice that could help inform and advise policy makers. In response to pressure from private parties, the Union Cabinet of India passed a bill on microfinance in February 2007. One key change was that NABARD was now empowered to regulate the microfinance sector in India. In addition, the minimum capital requirement was capped at Rs 1 lakh ($2,300), at least 50% of which had to come from MFI promoters.

Since its inception, however, the microfinance bill has received criticism from many stakeholders, especially SHGs. First, many challenge the election of NABARD as the regulating entity. Because NABARD is the largest lender to SHGs and MFIs, its regulation of them is seen as posing a conflict of interest. Moreover, the minimum capital requirement, given the size of the industry, is viewed as quite low; it is feared that it will attract unqualified organizations to the industry. Some SHGs wish the bill had capped the interest rates that can be charged instead of allowing them to float with the market. The exemption of MFIs not registered as NGOs and of NBFCs from regulation has also been strongly criticized. On the other hand, being exempt makes it harder for MFIs and NBFCs to take customer deposits.

Overall, the bill is a step in the right direction, as it has created more structure around the industry, and discussions among government officials and other stakeholders continue. Sa-Dhan, an association of community development financial institutions, is trying to create an enabling legal and regulatory environment for microfinance services within India. Its mission is to further the collective needs of "unorganized" microfinance organizations. Its membership has grown rapidly over the years, and it now represents more than three million SHG members and outstanding loans in excess of $100 million. Sa-Dhan's diversity is also growing: its member organizations include not only traditional MFIs but also capacity-building organizations, technical service providers, network organizations, bulk lenders, and commercial banks that represent an array of stakeholders in the microfinance sector. Yet, as the microfinance sector in India emerges from its nascence, it is becoming increasingly important to have a set of standards to ensure orderly growth and to build credibility with banks and policy makers. A comprehensive, clear, and uniform regulatory system is needed.

The Growth of Private Investment

Despite the aforementioned growth barriers, research suggests that the growth of MFIs in India is the fastest in the world. Vijay Mahajan of Basix, a leading microfinance lender in Hyderabad, estimates the size of the market to be about $30 billion. Many MFIs are entering the market, and their market share of small credit has grown from 28% in 2002 to 47% in 2007. The average size of a loan has also increased—from $161 to $201—and some leading MFIs have recorded annual rates of growth as high as 80% in 2006 to 2007. The transition from an NGO-driven culture is being fueled by rising involvement of capital markets. The entrance of private-sector investment is increasing access to capital as well as increasing scale and penetration of microlending models. The private sector will bring with it a significant level of professionalism and a business mind-set. Many hope that private interest will foster better governance and regulation, followed by innovative financing, product offerings, and improved technology. Lastly, these changes in the industry will invite competition and should lead to better service for poor lenders.

Leading the pack in pursuing this opportunity is ICICI, India's largest private bank. ICICI has a growing number of customers who qualify as deeply poor and an associated loan portfolio through its MFI/NGO partners. It works closely with MFIs and NGOs to adapt its products to suit their needs. Additionally, ICICI has been working with its insurance subsidiaries to expand its offerings of microinsurance products. Microinsurance is a relatively new product offering in which a group of poor people who may not be able to get individual insurance can come together and get group insurance.

Grameen Capital India (GCI) represents the newest player in microfinance in India. GCI is a collaboration among the Grameen Foundation, IFMR Trust, and Citicorp Finance (India) Limited to enable MFIs to develop wider access to the capital markets, primarily the domestic ones. The entry of GCI is targeted toward developing a commercial market for microfinance receivables. It will work with MFIs to access primary and secondary debt markets and private placement of MFI portfolios with banks. It will also provide credit enhancements to the portfolios of MFIs through capital advisory services and rating agencies to help the MFIs gain access to bank funds. Aggregation of loans allows GCI to diversify investment risk, thus improving on the usual practice of investing in a single MFI or region.

The entry of GCI signals the beginning of a new chapter in the microfinance sector. By providing access to new, larger sources of capital, GCI will most likely change the fundamental microfinance structure in India. GCI will aggregate regional loan portfolios across India, repackage them in diversified portfolios, and sell portions of these portfolios to investors and financial institutions. Repackaging reduces risk by introducing diversification. In addition, it allows for more-efficient capital markets by increasing the number of potential investors. GCI will also focus on collecting comprehensive data from MFIs and disseminating accurate information to its investors, including the use of credit ratings.

Unitus is another example of a private entity that has entered the market and plans to take a leading role in addressing challenges facing MFIs. In 2005, Unitus partnered with Accion International to grow the microfinance industry in India through the Unitus-Accion Alliance for India. Accion is a private nonprofit organization with the mission of giving poor people the financial tools they need (e.g., microenterprise loans, business training, and other financial services) to work their way out of poverty. Its goal is to deliver microfinance services to fifteen million of India's underprivileged citizens by 2015. Unitus identifies the highest-potential MFIs in developing countries and then helps accelerate their growth through capital investments and capacity building, thus empowering them to help exponentially more poor people worldwide. In doing so, Unitus aims to demonstrate that MFIs can be run as profitable, large-scale, poverty-focused businesses with links to local capital markets.

As part of this partnership, Accion focuses on assisting commercial entities such as banks and finance companies in extending microfinance products and services and providing technical assistance and training. Unitus, on the other end, focuses on identifying high-potential MFIs to transform or commercialize them from an unregulated nonprofit or NGO into a regulated for-profit institution. The transformation is expected to enable the MFIs to expand their product offerings, increase their access to finance through debt and equity, and provide greater transparency. This strategic partnership, thought to be the first of its kind, is designed to catalyze the creation of a large-scale, profitable microfinance industry in India.

In 2007, venture capitalists invested $50 million (Rs 200 crore) in microfinance activities—a considerable jump from almost nothing in 2006. According to Kate Cochran, vice president of finance and operations at Unitus, her organization provided their Indian MFI partners with $2 million in grants, $14 million in equity, and $20 million in debt. For instance, Unitus provided SKS Microfinance with $90,000 in grants, $500,000 in debt, and $490,000 in equity (13% of SKS equity). SKS raised additional equity from other major investors. Unitus will typically exit partnerships after MFI partners achieve scale and have the capacity and financing to continue their growth.

Concerns over Private Investment

The entry of these companies and of Indian banks such as ICICI and Yes Bank provides substantial benefits by bringing a huge influx of capital to a fragmented, undercapitalized industry. There are concerns, however, that this private investment will move MFIs away from their original social missions toward investor returns. One MFI claimed that real, tangible results on quality of life in a village are not seen until five to ten years after an initial loan is made to one of its SHGs. In fact, it stated that significant changes to poverty alleviation are not exhibited until the next generation. Loans made to help women save for advanced school fees for their children start to repay in social capital much later than when the loans were repaid in hard currency. Stakeholders who are physically and emotionally removed from the villagers could choose to advocate decisions that yield more-immediate, tangible financial results rather than investments that may pay off five to twenty-five years out.

While MFIs currently do not experience much interference from their local funding sources, who readily understand the social aspects of microfinance, private and commercial banks entering the highly profitable microlending market bring in more players on the MFI level. Aggregators will promote the creation of more MFIs to further diversify their portfolios. If competition at the MFI level becomes a reality, the power of rural villagers will increase, as they will now have a choice of microfinance providers. Experience suggests that, with access to alternative sources of credit, MFIs will lose leverage and the rate of repayment will decline. Although some MFIs are concerned about the commitment of private banks to the social goals of microfinance, competition can serve as a gauge of social responsibility. Indeed, it may ultimately force interest rates to become so competitive that the benefits of better access and lower cost of capital shift from investors to the villagers. Increased competition at any level can make the capital markets even more efficient, and if investors and aggregators remain vigilant, the introduction of capital markets could provide both positive financial results as well as social welfare gains. Prudent industry regulation from the Indian government would enable growth and assist MFIs in keeping the industry committed to the social mission of microlending.

The Future of Microfinance in India

The current system of microfinance in India has served its purpose well. During this nascent period, MFIs have provided first-generation Indian SHGs with a link to medium-sized sources of capital. The system works in this basic form because each entity benefits: SHGs receive much-needed seed money, MFIs can achieve their social goals and facilitate credit flow to the poorest sectors, and banks receive an interest rate more than commensurate with the risk they assume. MFIs have provided an effective method for small-scale channeling of capital to the rural population, and investors have captured premium returns on loans with a default rate of less than 1%. In short, the microfinance sector in India is booming.

However, times are changing in India. The value chain will expand, with firms like GCI providing the primary source of capital to the microfinance sector. Furthermore, organizations such as Sa-Dhan will evolve to play a much more active role as they increase membership and gain credibility. Eventually, they could also assume regulatory responsibility within the sector. Whether that responsibility would be formal or informal would depend on the actions of the government.

In addition, the MFIs' networks across communities represent an opportunity for companies that hope to reach India's vast rural population. SKS, for example, uses its network of field agents and clients as a distribution channel for moving a wide variety of products and services—such as mobile phones, insurance, and foodstuffs—on behalf of business partners, such as Nokia or large regional merchants and shops. Grameen Bank's Muhammad Yunus sees his microlending network as a starting point for all sorts of economic activity. He has formed a number of joint ventures with large multinationals to improve the health and livelihoods of India's poor. One of the ventures, Grameen Danone Foods, sells affordable, single-serving packages of nutrition-enhanced yogurt; the distribution is handled by Grameen Bank's customers.[2]

India is in the early stages of a transformation that will fundamentally alter the face of its microfinance sector. The primary challenge will be balancing the needs and desires of corporations, MFIs, SHGs, associations like Sa-Dhan, and the federal and state governments in a sustainable way that allows all parties to benefit while still focusing on the uninterrupted flow of credit to those below the poverty line. This transformation will give microfinance a tremendous opportunity to help hundreds of millions of people overcome a centuries-old legacy of poverty.

Public-Private Partnerships

Extending Corporate Social Responsibility into the Education Sector

An increasing number of private-sector companies see their responsibility as good corporate citizens to help governmental and other public organizations alleviate some of the most pressing social grievances in India. Commenting on Bharti's motivation for entering the social sector, Badri Agarwal, president of Bharti Foundation, stated that "it was the firm's social duty to give back to the community and support the aspirations of the under-privileged in the country."[3] He also noted that building strong bonds with rural communities is in the best interests of the firm's profitability, because, simply put, a company with a positive image will probably be more profitable than a company without it. Dileep Ranjekar, chief executive of the Azim Premji Foundation, stated that Azim Premji (chairman of the Indian IT services company Wipro Technologies) decided to begin the foundation in 1998 to "leave a legacy."[4] Education-related social efforts are particularly suitable for joint efforts of private firms and public organizations. The improvement of educational opportunities in rural India is broadly considered not only a priority, but a necessity: a better-educated population is key to India's continued economic growth, for it benefits firms by providing them with capable future employees and emancipated and aspiring consumers.

Most Indian firms are at least partially motivated in their philanthropic efforts by community relations. However, there is also a pressing political imperative to invest in the rural poor. On April 18, 2006, Prime Minister Manmohan Singh warned the business sector that the government was thinking of instituting quotas for the number of people hired from the poorly educated bottom of the Hindu caste system. Though Singh's warning suggested that the government would seek voluntary compliance with such quotas, many corporations believe that without widespread compliance, the government will make the quotas compulsory. Corporations fear that such mandatory employment of poorly educated workers would affect profitability, discourage foreign direct investment, and potentially burst India's economic bubble. Corporate investments in education can therefore be seen as preemptive measures, as attempts at solving a social and political problem before it becomes a business problem.

In addition to these political factors, the private sector is facing pressure from a public relations standpoint. Firms in Bangalore, India's Electronic City, that have profited significantly from the IT and outsourcing boom during the last years are now suffering a political backlash from Indian communities as the disparity between the wealthiest firms and their poor neighbors increases. This backlash has increased incentives for Indian firms such as Wipro and Bharti to create positive community relations through private-public partnerships that address social issues such as education.

The Problems of Rural Primary Education

Education for India's poor remains one of the most worrisome obstacles to India's continued growth. Recent surveys show that while the government's push for rural education has succeeded in increasing school attendance to unprecedented heights, the quality of education remains low and is even sinking in some subjects, such as mathematics.[5] Only 3% of the government's budget is allocated to education, falling short of the 6% target announced in 2004. Various states are trying to address the quality (and funding) gap through a host of schemes that include active participation by NGOs and corporate foundations—all of the schemes aimed at meeting the basic challenges of access, retention, and quality at the rural primary education level.

Why rural primary education? With an annual economic growth of 6%, India has seen the number of job openings in the country grow exponentially. This booming economy has run into a tremendous shortage of skilled workers, and the root cause of this shortage is the lack of educational opportunities for a large portion of India's population. When one considers that 20% of the world's population under the age of twenty-five is living in India, one can only see this lack as a waste of future human capital. And unless the cycle of cross-generational illiteracy is broken, the vast bulk of India's poor will fail to see the value and relevance of education in their lives and will be excluded from India's economic growth. According to Marshall Bouton, president of the Chicago Council on Global Affairs, "The challenge in India is to provide a basic level of education, accessible to this large population at a cost that fits their socioeconomic status and meets the needs of the rural community."

Tragically, educational opportunities remain beyond the grasp of large numbers of India's rural poor, especially girls, and illiteracy rates continue to be as high as 50% in some states. Politicians continue to pay lip service to prioritizing primary education, but the sector continues to be plagued by severe problems. Several factors seem to be at work in keeping access to, retention in, and quality of rural primary education at persistently low levels. Conversations with Bharti Foundation's Agrawal pointed to a nexus of teacher, student, and parent issues that lead to poor or little education for the vast majority of India's children. Budgetary constraints have meant abysmally low salaries and inadequate training for teachers, who may be certified but lack qualifications. And the lack of any clear, visible career growth path discourages long-term commitment to the profession that teachers might have had upon entry.

Additionally, lack of student motivation, together with an unstructured curriculum and with responsibilities to meet at home, creates little incentive for education. Because of their social background and uneducated parents, students do not realize the importance of education and its impact on their quality of life. Since many of these children come from a part of India that has not seen development, they do not have role models or success stories to influence them. The gap between what is taught and how it is taught leads to a compromise on the quality of the curriculum. The inadequacy of the curriculum, coupled with health problems due to poor hygiene and sanitation, causes the students to lose interest in school. Often, these children are pressured to work at home for long hours on activities critical to the family's daily life. For instance, even a five-year-old child may be burdened with looking after a younger sibling. The responsibility of earning a living for the household is shared by children and parents alike. Therefore, many children drop out of school or do not get enrolled. Compounding the problems of poorly trained teachers and unmotivated students are parents that are constrained by a lack of monetary resources. For these parents schooling may represent a loss of labor and an unaffordable expense, as they have no means to pay school fees and buy books and uniforms for their children.

Even as the national and state governments, handicapped by insufficient monetary resources, struggle to deal with issues of access, retention, and quality, efforts at implementing change continue to be sporadic. Since the state governments in India change frequently, the focus on education—assuming there is one—changes frequently too. Consequently, long-term policies are virtually impossible to implement, and any gains made by one government may be nullified by the next.

Making a Difference Through Private-Sector Involvement

Despite the lack of government leadership, the last couple of decades have seen a significant increase in real per capita expenditures on education in rural India. In 1993 to 1994, the expenditure was 1.5% of total consumption expenditure, and by 2001 to 2002, it was 2.5% in constant prices. For the top 5% of all rural households, the expenditure had doubled. Given that government schools charge no fees, the growing expenditure on education points to the growing demand for private schooling in rural India.

This positive trend may be partly attributable to the efforts of companies in the private sector. To understand how the private sector is making a difference in rural primary education, we looked at three well-established companies with educational programs: Tata Industries, with ninety-eight companies in seven business sectors; the Azim Premji Foundation, with financial resources contributed by Azim Premji, chairman of Wipro Technologies; and Bharti Foundation, which was established to lead the corporate social responsibility agenda of the Bharti group of companies in 2000, with the telecom giant Bharti Airtel serving as the flagship. We chose these organizations because of their strategic interest in growing their already considerable customer base. With their attention on growing this base, these firms have a high stake in India's economic and demographic structures.

Tata Industries: Focus on Community

Tata Industries focuses on community involvement and relies on partnerships to affect change. Their approach stresses that the community knows the needs of the community better than any outsider. By emphasizing the community as the central motivator, they easily capture community buy-in and avoid many challenges that other companies and foundations face. The Tata Council for Community Initiatives (TCCI) is an umbrella organization that helps Tata companies shape their community development projects.

According to Kishore Chaukar, head of TCCI and member of the Tata Group's Corporate Centre, the purpose of TCCI is to "improve the quality of life of the communities we serve through leadership in sectors of national economic significance." To this end, TCCI focuses on vocational education, which can benefit communities relatively quickly by increasing rates of higher education and employment.

The Tata Group's statement of purpose testifies to its dedication to build a community-oriented business model. Responsibility is part of the Tata code of conduct. The community aspect of that responsibility was integrated into the objectives of the business that would become the Tata Group since its inception. The Tata Group has launched programs to provide medical assistance and schooling since 1915. The inclusion of "Corporation Social Responsibility" in the firm's memorandum of association and articles of association allows the company to draw funds for community projects from the operational profit and loss accounts of the Tata Group.

The Tata Group works in a number of social fields that span different educational needs. Many of the Tata companies invest individually in building and supporting primary schools in the areas where the companies are located, such as Singur and Jamshedpur. Primary education is a common way in which the companies contribute to rural communities. For instance, Tata Infotech, in partnership with NGOs, is providing free computer and life skills education to children in municipality schools in Delhi and Mumbai. This initiative has given more than two thousand children access to a computer for the first time. Tata Infotech donates all the required hardware and software, and it assigns its faculty members to train the students.

Tata has developed a computer-based literacy program that targets the fifteen- to thirty-five-year-old age group in rural India, about 28% of whom the government estimates are illiterate. This program—which was developed by Tata Consultancy Services (TCS), Asia's largest software enterprise—uses teaching software and multimedia presentations to teach a person to read in a fraction of the time it takes to do by conventional means. Standard adult literacy projects teach reading, writing, and arithmetic. Typically, they are expensive, as they require classrooms and trained teachers and take six months to two years to complete. The TCS program focuses exclusively on reading and drastically reduces the time it takes a person to learn to read—thirty to forty-five hours spread over ten to twelve weeks. The emphasis is on words rather than alphabets, and the process is styled to suit the learner. Because the program is multimedia driven, it does not need trained teachers, which reduces the cost of eradicating illiteracy.

Today, the program operates in more than one thousand centers in several states and has helped more than twenty thousand people learn to read. More centers are being set up, and it is in this context that NGOs become valuable. They can motivate people to join the program by offering various incentives, like combining this literacy program with income-generation initiatives and self-help group activities.

Bharti Foundation: Focus on Innovation and Quality

Bharti Airtel has been at the forefront of India's telecom revolution and has helped even the most remote parts of India by linking them to the rest of the world through cell phones. Bharti now wants to leverage its infrastructure to help the underprivileged. Bharti Foundation was established in 2000 with a corpus of Rs 200 crores ($50 million) and has since won the Golden Peacock Award for Corporate Social Responsibility. The foundation relies on partnerships with local governments and with other NGOs already servicing the rural communities. In doing so, the foundation effectively avoids duplicating the efforts of other organizations. The foundation focuses on rural primary education, using a two-pronged approach of developing its own private schools in villages and adopting poorly performing government schools to improve their operations. This program is commonly referred to as the school improvement program (SIP).

The program focuses on education in rural India because the foundation believes education is a solution to India's socioeconomic ailments, especially the need to educate rural girls. The foundation's own experience and research show that the stigma borne by educated women in rural India has faded dramatically over the last ten years. Additionally, the program's focus is backed by studies showing that educated women have a deeper impact than others on the quality of life (i.e., health, hygiene, and further education) of the entire household.

Bharti Foundation's leaders feel very strongly about owning the implementation of projects funded by the corpus. They realize that even though the government provides tremendous support for education in India, it fails to reach its goals because of faulty implementation. In the foundation's plans to build, own, and operate one thousand schools across the country, it is willing to partner with public schools and NGOs. In the last year or so, the foundation set up about twenty schools, and it planned to have about one hundred in operation by the end of 2008. Interest in the areas where the schools have been established is high, and parent feedback surveys have been promising.

A key part of Bharti Foundation's elementary school initiative has been its computer-aided learning project, aimed at increasing interest in learning and performance and at ensuring steady enrollment in school. Bharti Computer Centres were initiated in 2004 to make computers accessible to underprivileged children. The centers use the computers to supplement teaching and learning in schools in order to stimulate children's interest in their own education. The foundation has partnered with leading NGOs to implement the program across several states. Children using the centers have shown remarkable improvement in number recognition and simple mathematical functions. In addition, the centers have increased enrollment and attendance at the schools they support. Moreover, the centers' success has sparked the interest of communities in having these centers at their schools. Bharti Foundation's SIP aims to substantively improve the quality and functioning of schools across the country. To achieve this goal, the foundation will partner with state governments and with other agencies to adopt a number of primary schools for an extended period of time. The program will begin with a detailed assessment of the needs of each school, including infrastructure such as classrooms, blackboards, toilets, and drinking-water supply. The program will also evaluate the functioning of each school, including key elements of its academics, such as teacher training, teaching-learning material, and assessment of children and curriculum. Where it finds problems, it will work with the government to resolve them. A start in this direction has been made in Rajasthan, where the foundation has partnered with the state government in the Rajasthan Education Initiative to implement the program in fifty schools over a ten-year period.

This SIP has the far-reaching objective to raise the overall quality of education in primary schools by improving all school processes. Most importantly, improvements are designed to be sustainable so that their benefits accrue to the schools even after completion of the program. To achieve the SIP's goals, the involvement of the local community, especially the Panchayat, the village council, is essential. The SIP needs to get community members to participate in the program in order to create a sense of community ownership of the schools.

To raise the overall quality of education, the foundation plans to focus on teacher training. It aims to raise expectations for existing government schools by providing them with ideas and teaching methods the foundation has developed and proven in its own schools. The biggest challenge the foundation faces in implementing its program is teacher motivation. Although there is no shortage of teachers for government schools, the quality of these teachers is dismal. Inadequate incentive packages for teachers have been identified as the key problem in the performance of schools. Although the foundation continues to make improvements, it is still trying to overcome this challenge.

The Azim Premji Foundation: Focus on Accountability

The Azim Premji Foundation focuses on improving the quality of elementary education in order to attract children to school and retain them. Since the government is the key provider of elementary education—especially in rural India, where more than 75% of all children study in government schools—the foundation mainly seeks to change government policy and awareness. The foundation's leaders believe that the key to improving the quality of elementary education is building accountability at every level of the delivery system. This accountability, which needs to apply to everyone from the teachers in the schools to the education minister of each state, is based on clear outcomes.

Instances of the foundation's attempt to raise awareness and influence policy can be seen in the National Learning Conference organized by the foundation in partnership with the Ministry of Human Resource Development in 2005. This, the second such jointly organized conference, focused on improving the quality of teachers. One issue that emerged during the conference was teacher accountability: it cannot be achieved if the education system does not support the teachers in doing their work of delivering quality learning to every child. The identification of the accountability issue was followed by workshops organized with the departments of education in the states of Rajasthan and Karnataka. The workshops facilitated discussions about specific solutions that could be implemented in the government school system. Workshop participants included senior education officials, individual experts, NGOs, and educators.

In its approach to change schools, the foundation has part-nered with the public, government, and other NGOs in the field of education. The objective of these partnerships has been to demon-strate a sustained, comprehensive improvement in the quality of education. Efforts have been made to provide a healthy and clean school environment, teacher training, and child-centered learning.

The Azim Premji Foundation has also shown how low-cost technology can be deployed in the form of educational programs, CDs, and low-cost computers. Computer-aided learning combines curricular content that is child centered, interactive, and playful with assessment tools that are fun. Such programs focus on engaging and educating teachers to use interactive content as an effective supple-ment for classroom teaching in order to simplify difficult concepts and make learning enjoyable. The programs also target children with specific learning disabilities while building confidence and IT awareness among children.

Areas are chosen for the introduction of these programs on the basis of the number of children, particularly girls, who are out of school. Other criteria are the ratio of teachers to children in school, access to school, learning levels, and the level of economic development in the area. Poor scores on all of these counts qualify an area for the introduction of these programs.

As of January 2006, thirteen states have participated in the foundation's collaborative programs. More than 14,000 schools, 2.5 million students, and almost 43,000 teachers have benefited from the introduction of these programs in their local community. Pilot programs introduced in the schools have significantly raised enrollment and school attendance, as well as scores on language and math tests. The performance of children in the lowest quartiles has improved greatly.

The Future of Public-Private Partnerships

There are almost a million primary schools in India; 85% of these are government schools providing education mainly to the underprivileged. Clearly, many more private entities must partner with both local and national governments as well as NGOs to make a real and lasting change. However, the three aforementioned private organizations have made inroads into education problems in rural India, using different approaches. In each case, the results are tangible. Whether private entities rely on their own strong community ties or choose to forge partnerships with state governments and local NGOs, when a program directly addresses what the community has already identified as a problem, implementation is smoother and more likely to show positive, sustainable results beyond the drive of the outside organization. Improvements encourage community buy-in, enabling long-term programs to remain in place. In addition, technology has proven to be a key means of increasing interest, attendance, and educational performance. By using the right approach—whether it's an explicit focus on the needs of the local community, a modernized curriculum that teaches literacy through technologically mediated learning modules, or a system of

accountability that ensures a minimal standard of quality education—these three organizations are convincing a large segment of
the Indian population of the worth of education in their lives.

The major concern about corporate philanthropic efforts, and
public-private partnerships in particular, relates to the sustainability
of the programs such efforts have helped initiate. Critics warn that
investments in education are not a core business for Indian firms
but function rather as expedient strategies that primarily serve
image, PR, and political goals. Consequently, these critics say,
firms' commitment to these efforts might waver if the firms' goals
and political or economic circumstances change. If firms withdrew
their financial support, many of the programs they have instituted
would falter.

Political volatility, too, could endanger education efforts that
originated in public-private partnerships. For example, a philanthropic endeavor by Infosys, which backed a political initiative to
improve governance and infrastructure in Bangalore, ended abruptly
when Infosys's government partner was pushed out of power.

The three organizations we examined above have emphasized
in their public statements that to them improving the quality of
elementary education is a mission. Moreover, they have managed to
sustain their efforts despite the volatile rural political environment.
As the impact of their programs increases, they may even provide
the blueprint for quality education at an affordable price. But to
ensure the lasting impact of their public-private initiatives, firms
must ensure that their efforts empower rather than simply service
local communities. To succeed, their efforts may require increased
coordination among individual private partners' projects. In this
regard, joint public-private initiatives would benefit from following
the lead of MFIs, who have increased opportunities for the poor and
empowered them through interorganizational coordination, consolidation, and standardization of practices, and through sharing of
information and lessons learned. Perhaps the education sector would
benefit from an association such as Sa-Dhan—one that consisted
of organizations involved in providing education. Such an association could help disseminate valuable information about innovative
practices or partnerships, monitor outcomes, develop accountability

measures to ensure quality, and provide a collective pool of learning resources to help standardize learning, reduce cost duplication, and ensure the sustainability of the educational programs.

Conclusion

The Indian government will not be able to address the needs of its poor on its own; it must partner with and create incentives for social entrepreneurship to help create and be part of the solution. Microfinance institutions enable India's poor to help themselves and mobilize their entrepreneurial spirit. Private organizations bring efficiency, innovation, and additional capital to public initiatives. Successful partnerships like the one between the Azim Premji Foundation and local governments should be encouraged, as they allow for strong community buy-in and improved implementation of solutions. They rely on the government as the regulator rather than the implementer. Increased collaboration between the various organizations striving to help India's poor will allow sharing of best practices, capitalizing on synergies, and limiting duplication of effort. Networks of MFIs and private-public partnerships can bring solutions to difficult-to-reach communities. Furthermore, for-profit firms can use the insights gained from their own and other's social initiatives to improve and strengthen their corporate social responsibility programs. The benefits would accrue to India's population and its business community. After all, a healthy, educated, and thriving population is the best environment for business.

Notes

1. Steve Hamm, "Capitalism with a Human Face," *BusinessWeek,* December 8, 2008, 48ff.

2. Hamm, "Capitalism," 48ff.

3. "Bharti Foundation Unveils Its Vision" (press release), May 3, 2006, http://www.bharti.com/129.html?&tx_ttnews%5Bpointer%5D=3&tx_ttnews%5Btt_news%5D=184&tx_ttnews.

4. "Azim Premji, Boss of Wipro," *The Economist,* October 21, 2004. The motivation to leave a legacy does not mean that firms always use these efforts for publicity. In fact, most Indian firms do not widely publicize their philanthropic efforts. Tata executives note that in some cases Tata Industries went so far as to hide the names of its community partners, as this sort of publicity might offend its stakeholders. The Azim Premji Foundation is a stand-alone effort not at all connected to the business side of Wipro.

5. Somini Sengupta, "Education Push Yields Little for India's Poor," *New York Times,* January 17, 2008, A1.

Bibliography

Arora, Sukhwinder Singh. 2005. "The Future of Microfinance in India." *Microfinance Matters,* October. http://www.uncdf.org/mfmatters/.

Autospectator.com. 2008. "Tata Motors Takes Forward Its Initiative to Support Primary and Secondary Education in Singur," February 12. http://www.autospectator.com/cars/tata/.

Bajaj, Kapil. 2007. "Microfinance Muddle." *Business Today,* November 4.

Bharti Foundation. 2008. "School Improvement Program." http://bhartifoundation.org/programs/school-improvement-program.html.

Businesswireindia.com. 2007. "Unitus Announces Three New Partnerships in India," May 14. http://www.businesswireindia.com/.

Chopra, Sunil. 2007. Lecture to GIM-India, Kellogg School of Management, Evanston, Ill. February 23.

Corporate Social Responsibility Newswire. 2006. "Accion Establishes Partnership with India's Yes Bank to Launch Yes Microfinance India," December 8. http://www.csrwire.com/News/7032.html.

Economist. 2007. "One Eye on the Ballot Box: India's Budget," March 3.

———. 2006. "Caste and Cash." April 27.

———. 2006. "Defiantly Poor," April 20.

———. 2006. "Light and Shade," August 10.

———. 2006. "Now for the Hard Part," June 1.

———. 2005. "Microcredit in India: Helping Themselves," August 11.

———. 2004. "How Not to Spend It," October 21.

Hamm, Steve. 2008. "Capitalism with a Human Face." *BusinessWeek,* December 8.

Hindu. 2007. "Unitus' Success in Microfinance in India," March 6. http://www.hindu.com/2007/03/06/stories/.

ICICI Bank. 2008. "About Us." http://www.icicibank.com/pfsuser/aboutus/overview/overview.htm.

Jyoti, Sunita. 2005. "ICICI Bank, Grameen of USA Set Up JV for Microfinance." *Financial Express,* November 15. http://www.financialexpress.com/.

Kuber, Girish, and Preeti Iyers. 2007. "Microfinance Bill Puts Nabard in Regulatory Seat." *Economic Times,* February 26. http://economictimes.indiatimes.com/.

Lakshman, Nandini. 2006. "India's Banks Are Big on Microfinance." *BusinessWeek,* August 22.

Moneycontrol.com. 2008. "Grameen Capital to Enable MFIs to Develop Access to Capital Markets," January 24. http://www.moneycontrol.com/india/news/.

Prahalad, Coimbatore Krishna. 2005. *The Fortune at the Bottom of the Pyramid: Eradicating Poverty Through Profits.* Upper Saddle River, N.J.: Wharton School Publishing.

Prahalad, Coimbatore Krishna, and Stuart Hart. 2002. "The Fortune at the Bottom of the Pyramid." *Strategy + Business* 26:54–67.

Puranam, Phanish, and Parul Sharma. 2006. "Wanted: A Profitable Business Model for Schooling in Rural India." *ISB Insight,* September.

Sachin, Dave. 2008. "Microfinance Business to Touch $2 bn by 2009." *Economic Times,* January 28.

Sa-Dhan. 2005. "Microfinance and Poverty." Perspective Paper Series. http://www.sa-dhan.net/Resourcepublication.htm.

Sengupta, Rajdeep, and Craig P. Rajdeep. "The Microfinance Revolution: An Overview." *Federal Reserve Bank of St. Louis Review* 90 (1).

Sengupta, Somini. 2008. "Education Push Yields Little for India's Poor." *New York Times,* January 17.

Stay, Tim. 2008. "Unitus Expands Across India." http://unitus-microcredit.blogspot.com/.

Subramanian, Samanth. 2008. "Live Mint NGOs Struggle as They Venture into Microfinance." *Livemint.com,* April 20.

Tata Power. 2008. http://www.tatapower.com/.

United Nations Capital Development Fund. 2005. "Banking the Missing Middle in India: Symposium on Challenges in Involving Commercial Banks in Microfinance," October. http://www.uncdf.org/mfmatters/.

———. 2005. "Voice of Microfinance," October. http://www.uncdf.org/mfmatters/.

Unitus. 2008. "About Us." http://www.unitus.com/about-us/.

Chapter 9

THE TATA NANO: INNOVATING FROM THE GROUND UP

*Archit Gadicherla, Alexis Jhamb, Raj Kapadia,
Carlos Vasquez, John Wanner*

On March 23, 2009, Ratan Tata, chairman of the Tata Group, launched the most inexpensive car in the world—the Rs 1 lakh ($2,500) Tata Nano. The Nano's launch was a significant milestone in the five-year development of Tata Motors' "people's car." It garnered significant international media attention and drew large crowds of prospective customers to Tata Motors' showrooms across India. But the Nano was not merely celebrated as a major product launch for the Tata Group or the Indian car industry. Commentators saw the Nano instead as a "launch of a million possibilities," heralding a new age of innovation in India.[1] The Nano has shown the world that MADE IN INDIA "is no longer [only] about off-shoring or about inexpensive services."[2]

The Tata Nano is a noteworthy case on three levels. First, it is a remarkable disruptive innovation whose development is an instructive example of best-in-class cost discipline, design ingenuity, and supplier collaboration. Second, the Nano is based on a pathbreaking business model of decentralized assembly, sales, and servicing. This business model enables the creation of hundreds and thousands of jobs, and makes the Nano truly a "people's car." Third, the Nano serves as a powerful and inspiring example of the potential of Indian entrepreneurship and engineering both to domestic companies and to foreign investors. We will examine all three points in this chapter.

221

The Origin Story

The story goes that on a rainy Indian afternoon, Tata Group chairman Ratan Tata spotted a family of four on a motorcycle, ducking for cover and trying to make their way through dense traffic. This spurred him to envision a basic, affordable, and safe car for the common Indian consumer. Priced as low as Rs 1 lakh ($2,500), the car has provoked strong responses worldwide, ranging from awe to skepticism. Not surprisingly, questions have been raised about the design, safety, and viability of the Nano for both domestic and international markets, whether the price point will be sustainable, and ultimately, if Tata Motors' bet on the strength of the bottom-of-the-pyramid market will be successful. In this chapter, we examine how the Nano has managed to achieve its unimaginably low price point, the domestic and international market opportunities for this unique product, and the competitive response to the entry of the Nano into the auto market.

Necessity as the Mother of Invention

For decades, Tata Motors had been the dominant commercial vehicle maker in India, and because Indian consumers had little choice before the government deregulated the economy in 1991, the company concerned itself very little with consumers' needs and preferences. When it decided to enter the passenger car market, it did so to insulate itself from the cyclical commercial vehicle business. But the industry deregulation, the economic slowdown in the late 1990s, and the cost of development for the passenger car hit the company hard. The loss amounted to $110 million in fiscal year 2000—the first loss since the company's founding in 1945, and the largest loss in India's corporate history to that point.

The crisis shook up the company. In the spring of 2000, Ravi Kant, managing director of Tata Motors, recognized the problems the company was in and assembled his most talented engineers to brainstorm for ideas to stop the losses in commercial vehicle production. He demanded a 10% cost reduction at a time when raw material costs were steadily rising. His team came back with ideas for bench-marking; purchasing from Internet auctions; outsourcing parts to more-efficient suppliers; boosting revenue by selling Tata-made dies to Jaguar, Ford, General Motors, and Toyota; and allowing made-in-India Mercedes to be run through Tata Motors' paint shop. Hundreds of small cost-saving measures and process tweaks later, Tata's efficiency was significantly improved: the time to change a die on the passenger car assembly line was reduced from two hours to less than fifteen minutes, and turned the company's break-even point for capacity utilization into one of the best in the industry world-wide. Tata Motors returned to profitability by fiscal year 2003.

By then, the company's leadership, facing tough competition from foreign manufacturers to its large commercial vehicles and its passenger cars, started to think about ways to build vehicles for the largely untapped low end of the market. In 2003, Ratan Tata first mentioned his dream of building a very low-cost car. "They are still saying it can't be done. . . . Everybody is talking of small cars as $5,000 or $7,000. After we get done with it, there will hopefully be a new definition of 'low-cost.'"[3] The press labeled Tata's goal the "Rs 1 lakh car" (Rs 100,000 car). Ratan Tata kept the name as a stretch goal.[4]

The first step in the low-cost direction, however, was the devel-opment of a truck cheap enough to compete with three-wheeled auto rickshaws. Tata engineers—for the first time—talked to their target customers, the rickshaw drivers. They learned what these customers really needed to transport chickens, eggs, or potatoes from the village to the market. They found out that four wheels were better than three, because four improved the drivers' status and gave them better marriage prospects. When Tata Motors brought out the bare-bones Ace truck in May 2005 for $5,100, it was a smash hit, selling one hundred thousand units in twenty months. It was proof of the potential hidden at the bottom of the pyramid.

Less Is More: Innovation in Development and Design

It was this experience of extreme frugality and customer insight with which Tata Motors approached the Nano. The firm's engineers had learned to question all assumptions about how a car was supposed to be designed and built. They also discovered that the best approach to the low-end market was to start from scratch. According to Rohit Pathak, associate partner and leader of the automotive practice at management consulting firm McKinsey & Company in India, Tata was innovative in their initiative to "start from the ground up to create a bare-bones basic car." He believes that having an ambitious cost goal from the initial planning stages and developing an original design for the bottom of the pyramid were distinct from the traditional automaker approach. Typically, automakers designed off a standard platform that would yield numerous derivatives, with all derivatives tailored to the needs and desires of current customers. Tata's approach began with the image of a family of four traveling on a two-wheeler, exposed to the road and the elements. This approach from the ground up enabled Tata to challenge conventional wisdom and expectations.

In 2006, Tata Motors set up a small development team of four people—by 2008 it had grown to about five hundred—to develop a workable design. The team initially considered modeling the vehicle after an Indian rickshaw or scooter, then thought about designing a car made from engineering plastics. Many early concepts were discarded as the team realized that "the market does not want a half-car. The market wants a car."[5]

Ravi Kant, the managing director who oversaw the project, eventually turned to California-based consulting company Ariba for help. The company helps clients reduce manufacturing costs by minutely analyzing the commodities, labor, and expenses of their clients' suppliers. Ariba proposed early on to outsource large parts of the Nano's design process to suppliers as a way of driving down costs. Tata's team would provide a basic modular architecture for the car and set parameters and goals but would leave it to suppliers to come up with novel yet simple, low-cost solutions for the car's components. To guide the basic architecture and specifications, Tata used the Maruti 800—then the cheapest car in India and the Nano's closest competitor—as a benchmark to match or exceed in performance, capacity, and comfort.

Deep Supplier Collaboration

Close collaboration with suppliers is nothing new for the automotive industry. Major OEMs (original equipment manufacturers) world-wide turn to their suppliers to add innovations to their cars and help them differentiate their models from the competition with unique features. Often, however, this OEM-supplier collaboration results in additive, incremental innovations (better breaks, comfier seats, custom paints, more-sophisticated in-car entertainment) commonly coupled with modest cost reductions—more for less. Rarely do car manufacturers push their suppliers as hard as Tata did to come up with disruptive innovations for low-frills components at unprece-dentedly low-cost levels—to deliver less for much less.

Tata also gave its suppliers more responsibility for designing components than other OEMs had. With highly engineered components, about 70% of the cost is determined by the design; it cannot be reduced significantly by higher process efficiencies or lower material costs. Therefore, getting the initial design of indi-vidual components right largely determines the total cost of the car. Traditionally automakers have their own engineers come up with designs for the most critical components and provide bidding suppliers with precise specifications. Thus, they automatically set a certain cost range for the components. The Tata-Ariba development team instead laid out only the overarching imperative of "Make it simpler, make it light" and provided general goals for each part; then the team asked suppliers to develop prototypes to meet or exceed the targets. Ariba assessed the competing designs and helped Tata select the best ones. The early involvement of, and collabora-tion with, suppliers is seen by many as a fundamental change in the traditional R&D process. The connection with the most cost-competitive suppliers up front, and the leveraging of their low-cost design expertise, allowed Tata to push costs down significantly.

Encouraged by Tata, suppliers fundamentally rethought the design of basic components and how they were manufactured. A lot of the savings were generated by reducing the amount of work done on individual parts, simplifying processes, using fewer welds, and finding alternative ways of putting together subassemblies. Bosch's

35-amp generator for the Nano weighed eleven pounds—two pounds less than a standard 40-amp, and it cost less because Bosch simplified the design and used an external cooling fan. Delphi modified its production process to reduce capital investment for the Nano instrument cluster. Traditionally, the pointer for an instrument would be added by a robot in North America; for the Nano the process was changed so that the pointer could be added manually, with precision and with less capital intensity.[6]

While Tata Motors gave its one hundred vendors a lot of room for creative solutions, it closely supervised, coordinated, and at times redirected their activities. The car's design, for example, was outsourced to Italy's I.DE.A Institute (Institute of Development in Automotive Engineering), but Ratan Tata himself ordered changes along the way.

Indian suppliers and European suppliers with production capacity in India had a big advantage over rivals when Tata Motors started to look for partners. One reason the Nano is the cheapest car in the world is because 97% of its parts are sourced locally. This means that costs are lower because of low local wages, and the shorter supply chain cuts inventory and safety stocks.[7] To optimize the supply chain, half of all one hundred vendors for the project are locating with Tata in its 350-acre vendor park in Singur (a suburb of Kolkata, in eastern India), next to the plant that will produce the Nano.

Why did suppliers bend over backward to come up with low-cost components that have paper-thin margins, at best? The incentive for most manufacturers was to grow into a new segment. By 2020, the global market for vehicles priced below $5,000 is estimated to grow to 15.7 million units annually (about the size of the entire U.S. new-vehicle market in 2007) from just 1.9 million in 2008. One of the Nano's suppliers said being known as Tata Motors' partner establishes the company's credentials as an ultralow-cost supplier. Germany's Continental, too, sees its Nano contract as a modest but profitable start in the low-cost sector.

In addition, Tata rewarded the majority of its suppliers with exclusive contracts for the entire life of the model, with the option to provide more-complex and more-profitable parts for an upgraded

Nano. For example, Shivani Locks in Faridabad, India, which supplies the manual window lifters for the Nano, is already developing electric window lifters for the upgraded Nano. The firm's general manager clarifies: "We don't make a lot on the manual lifters, but we will do well on the upgrades. And the program is for a million."[8]

The No-Frills Charm of the Nano

The result of Tata's extreme frugality and design prudence, and its suppliers' creative design solutions, is "the world's most frill-free car."[9] Its huggable, cheerful design is reminiscent of Daimler's smart car and the old Italian Isetta. It has four doors, is a little more than ten feet long, and is nearly five feet wide. A 623cc two-cylinder engine at the back powers the car with 33 horsepower, accelerating it slowly but steadily to 65 miles per hour. It meets all Indian standards for emissions, pollution, and safety; and with its low vehicular weight and its tiny engine, the car's fuel economy of 54 miles per gallon comes close to that of Toyota's Prius.

The Nano's four small wheels are at the absolute corners of the car, and the battery is tucked under the seat—to improve handling and maximize interior space. Compared with the Maruti 800, its closest competitor, the Nano is smaller but offers 20% more seating capacity. It can comfortably accommodate the six-foot-tall Ratan Tata—a key design requirement—and has a trunk big enough for a duffel bag. However, the base model has no power steering, radio, passenger-side rearview mirror, sun visors, or air-conditioning. The Nano has only one windshield wiper.

A lot of the Nano's design and engineering ingenuity is revealed only at second glance. For example, the Nano uses the same lock on all four doors rather than separate left and right door locks. Ratan Tata further points out, "When you see the car, what will strike you is that we have packaged it really tightly. Most of the benefit we got on cost is because we used less steel. We just made the car smaller outside, yet big inside."[10] The vehicle sits on a basic suspension system, has a single balance shaft (instead of two) per cylinder, and only three lug nuts per tire. In addition, Tata shrewdly located the instrument cluster in the center of the dashboard so that the same dashboard could be used for left- or right-side driving versions. The Nano's most publicly discussed patent is for the significant cost saving achieved by using structural adhesive instead of welding, a process that is not new to the industry and typically is preferred in countries that have abundant cheap labor. The only significant technologies advanced through the Nano are Euro 4 emissions compliance and crash safety structural design at low weight. Thus, the Nano would not register as an innovative car by traditional measures. There are no clear technological breakthroughs in its design, components, or assembly. Only thirty-four patents were filed in its development, a small number compared with the 280 or so patents awarded to General Motors every year. What makes the Nano unique is not its features; it is the product concept and the mind-set of extreme frugality that drove its disciplined execution.

Tata plans to scale up from the basic Nano to an upgraded model priced between $2,500 and $7,000. The car is deliberately designed to be upgraded with higher-priced equipment. During the design phase, Tata had these extension plans in mind and focused on reducing the life-cycle cost of the parts. The front-door steel, for example, was originally designed for the stress of manual window lifters. But the designers knew they would add a power lifter later, which puts stress in a different place, so they redesigned the door to handle both.[11]

Can the "People's Car" Translate into Sustainable Profits?

Innovatively starting from the ground up with the bottom of the pyramid in mind, Tata has been remarkably successful in designing the world's lowest-cost car. Demand for the car is shaping up to be remarkable: when Tata Motors presented the Nano in its showrooms in April 2009, eager customers, from first-time buyers to families looking for an affordable second car, were queuing up to put down deposits and apply to be among the first owners. Tata will hold a lottery to pick the first 100,000 Nano owners; all others will be put on a waiting list.

As McKinsey's Rohit Pathak observes, the three most critical issues to the Nano's success are getting the quality right at launch, creeping up the price point over time, and dealing successfully with new market entrants.

A critical challenge ahead for Tata will be the issue of convincing consumers, both domestically and globally, that despite the Nano's basic features and affordable price, they will not have to sacrifice quality and standards. Indian consumers from the bottom of the pyramid could prove more discerning than others, because they may be more acutely value conscious and will be stretching financially to purchase a car. Tata experienced quality control problems with the launch of its passenger car Indica, but the market forgave them at the time since it was India's first wholly indigenous car. With more brands at stake under the Tata umbrella now, the market may not be as kind. It is therefore imperative for Tata to get the Nano right the first time.

While McKinsey's Pathak applauds Tata's commitment to the Rs 1 lakh ($2,500) price point, he is convinced that "the base version of the Nano may not prove profitable due to increasing commodity prices and will not be sustainable [for the supply base] without significant realized economies of scale." Furthermore, he mentioned that Tata Motors' sales mix would perhaps comprise 40% by volume of the base model and 60% by volume of the deluxe model, which could help make the Nano profitable enough to remain relevant and competitive.

Discussing strategies for enhancing profitability, Pawan Munjal, managing director and CEO of Hero Honda, believed that Tata could follow a similar strategy to Hero Honda's: selling small bikes at low prices and then upgrading owners to higher-priced permutations. But some market experts are unsure whether higher-priced Nano versions would be possible, given the basic dimensions of the vehicle. For instance, the Nano has 21% more cabin volume than the Maruti 800, which might make it difficult to provide sufficient air-conditioning with a 600cc engine. Munjal did see the necessity of Tata sticking to a Rs 1 lakh price for a while because of the media hype around this price point.

Who's in the Market for the Nano?

Even though the Tata Nano is the world's cheapest car, its price of $2,500 is still 300% of India's per capita income. In comparison, the cheapest vehicle in the U.S. market, the $11,000 Chevrolet Aveo, represents only 25% of U.S. per capita income. So, who among the 300 million Indians at the bottom of the pyramid is in the market for the Nano? And how experienced is the company in reaching its target segment?

K. Sunil Kumar, senior sales manager at Arvind Motors, Tata's oldest dealership in the state of Karnataka, is confident that Tata can reach the low end of the market, judging from Tata's previous success in that segment with the Tata Ace, India's first minitruck. The first-time car buyers, usually trading up from three-wheelers, represented 20% of total sales for the Ace. For the Nano, Kumar expects most of the sales to come from first-time car buyers whose annual income ranges from $4,500 to $10,000 and who require a practical, simple means of urban transport for their families. This segment constitutes approximately 40% of India's working population and greatly overlaps with current motorcycle customers. For these families, the safety and comfort of female drivers may be a particular concern. In addition, the Nano has turned out to be attractive to families in the upper middle and upper classes seeking to purchase a second vehicle for their household.

Tata Motors expects that the Nano will cannibalize some of the existing low-end cars, including Tata's own Indica, two-wheelers, and three-wheelers.[12] According to some industry analysts, if just 10% of current motorcycle owners switched to the Nano, it would mean a demand of 700,000 units, far exceeding Tata's estimated production capacity of 250,000 units for the first production year. If the government authorized the Nano as a taxi vehicle, it could replace some of India's tens of thousands of auto rickshaws. Putting such growth predictions into perspective, Hero Honda executives noted that at the bottom of the pyramid, the monthly operational cost of a vehicle, including fuel consumption and maintenance, matters more than the initial price tag. They estimated that switching from a motorcycle or auto rickshaw to the Nano would mean six times higher gasoline bills for owners. The higher status and better marriage prospects that come with buying a four-wheeler may make the higher fuel expenses appear worthwhile, though.

Over the long term, the Nano might also significantly increase Tata Motors' exports. While Tata has no plans to begin exporting the Nano for the next two years, until demand in the Indian market has been satisfied and quality is assured, it considers Brazil and Argentina, Africa, and Far East markets such as Malaysia and Indonesia as attractive growth options for the future.[13]

The Tata Nano Business System

One of the most remarkable—and most frequently ignored—features of the Nano is its modular, open design. The car is constructed of components that can be built and shipped separately to be easily assembled in a variety of locations. Some have called this the McDonaldization of the car industry.[14] It means that the Nano can be sold as kits that are distributed, assembled, and serviced by local entrepreneurs. Not only would this feature help lower distribution costs and seed the Nano in remote rural areas, but it could invigorate entrepreneurship throughout the country. "My aim was that I would produce a certain volume of cars and then I would create a very low-cost, low-break-even plant that a young entrepreneur could buy and that a bunch of young entrepreneurs could establish [as] an assembly operation," says Ratan Tata.[15]

The Open Distribution Model

In an interview with the *Economic Times* in January 2008, Ratan Tata sketched out what a decentralized system of distribution and servicing could look like.[16] Tata Motors and its suppliers would produce all the mass items and sell them as kits. Tata would also create the tools and equipment to assemble the car. It would effectively sell small-scale, low-cost, low-break-even assembly plants. The company would then bring together aspiring entrepreneurs from around India to help them set up satellite assembly and dealership operations. To ensure the quality of the end product, Tata Motors would train and certify independent quality assurance people to oversee the operations of these entrepreneurs. "The service person would be like an insurance agent who would be trained, have a cell phone and scooter, and would be assigned to a set of customers," explains Mr. Tata.

The article adds, however, that industry experts estimate that each small setup would have to invest about Rs 15 to Rs 20 lakh ($32,500 to $43,300), which, given the low price point customers expect of the Nano, means that entrepreneurs would operate at very thin margins and would need to compensate with very large volumes. But if the demand for the Nano reaches its current projections, such a decentralized assembly operation could be a viable strategy to expand Tata Motors' limited production capacity and distribution network. Local entrepreneurs could further improve their margins by providing services such as financing, insurance, and after-sales service. The last area in particular promises to be a profitable business.

Details of this plan remain blurry, and Ratan Tata has recently stated that he will rely on tried and tested central assembly until Tata Motors has "stabilized [its] production."[17] But the concept shows the entrepreneurial potential that could be unleashed by opening up the business model to local entrepreneurs. *BusinessWeek* called this model "open-distribution innovation" because it mobilizes large numbers of third parties to reach remote rural consumers, tailors products and services to more effectively serve local needs, and adds value to the core product or service through additional services.[18] The networks Tata would establish following this approach could be highly beneficial to the company in the long term, generate deeper insights into consumer needs and desires, and point toward further business opportunities.

The Product Is No Longer a Black Box

The Tata Motors modular approach for the Nano contrasts starkly with the strategy of most other car manufacturers in another respect. During previous decades most automakers have integrated each new model ever more tightly, and they have used increasingly highly embedded systems in their cars that represent a complete "black box" to the customer. For most modern car models, customers could not fix many of the simplest problems even if they had some engineering savvy. Intentionally so, one might add, since a whole industry rests on the car drivers' helplessness and dependence on professional, certified repair shops. The days of customizing cars and tweaking their performance seem to be all but over.

The Tata Nano's open modular design, however, seems to be harking back to the early days of automotive history, when a large percentage of drivers were able and happy to maintain their VW Beetles, Citroën 2CVs, or Minis. This ability empowered customers, gave them a deeper appreciation of the products they owned, and in many cases made them demand more customization and value-added services to meet their evolving needs—needs that could be met profitably by Tata and its system of satellite entrepreneurs.

The Tata Nano as a New Model of Innovation for India

With the Nano, Tata Motors—a car manufacturer with only a few years of experience in the passenger segment, a manufacturer dwarfed by most of its rivals—has succeeded where all Western and Southeast Asian carmakers have failed or have not dared venture. It made what many industry veterans declared impossible, possible. Anand Mahindra, managing director of Mahindra & Mahindra, Tata Motors' primary competitor, said before the Nano's unveiling, "I think it's a moment of history and I'm delighted an Indian company is leading the way."[19]

The Nano is not just a success for the Indian auto industry; it has broader significance for the Indian economy. Indian entrepreneurs and industrialists have long been perceived in the West as skilled at making money, copying or adapting business ideas, or executing foreign templates. Traditionally, they have not been seen as pathbreakers or innovation leaders. The Nano has the power to change such perceptions. It has demonstrated the insight and ingenuity of Indian engineers and entrepreneurs, and their ability to orchestrate a complex network of domestic and foreign partners to bring to life an innovative business idea that has been rejected or has failed in many other countries. It shows the tremendous potential of business models that are tailored to the Indian market, specifically to the large untapped market at the bottom of the pyramid, and it proves that Indian firms can transcend foreign templates and blueprints to develop a uniquely Indian way of business.

The Nano case brings together many strands of the previous chapters. Tata Motors has taken the Indian consumer seriously and developed an intimate understanding of the potential of India's different consumer segments and their wants and needs. Like India's telecom companies and India's airline industry, Tata has taken up the challenge to design a product for the large and largely untapped lower-income segment. And it seems to have found a sustainable business model to service this segment profitably —a model most of India's airlines are still trying to find.

Like India's national retailers, Tata seeks to spread the benefits of India's economic growth and technological emancipation to India's rural areas. Where the retailers seek to bring the amenities of low prices, consistently high quality, and a broad selection of consumer goods to the population, Tata aims to bring the benefit of mobility to those who had no previous access to it. And just as the retailers, whose investment and expansion holds significant potential for farmers, traders, and other market players, Tata's open business model also has the potential to give rise to business opportunities for local entrepreneurs.

On top of all that, Tata with its Nano has accomplished what few other Indian companies have: it has sparked an unprecedented interest by foreign companies in India, not just as a consumer market but as a rich pool of talent and competence, a place where radical innovations for the world's emerging markets can be hatched and brought to fruition. "With the recognition of the Nano, there's a tremendous amount of interest that's starting to build," points out Warren Harris, CEO of Incat, a Tata Technologies unit that was involved in the Nano's development. Other manufacturers are now studying and adapting the approach that Tata Motors took to develop the Nano, and they are planning to set up development operations in India and enter the low-cost vehicle segment. McKinsey believes that the country could become a global hub for small-car production, as the United States is for pickups.[20] Foreign firms' confidence in Indian engineering capabilities certainly seems to have received a strong boost. Incat has recently signed on for so-called "Class A jobs," which involve engineering work on all exterior surfacing, for one of its North American customers. Harris confides that "they didn't think we could do it in India."[21] Now they do.

Conclusion

The Nano may become one of the most groundbreaking products to come out of the automotive sector in decades. Its price point, at one time mocked by industry giants and automotive experts, caters to India and the world's bottom-of-the-pyramid markets. The Nano has great potential for the Tata brand. The vehicle has already brought pride to India—and not only to the manufacturing sector, but to the economy as a whole. In a meeting with Munjal, the CEO of Hero Honda, he said, "As an Indian, I am very proud of the fact that an Indian company has done this. The Nano has put India on the map and showed the world that there's more than just China."

From a technology standpoint, the little Nano, a result of innovative and collaborative design processes, has not only afforded Tata a cost advantage, but has directed the world's attention to a new way of thinking about innovation—one that challenges conventional wisdom by starting from the ground up rather than emphasizing a product's breakthrough technological features. Admittedly, skeptics wonder whether this vision of a "people's car" will translate into profitability for Tata in the near term, but it is no small achievement that one man's vision of a "people's car" has revolutionized not just how we conceive of a four-wheeler for an aspiring family, but also how we can conceptualize the design process. The Nano encourages Indian entrepreneurs in all sectors of the economy to develop path-breaking innovations—and it encourages us to look forward to the many fresh ideas and revolutionary products that will be MADE IN INDIA in the coming years.

Notes

1. Suhel Seth, "Why India Needs a Nano," *Financial Times,* March 22, 2009, http://www.ft.com/.

2. Seth, "Why India Needs a Nano."

3. Robyn Meredith, "The Next People Car," *Forbes,* April 19, 2007, http://www.forbes.com/ (accessed March 25, 2009).

4. Jesse Snyder, "How Tata Built the $2,500 Car," *Automotive News,* January 14, 2008, 3.

5. John Lorinc, "Compact Explosion: India's Tata Nano Launches the Race for the World's Cheapest Car," *Globe and Mail,* April 25, 2008, 58.

6. Snyder, "How Tata Built the $2,500 Car."

7. Snyder, "How Tata Built the $2,500 Car."

8. Jesse Snyder, "Tata Nano Changes Low-Cost Development," *Automotive News,* April 14, 2008, 16D.

9. John Lorinc, "Compact Explosion," 58.

10. T. Surendar and J. Bose, "I'm in a Lonely Phase of My Life: Ratan Tata," *Times of India,* January 11, 2008.

11. Jesse Snyder, "Tata Nano Changes," 16D.

12. Surendar and Bose, "I'm in a Lonely Phase."

13. Richard S. Chang, "Tata Nano: The World's Cheapest Car," *New York Times,* January 10, 2008, http://wheels.blogs.nytimes.com/.

14. Ritwik Donde, Lijee Philip, and Jacob Cherian, "Tata's Small Car: Small Size, Big Opportunity," *Economic Times,* January 11, 2008, http://economictimes.indiatimes.com/.

15. Donde, Philip, and Cherian, "Tata's Small Car."

16. Donde, Philip, and Cherian, "Tata's Small Car."

17. Nandini Lakshman, "Tata: Making the Nano More Affordable," *BusinessWeek,* March 24, 2009, http://www.businessweek.com/globalbiz/content/mar2009/.

18. John Hagel and John Seely Brown, "Learning from Tata's Nano," *BusinessWeek,* February 27, 2008, http://www.businessweek.com/innovate/content/feb2008/ (accessed April 6, 2009).

19. Chang, "Tata Nano."

20. James B. Treece, "Nano Brings Credibility to Indian Engineering," *Automotive News,* April 14, 2008, 16L.

21. Treece, "Nano Brings Credibility," 16L.

Bibliography

Automotive News. 2008. "Panel: Adapting to Ways in China, India, Russia," January 28.

Automotive News Europe. 2008. "After Africa, Southeast Asia, Europe Could Get Nano," January 21.

Aztec, S. A. 2008. Personal interview, March 26.

Bunckley, Nick. "At Auto Show, Chinese Are Sidelined but Not Ignored." *New York Times,* January 16.

BusinessWeek. 2007. "The Race to Build Cheaper Cars," April 27.

Chang, Richard S. 2008. "Tata Nano: The World's Cheapest Car." *New York Times,* January 10. http://wheels.blogs.nytimes.com/.

Donde, Ritwik, Lijee Philip, and Jacob Cherian. 2008. "Tata's Small Car: Small Size, Big Opportunity." *Economic Times,* January 11. http://economictimes.indiatimes.com/.

Edge (Malaysia). 2008. "Corporate: Naza in Talks with Tata," January 28.

Foster, Peter, and Pallavi Malhotra. 2008. "Ultimate Economy Drive: The Pounds 1300 car." *Daily Telegraph,* January 11.

Gibbs, Edwina, and Kiyoshi Takenaka. 2008. "Toyota to Make Low-Priced Cars in India." *Reuters,* April 12. http://in.reuters.com/article/basicIndustries/.

Hagel, John, and John Seely Brown. 2008. "Learning from Tata's Nano." *BusinessWeek,* February 27. http://www.businessweek.com/innovate/content/feb2008/ (accessed April 6, 2009).

Incantalupo, Tom. "Nano Car Has a Nano Price—Just $2,500." *Newsday,* January 11.

Johnson, Jo. 2008. "Optimism Outpaces Hesitant Reforms." *Financial Times,* January 24.

Kumar, K. Sunil. Personal interview, March 25.

Lakshman, Nandini. 2009. "Tata: Making the Nano More Affordable." *BusinessWeek,* March 24. http://www.businessweek.com/globalbiz/content/mar2009/.

Lorinc, John. 2008. "Compact Explosion: India's Tata Nano Launches the Race for the World's Cheapest Car." *Globe and Mail,* April 25, 58.

Meredith, Robyn. 2007. "The Next People Car." *Forbes,* April 19. http://www.forbes.com/ (accessed March 25, 2009).

Munjal, Pawan. 2008. Personal interview, March 29.

Pande, Anadi. 2008. Personal interview, March 29.

Pathak, Rohit. 2008. Personal interview, March 26.

Phelan, Mark. 2008. "Nano Could Put Tata over the Top." *Ventura County Star,* April 5.

Ramesh, Randeep. 2008. "India Gears for Mass Motoring Revolution." *Guardian* (London), January 11.

Reed, John, and Bernard Simon. 2008. "Honda Disputes Cheap Car Logic." *Financial Times,* January 13.

Seth, Suhel. 2009. "Why India Needs a Nano." *Financial Times,* March 22. http://www.ft.com/.

Snyder, Jesse. 2008. "How Tata Built the $2500 Car." *Automotive News,* January 14.

———. 2008. "Tata Nano Changes Low-Cost Development." *Automotive News,* April 14.

Stoll, John. 2008. Personal interview, April 7.

Surendar, T., and J. Bose. 2008. "I'm in a Lonely Phase of My Life: Ratan Tata." *Times of India,* January 11.

Swift, Allan. "Tiny Cars Spark Speedy Growth." *Gazette* (Montreal), January 24.

Tata Motors. 2008. April 24. http://www.tata.com/.

Time. 2007. "Autopian Vision," September 27.

Treece, James B. 2008. "Nano Brings Credibility to Indian Engineering." *Automotive News,* April 14, 16L.

Whitelaw, Jackie. 2008. "India Faces Roads Meltdown." *New Civil Engineer,* January 17.

Winding Road. 2008. "Tata Motors Eying the Thai Market," April 24. http://njection.com/blogs/windingroad/archive/.